Confronting Pornography

Confronting Pornography

A Guide to Prevention and Recovery for
Individuals, Loved Ones, and Leaders

edited by **Mark D. Chamberlain**, Ph.D., **Daniel D. Gray**, LCSW,
and Rory C. Reid, MSW

᚛ᚕᚏ᚜
DESERET
BOOK
SALT LAKE CITY, UTAH

Library of Congress Cataloging-in-Publication Data

Chamberlain, Mark D., 1964–
   Confronting pornography : a guide to prevention and recovery for
individuals, loved ones, and leaders / [edited by] Mark D. Chamberlain,
Dan Gray, Rory C. Reid.
       p. cm.
   Includes bibliographical references and index.
   ISBN 1-59038-235-8 (pbk.)
   1. Pornography. 2. Men—Sexual behavior. 3. Sex addiction—Religious
aspects. 4. Sex addicts—Rehabilitation. I. Gray, Dan. II. Reid, Rory C. III. Title.
   HQ471.C44 2005
   241'.667—dc22   2004030156

Printed in the United States of America   54459
Malloy Lithographing Inc., Ann Arbor, MI

10   9   8   7   6   5   4   3   2   1

Contents

Acknowledgments

This book has been a collaborative effort. We want to specifically acknowledge the efforts of Becky Harding, Warren Tenney, and Katherine Gille, who have been invaluable in helping us edit and condense chapters.

Pornography—A Consuming Fire

Mark D. Chamberlain

Leonard Gregg had been fascinated by fires since he was a child. As he watched firefighting planes drop slurry on wild-fires, he dreamed of becoming a firefighter himself someday. In fact, his older brother, Wilson, remembers watching Leonard play make-believe: "He put boxes in a line and would pretend he was dropping slurry on those boxes" like the big firefighting planes did.[1]

Leonard eventually achieved his goal and became a firefighter, but at age twenty-nine his dream became a nightmare. He was out of work and trying somehow to support his girlfriend and her six children. He knew that he could make some money, if only there was a fire to fight—so he decided to try to start one himself. On June 18, 2002, near the Fort Apache Indian Reservation town of Cibecue, Arizona, he used matches to light some dry grass on fire in two different areas. One of the fires was put out that day, but the other spread quickly up steep terrain and into the surrounding White Mountains.

Crews fought the blaze, but it continued to grow in the hot, dry, and sometimes breezy weather. On June 23, the fire merged with another that had been started by a lost hiker to signal a helicopter, and the wildfire became the largest in Arizona history. At its worst point, 4,400 firefighters were battling a fifty-mile-wide wall of flames. Thirty thousand people from nine communities had to be evacuated.

By July 9, the fire was finally contained as crews doused the final smoldering embers. In the intervening twenty-six days, 467 homes had been destroyed and over 732 square miles of ponderosa pine and juniper forest were blackened. The blaze itself caused at least $28 million in damage, and the cost of fighting it was estimated at $43 million. The region's economy, largely dependent on the forest, was devastated and will likely take years to recover. To a judge in a Flagstaff courtroom, all Leonard could say was, "I'm sorry for what I did."

When I consider Leonard's remorse, and his astonishment about how quickly the problem he created spread beyond the limits he initially intended, I can't help but think of some of the people I have talked with about the consequences of their involvement in pornography:

I think of *Seth,* a 57-year-old business owner and former bishop, who described how his on-and-off involvement with pornography fueled his sexual appetite in ways that left him ever less satisfied with his wife, with her body, and with the frequency and intensity of their sexual encounters. "At first I justified entertaining my lust because my focus was 'only' racy stuff on TV and provocative ads in 'mainstream' magazines. When I started to masturbate to those images, I rationalized, 'If my wife even had an average level of sexual interest, I wouldn't need to resort to this, but every normal man needs a healthy sexual release now and then.' I'm ashamed to say that I even used certain scriptures to convince myself that I was being wronged when she wasn't interested in sex and that this whole problem was really her fault." Over time, Seth sought out material that was more and more explicit, always feeling guilty and vowing to abstain in between his lapses into pornography. When I asked him what led him to finally seek treatment, he said, "I knew how drastically pornography had changed me one day when I found myself feeling bad—like I had missed out on some great thing—because I had never had sex with a prostitute."

I think of *Brad*, a forty-eight-year-old father of five who tearfully described the day he loaded all of his personal belongings into his truck and drove away from the family home he and his wife had purchased some twenty years earlier. "As I turned off our street, I looked in the rearview mirror and caught a glimpse of the treehouse in the giant maple to the side of our house. At that moment, my heart broke. I knew I was leaving behind everything I had tried to build for her, for the kids, and for myself. Later I thought, I planted that tree and nurtured it well. Too bad I couldn't have done the same for my marriage." For fifteen years his wife worked patiently at his side as he battled an addiction to pornography and masturbation. She had finally decided to end their marriage when he got involved with a woman he met on a business trip.

I think of *Kevin*, an eighteen-year-old young man who was first appalled when he looked at pornography that featured young children. "My reaction was, 'How could anybody look at that stuff?!' and I immediately got off of that website. But then some curiosity lingered, and I went back to check out the material. My fascination for it grew, at first out of disgust and disbelief, but then gradually it got to the point where I was entertaining those kind of fantasies myself." Then one day when he was tending his three-year-old cousin, he impulsively reached over and fondled her for a few seconds. As soon as he did, he was horrified and immediately called his parents and then his aunt and uncle to tell them about it. From there he went through a police investigation and a court hearing and was sentenced to a year of probation, which prevented him from leaving the state to attend the college of his choice as a freshman. He acknowledges, however, that the effects of his actions on his own life have not been the most difficult consequences to face. "The hardest part was apologizing to this sweet little girl about something she shouldn't even have to worry about at her age—or ever in her life, for that matter. She looked up at me with big eyes and with a quivering voice said, 'Kevin, you did something you not supposed to.' It tore me up inside to think about what I had done to her. I despise what I had become, to be able to do something like that. I damaged her innocence. It's tough even now when I see how low I sank, to the point where I can't even be trusted to play with my nieces and nephews without supervision."

Finally, I think of *Terry,* a twenty-seven-year-old young man whose wife recently gave birth to their first baby. He described how he began exploring pornography on the Internet six months ago "just to see why everyone's making such a big deal about it." After a couple of months of occasional looking he stopped and stayed away from those kind of websites from then on, but he has found that he can't seem to erase those images or completely reverse the effect that "just looking" has had on him. "If only I could enjoy my relationship with my wife without those images flooding into my mind," he said. "I don't think I'll ever get caught up in that again, but there are certain things I would rather not even know are out there. I wish I could go back to being naïve."

Leonard, the part-time firefighter, never suspected that his youthful obsession could explode out of control and wreak such devastation once it was unleashed. In a similar way, the flames of sexual fascination can easily escalate beyond our control and devastate our lives. As Isaiah prophesied, "Wickedness burneth as the fire . . . and the people shall be as the fuel of the fire" (Isaiah 9:18–19). Some curiosities cannot be pursued in "harmless" or "manageable" ways—we are wise to avoid them altogether. The modern plague of pornography is one such danger. Church leaders have done all they can to warn us of its dangers. One purpose of this volume is to echo these voices of warning.

As important as prevention is, there is also other work to be done. Despite warnings, many find themselves surrounded by pornography's flames. To these, we wish to convey hope and help them find their way back to freedom and safety. In addition, there are also many who have previously struggled who now relish the knowledge that they have overcome pornography and the freedom they now enjoy. The lives of individuals like these stand as a bold witness that repentance and change are possible through the atonement of Jesus Christ. A fire can continue to burn only as long as there is fuel to feed it. Fortunately, after the fire has been managed and then extinguished, there are few scars that cannot be healed by the miracle of rebirth and regrowth. Later, the journey of recovery will be described in greater detail, but let me offer these brief illustrations that success is possible:

I admire *Devin,* who now serves as a high councilor in his stake. He supports and counsels five brethren in his stake as they work to overcome pornography problems themselves. It has been eleven years since Devin viewed pornography. He conquered the problem through effort and fasting and prayer and relying on the Lord. He recalls: "As I tried to do my part and earnestly sought the Lord's help, I was able to abstain for longer and longer periods. It was hard when I'd falter after doing so well, but I tried not to let discouragement creep in as an excuse to indulge myself again. My wife was deeply offended, but she didn't give up on me. More and more I found pride in being able to announce to her at the end of a business trip, 'These eyes are only for you. Your old man isn't trying to turn himself on by looking at other women.'" When asked about what helped him and what he has seen help others, Devin responded, "Some of the men I work with seem to have a harder time than others. I haven't seen any one key thing that enables people to overcome this—just that those who keep trying and don't give up seem to eventually get there with the Lord's help."

Lyle and Evelyn were shocked and dismayed when they discovered that their son, *Trent,* had developed a habit of looking at pornography on the Internet. That was three years ago; Trent is now eighteen. "After getting over the initial reaction—'this can't be happening to *our* son'—Lyle and I became proactive," Evelyn recalls. "No one would expect a young warrior to go into battle without preparation and protection. When we thought about what a struggle it must be for youth to stay morally clean today, we realized that Trent and his younger brothers would need more mentoring and armor than we required at their age."

Evelyn and Lyle started having regular talks with their boys in an effort to provide better support and consultation regarding morality and sexuality. They installed filtering and monitoring software on their computer. They are trying to help their boys learn to manage their own computer use and other habits to avoid excesses of all kinds. They've had interesting discussions with individual boys about everything from the outrageous lifestyles of celebrities to the content of novels in English class and the difference between art and obscenity.

Lyle concluded: "We're seeing our boys develop their own, internal moral filters over time. When Trent accessed pornography, that was a real slap in the face, but some good has come from it. We're not just assuming that our boys will develop the understanding, values, and self-restraint they need to survive in today's world. We're doing more to stay in touch with and help each of them."

Randall continued to experience intense temptations to return to a pornography and masturbation habit that had been part of his life before his conversion and baptism. In fact, he did return to his old ways for brief periods many times during his first several years as a member of the Church. He struggled and suffered throughout those early years. He searched his soul and searched the teachings of the gospel for help. In the process, he read President Boyd K. Packer's promise that "true doctrine, understood, changes attitudes and behavior. The study of the doctrines of the gospel will improve behavior quicker than a study of behavior will improve behavior."[2]

Encouraged by this assurance from an apostle, Randall resolved to embark on an intense study of the Book of Mormon. He scheduled his reading so that he would make it through the entire book in a month. In faith and with high hopes, he began the process. One month later he finished the Book of Mormon. That month had not been without its challenges, but he also felt that he had learned more than ever about the Lord and had been buoyed up by the Spirit as never before. It had gone so well, in fact, that he decided to continue the process and read the entire Book of Mormon again, and to do so once a month eleven more times to make it a full year's worth of immersion at that depth.

Toward the end of that year, Randall was called as bishop of his ward. "That's what you get for reading the Book of Mormon every month," I joked with him later. During the call, he shared with his stake president the nature of his struggle. Randall's heart—the steadfastness of his desires—shone through the darkness of his difficulties. The stake president could see how much his ward would benefit from this good brother's strength and from how well he had come to know the Lord through his struggle. He had survived a fiery furnace and could bear special testimony of the saving power of the atonement of Jesus Christ.

As you might imagine, serving as bishop brought new stresses and challenges. Working through those has not been easy. At times, discouragement has prevailed, sometimes for days. However, the light of hope and promise always shines through as this man of honor is blessed by an ever-deepening conviction that his efforts, progress, growth, and service are acceptable to the Lord.

Some have aptly called pornography a modern plague. Fortunately, we are learning much about what we can do to facilitate prevention and healing. Part 1 of this volume explores important issues related to pornography and provides suggestion on how to prevent pornography-associated problems. Part 2 offers help for spouses, ecclesiastical leaders, parents, friends, or anyone else who supports someone who is struggling with a pornography problem. Finally, part 3 addresses how to proceed toward overcoming a pornography problem. We hope that all who are searching for help will find this material both enlightening and helpful.

NOTES

1. www.azstarnet.com/wildfire/20702WILDFIRE2fSUSPECT.html (accessed April 11, 2004). For more information on the Leonard Gregg story, see www.katu.com/news/story.asp?ID=48261 (accessed July 9, 2002) and www.cnn.com/2002/LAW107/03/arizona.wildfire.indictment/index.html (accessed July 9, 2002).
2. Boyd K. Packer, "Little Children," *Ensign*, November 1986, 17.

Understanding the Issues and Preventing Problems

CHAPTER ONE

The Pornography Trap

Victor B. Cline

D r. Albert Cooper, a staff psychologist and researcher at Stanford University, recently conducted a survey that identifies what he calls an explosion of individuals in the United States involved with pornography or sex on the Internet. Fully one-third of all visits by adult Internet users are to sexually oriented web sites, which also include many chat rooms and news groups with a similar focus. Porn compulsives also use many other kinds of erotic materials to feed their addiction, such as men's magazines, adult videos, phone sex, X-rated programs on cable and dish TV, and live strip clubs. Much research and clinical evidence suggests that this addiction has become a major public health problem, with many negative or harmful consequences for both adults and children. It also raises the questions of whether and to what extent this addiction is treatable—which questions this chapter will address.

DEFINING PORNOGRAPHY AND OBSCENITY

To ascertain something about pornography effects, we first need to define it. The word *pornography* comes from the Greek words *porno* and *graphia,* meaning "depictions of the activities of whores." In common parlance, it usually means "material that is sexually explicit and intended primarily for the purpose of sexual arousal."

INTERNET PORN

In the past five years, porn on the Internet has virtually exploded in volume and is now the leading source of pornographic materials worldwide. The Internet can be more devastating than other mediums in spreading pornography because of what some experts have called the three "A's." It's easily *accessible, affordable,* and *anonymous.* No one will ever know. Many get on the net when no one is home or after midnight when the family is asleep.

I have worked with boys in their early teens who got into this wasteland and suffered quite negative consequences. They told me they actively search for porn on the Internet using specific key words. Then, once they have found how to quickly access it, they go back again and again—just like drug addicts.

The main avenues for accessing porn are home computers and some libraries that have no protecting filters. Computer-wise young people are sometimes able to bypass filters. So wise parents should keep computers out of kids' bedrooms and in "public" areas where their on-line activities can be easily monitored.

This is commonly called "Cybersex addiction." Albert Cooper indicates that cybersex compulsives are much like drug addicts. Their "drug of choice"[1] is the Internet, and that "drug" often brings significant damage to their lives both at home and at work.

Dr. Mark Schwartz of the Masters & Johnson Institute in St. Louis, Missouri, agrees. "Sex on the Net is like heroin," he says. "It grabs them and takes over their lives. And it's very difficult to treat because the people affected don't want to give it up."[2] Some cybersex addicts develop such a conditioned response that they become sexually aroused simply by sitting in front of a computer. As the addiction progresses, the addict can develop a tolerance to the stimulation. He may take greater and greater risks seeking a new "high."

Dr. Jennifer Schneider, a Tucson, Arizona, physician, conducted a survey of nearly one hundred people affected by the cybersex addictions of others and found that the problem could develop even in loving marriages. "Sex on the Net is just so seductive and it's so easy to stumble upon it. People who are vulnerable can get hooked before they know it."[3] She compared the damage to that caused by compulsive gambling, alcoholism, or drug abuse. Cybersex addiction can leave a trail of evils behind it, including feelings of betrayal, deception, and abandonment. Victim spouses often feel devalued, ignored, and unable to compete with a fantasy. Among those studied was a woman married fourteen years to a minister whom she discovered had a cybersex addiction. She commented, "How can I compete with hundreds of anonymous others who are now in our bed, in his head. Our bed is crowded with countless faceless strangers, where once we were intimate."[4]

FOUR MAJOR CONSEQUENCES OF REPEATED PORNOGRAPHIC EXPOSURE

In some twenty-five years of treating mostly males with this problem, I've seen approximately four hundred patients so afflicted. I have found that there are four major things that happen to them when they get immersed in this pornographic milieu and become ill with it.

The first consequence is *addiction,* which has been discussed somewhat above. It usually starts when the person is a teenager or earlier, with a friend being a common source of their exposure— usually to men's magazines like *Penthouse* or *Hustler.* "Stumbling onto" pornographic popup ads or some other enticement on the Internet is increasingly becoming a common form of first exposure.

The problem may grow to include videos, phone sex, and erotic films on cable or dish TV. They look at this material initially out of curiosity and find it sexually stimulating and arousing. In time, they increase their frequency of exposure, often seeking it out and nearly always masturbating to it. The addiction grows or increases slowly as they keep going back to this material and repeating the cycle.

Nearly always, they experience some shame and guilt about it. They keep it a secret. They almost never discuss what they are doing with their parents or other adults. In a way, they have a love-hate relationship with it. They intuitively know they shouldn't be involved in it—but they still continue. And each time they go through the cycle of exposure, arousal, and then sexual release, it strengthens the hold the addiction has on them through standard Pavlovian conditioning.

If they are looking at materials that mix sex with violence or other major pathology (abuse of children, rape, exhibitionism, and so forth), then they are on the royal road to acquiring a major sexual illness. This is the way many sexual deviations are acquired.

The second thing that happens is *desensitization*. What was first shocking and revolting in time becomes commonplace and ordinary. Eventually it seems less extreme; they may even assume that "everybody is doing it." Conscience and constraint are diminished or turned off. They get hardened. Nothing bothers them. Viewing rape, abuse of children, incest, or group sex becomes merely titillating. In time, they become incapable of understanding the pathology and inappropriateness of the material they lust after. Some become impotent.

The third thing that occurs in time with many patients is *escalation*. In order to get their highs, the buzz, the kicks, and the erotic turn-ons, they develop a need for ever more aberrant materials—something more gross, more exciting, and more deviant. As with a drug, it takes more and more to achieve the same excitement they had in the past with lesser materials.

And the fourth thing that occurs is *acting out* behaviorally. Some eventually start acting on their fantasies. Their judgment is affected. In the workplace, they do things that their female co-workers call sexual harassment. As their illness escalates, they lose the ability to discriminate between what is appropriate and what may send them to jail. They and their employer may get sued. Some lose their jobs. But probably the worst consequence of all is the damage it does to their marriage or partner relationship, as well as their family as a whole.

CONSEQUENCES OF SCHOOL-AGE CHILDREN'S EXPOSURE TO PORNOGRAPHY

In a study reported to the Attorney General's Commission on Pornography by Dr. Jennings Bryant, "600 American males and females of high school age and above were interviewed about their 'out in real life involvement with pornography.' 91% of the males and 82% of the females admitted to having been exposed to X-rated, hard-core pornography. Two-thirds of the males and 40% of the females reported wanting to try out some of the behaviors they had witnessed."[5]

And among high school students, 31 percent of the males and 18 percent of the females admitted actually *doing* some of the things sexually they had seen in the pornography *within a few days after exposure.* This clearly suggests the model-effect or imitative-learning effect, as well as the "triggering effect," that pornography has on human sexual behavior in some individuals.

Additionally, it was found that massive exposure to pornography over a six-week period was able to change the attitudes and feelings of adult subjects in a laboratory setting, making sexual improprieties and transgressions seem less bad. The victims of such transgressions were also perceived to suffer less and to be less severely wronged. In other words, these adults had become to some degree desensitized as a result of the pornography exposure.

As Dr. Jennings Bryant comments, "If the values which permeate the content of most hardcore pornography are examined, what is found is an almost total suspension of the sorts of moral judgment that have been espoused in the value systems of most civilized cultures. Forget trust. Forget family. Forget commitment. Forget love. Forget marriage. Here, in this world of ultimate physical hedonism, anything goes."[6]

IMPRINTING THE BRAIN WITH SEXUAL IMAGES

The work of psychologist James L. McGough at the University of California–Irvine needs mention here. His findings (oversimplifying considerably) suggest that memories of experiences that occurred at times of emotional arousal (or possibly sexual arousal) get "locked into the brain or memory" by an adrenal gland hormone, epinephrine, and are difficult or impossible to erase. This may partly explain pornography's addicting effect. Powerful, sexually arousing memories of experiences or exposures from the past keep intruding themselves back on the mind's memory screen, serving to stimulate and erotically arouse the viewer. If one masturbates to these fantasies, the linkage between sexual arousal (including orgasm), and the particular scene, person, event, or image is reinforced and is quickly locked into one's memory. Thus, the brain creates its own "library" of erotica—much of it antisocial. This increases the likelihood of later acting out the fantasy.

CONDITIONING INTO DEVIANCY

Dr. Stanley Rachman conducted research in London that demonstrated that sexual deviations could be created in adult male subjects in a laboratory setting. Using highly erotic pictures in two separate experiments, he was actually able to condition 100 percent of his normal male subjects into a sexual deviancy (fetishism). This is one of the first studies in the literature that, using strict laboratory procedures, demonstrated how easy it is to condition deviancy through pornography exposure.

Psychologist Patrick Carnes, currently the leading U.S. researcher on sexual addictions, has published a series of research and data-based books that bring to national awareness the problem of out-of-control, compulsive sexual behavior. His latest volume documents a host of serious legal, marital, and health consequences of such compulsions.

He found that among 932 sex addicts studied, 90 percent of the men and 77 percent of the women report pornography as significant to their addictions. He also found that two common elements in the early origin of sexually addicting behavior are childhood sexual abuse and frequent pornography exposure accompanied by masturbation.

In my experience as a sexual therapist, any individual who regularly masturbates to pornography is at risk of becoming, in time, a sexual addict, as well as conditioning himself into having a sexual deviancy that may disturb or disrupt a bonded relationship with a spouse or girlfriend. The sexual side becomes, in a sense, dehumanized. Many of them develop an "alien ego state" (or dark side), whose core is antisocial lust devoid of most values.

In time, the "high" obtained from masturbating to pornography becomes more important than real-life relationships. It has been commonly thought and taught by health educators that masturbation has negligible consequences other than reducing sexual tension. Certainly one exception that is rarely mentioned is in the area of repeatedly masturbating to deviant pornographic imagery (either as memories in the mind or as explicit pornographic stimuli), which risks, via conditioning, the acquiring of sexual addictions and/or other sexual pathology.

It makes no difference if one is an eminent physician, attorney, minister, athlete, corporate executive, college dean, unskilled laborer, president of the United States, or an average fifteen-year-old boy. All can be conditioned into deviancy.

The process of masturbatory conditioning is inexorable and does not stop without significant effort. The course of this illness may be slow and is nearly always hidden from view. It is usually a secret part of the man's life, and, like cancer, it keeps growing and spreading. It rarely ever reverses itself, and it is also very difficult to treat and heal. Denial on the part of the addict and refusal to confront the problem are typical and predictable, and this almost always leads to marital or couple disharmony and sometimes divorce, if married.

ILLUSTRATIVE CASES

I remember Charlie, a very successful up-and-coming businessman in his early thirties. He'd gotten into porn in his early teens and somehow could never quite shake it. With the advent of the Internet, he found himself wildly out of control, with many negative experiences, especially when his wife found out about his problem. She soon discovered him lying repeatedly; as it worsened, she decided to leave the marriage, fearing the effects of the illness on the children as well as herself. She also found that her trust in her husband was totally absent now.

At this point Charlie decided to get professional help. He also joined a Sexaholics Anonymous twelve-step group and in time found himself 95 percent "sober." His one weak area was when away on business trips. He discovered that nearly every hotel in America provided easy access to adult porn channels on the in-room TV. This was his trigger—being away from home and in a room with instant access to porn. And he knew if he did access it, no one would ever know. He found he couldn't handle this level of temptation. So his therapist, as well as some of his friends in SA, provided the solution. When checking into any hotel while traveling, he was always to have the desk clerk block the porn channels on his room TV. In addition, he agreed to always call his wife at 9:30 P.M. to discuss how his day went. Since she was jointly attending all of his counseling sessions, she was able to give good support and help him retain his sobriety.

In the case of Richard, a twenty-three-year-old college student, as well as a porn and sex addict, the combination of therapist and SA support group, with its twelve-step program, led to gradually diminishing relapses. He had a strong motivation to be free of his addiction before he married or started seriously courting. After two years with some positively reinforcing spiritual experiences, he moved into long-term sobriety. However, he continues to attend SA, mainly to give help and support to newcomers who are painfully struggling with their addiction as he once was.

SEX AND PORN ADDICTIONS: THEN AND NOW

Twenty years ago, deciding whether pornography was harmful or not was a controversial issue among behavioral scientists. I spent much time and energy debating with my colleagues about this at professional meetings, seminars, on TV talk shows, and in the courts. But that is not the case now.

I hear almost nobody currently claiming that pornography is harmless and has no deleterious effects. It has now been five years since anyone would debate me on this issue. And it's not that I am that good as a debater—it's more what the preponderance of evidence now demonstrates.

The harmful effects of pornography and sex addiction have in recent years been repeatedly documented, with the publication of many research-based books and journal articles, presentations at professional meetings, and the simple fact that tens of thousands of victim-patients are being daily treated in major hospitals and clinics throughout the United States, including such places as the Menningers, the Meadows, and Sierra Tucson in Arizona; Del Amo Hospital in Los Angeles; River Oaks in New Orleans; the Masters and Johnson centers in St. Louis; as well as in outpatient clinics involving hundreds of therapists in all of the healing professions in every major city in America.

Television and radio talk shows often feature therapists who are treating these illnesses, along with their patients telling their stories. I was on the Geraldo Rivera TV show several years ago with two couples, where the husbands were recovering porn and sex addicts.

We told our story to a nationwide TV audience, detailing how their addiction nearly broke up their marriages and damaged their families and relations with their children; but the ultimate outcome was one of hope and healing. Porn and sex addictions are now a part of our popular culture. Nearly everyone knows about it or has family or friends struggling with it. The big question now facing us is not whether pornography and sex addictions cause harm— clearly they can and do—but how do we heal those who have been wounded? And how can we protect our children from pornography's toxic influence so they won't get addicted, especially with Internet porn so easily accessed now?

The Internet is now easily the main source of this material. The Internet, which is worldwide, cannot be policed. Our laws don't cross our borders. There is no limit to the pathology that is available on your computer monitor; all it takes is a few clicks of the mouse. Half of my clinical practice involves trying to repair the damage that flows from Internet porn.

Pornography on the Internet has totally changed the playing field. As I mentioned, nearly every hotel in America now sells porn on its in-room TV sets. Ironically, the hard-core porn they present and sell is contrary to the laws in most communities. But there is little or no enforcement of those laws. The only attempt to police or control its proliferation is with child pornography.

In America, it is illegal to download child pornography. But if your children download adult pornography at the library or school or home, it's the parents' problem. Unfortunately, in the majority of cases that I am seeing, most parents don't have a clue what their children are getting exposed to. It's very important for parents to have an open dialogue with their children about these issues and their possible exposure. Then your children can be given appropriate boundaries, ground rules, and protection.

This is a very "infectious" disease that can spread to your children from their peers, who may be deeply addicted. This is an illness that you don't "mature" out of. With time, it only gets worse, unless there is some very active intervention or treatment and the individual is committed to doing whatever it takes to get well. To complicate matters, pornography involvement often involves living a secret life because of shame, fear of discovery, and avoiding marital conflict.

HEALING

Porn and sex addictions are very difficult to treat, heal, or obtain sobriety with. Self-discipline, willpower, threat of job loss, divorce, jail, or even a genuine desire to quit rarely are enough. Thus very active therapeutic interventions are almost always necessary. While there is much we still need to know about effective treatment, I have found there are four major factors that most predict success in recovery.

First, the individual must be personally *motivated* to be free of his addiction and possess a willingness to do whatever it takes to achieve success. While freedom from addiction and renewed health are possible, you can never force a person to get well if he doesn't want to. The journey to health is his alone to make. He can't cut corners, miss appointments, or neglect homework given to him. It may take him several years to break free and get his agency back again.

Second, it is necessary to *create a safe environment,* which drastically reduces access to porn and other sexual triggers. It may require changing jobs. It will also require putting effective filters on all computers. But one should choose wisely, since filters vary greatly in quality and effectiveness. It also may require that only the parents or wife know the password to get Internet access. No computers should be allowed in the bedroom, especially of a child. And parents (or the wife) should regularly monitor the history of all family Internet computer use. Since most hotels provide easy access to porn, the individual, when traveling, should ask at the front desk that the room TV be disconnected from the porn channels. And it also helps for him to call his spouse at home nightly and discuss how the day went.

Third, he should *affiliate with a twelve-step support group* (which cost nothing) such as SA (Sexaholics Anonymous). They meet weekly and can be found in most medium or larger cities in America. Like their cousin organization, Alcoholics Anonymous, SA makes use of the twelve-step therapeutic programs that rely on a "Higher Power" to assist participants in becoming sober long-term. In surveys of recovering addicts, an affiliation with such a group has been shown to be most helpful in facilitating healing. After a participant attends several meetings, he chooses a "sponsor" (a member of their group with good sobriety, whom he can connect with), whom he can call twenty-four hours a day for help if he finds himself slipping, crumbling, threatening to relapse, or needing support. With a particularly virulent illness, he may choose to attend several different SA meetings weekly or even daily.

Fourth, the individual needs to *select a counselor/therapist* who has had special training and success in treating sexual addictions.

Most therapists know little or nothing about treating this illness. There are virtually no medical or graduate university programs that teach how to treat these addictions. Despite this, there are still some therapists who have received excellent training through private organizations and special seminars that may be of great help. If married, it's usually wise for him to involve his wife in joint treatment, for she will likely be wounded, perhaps depressed, in despair, and uncertain what to do. The couple will have enormous anger, trust, and marital problems that invariably have to be addressed. With his wife involved, the porn user has someone he can share his day-to-day concerns and ups and downs with. And, most refreshingly, he will no longer have any secrets to be hidden and lied about.

If parents have a son living in the home, and they discover he has a porn addiction, it's important to get it out into the open and discuss it with him. Since porn users often initially deny, minimize, or pretend to know nothing about it, it's best to have convincing evidence at hand so they don't blow you off. Evidence could include material downloaded from the computer or inappropriate materials found in the living area in the home. Since this is a problem that the son can rarely lick by himself, promises to quit and never do it again should be regarded skeptically. You might suggest counseling and joining an SA group.

If an individual has several different addictions, it's important to have them treated concurrently, not just one at a time. And if, while in the healing process, he has some slips along the way, he shouldn't get too discouraged. This is where a support group can be invaluable, shoring him up and giving him hope. A therapist can also help him identify the triggers that led to his slip and help him build a wall of protection around himself. It's like with most people who quit smoking: they usually quit many times before they finally really quit and get totally free of their habit.

THE FUTURE IS NOW

In sum, I see porn and sex addictions as very pernicious and challenging public health problems. They are illnesses that attack the very fabric of family life; and family is the core of our civilization. Since the Internet has no boundaries or limits, it cannot be tamed or managed, and thus the problem rages on.

What that means for now is that every family is on its own to protect its offspring, and even the parents may not be immune from pornography's influence. This means that we need to put resources into improving treatment and having a better understanding of the basic neurology and biology underlying the acquisition of these kinds of addictive illnesses. There will always be some who will not be willing to give up their illness and its addictive behaviors. But for those who do, there is both help and hope. Many addicts recover when actively engaged in a healing program with the help of competent therapists and support groups.

SUGGESTED READINGS

Patrick Carnes, *Don't Call It Love: Recovery from Sexual Addiction* (New York: Bantam Books, 1991).

Victor B. Cline, "Pornography Effects: Empirical and Clinical Evidence," in Zillmann, et al., *Media, Children, and the Family* (Hillsdale, New Jersey: Lawrence Erlbaum Associates, 1994).

————, *Pornography's Effects on Adults and Children* (New York: Morality in Media, 2004).

Victor B. Cline, ed., *Where Do You Draw the Line? Explorations in Media Violence, Pornography, and Censorship* (Provo, Utah: BYU Press, 1974).

Al Cooper, "Sexuality and the Internet: Surfing into the New Millennium," in *CyberPsychology and Behavior* 1 (1998): 181–87.

Al Cooper, David L. Delmonico, and Ron Burg, "Cybersex Users, Abusers, and Compulsives: New Findings and Implications," in *Sexual Addiction and Compulsivity* 7 (2000): 5–29.

Al Cooper, Irene P. McLoughlin, and Kevin M. Campbell, "Sexuality in

Cyberspace: Update for the 21st Century," in *CyberPsychology and Behavior* 3 (2000): 521–36.

James L. McGaugh, "Preserving the Presence of the Past," in *American Psychologist,* February 1983, 161.

Stanley Rachman, "Experimentally Induced Sexual Fetishism," in *Psychological Record* 18 (1968): 25.

Jennifer P. Schneider, "How to Recognize the Signs of Sexual Addiction," in *Postgraduate Medicine* 90 (1991): 171–82.

———, "A Qualitative Study of Cybersex Participants: Gender Differences, Recovery Issues, and Implications for Therapists," in *Sexual Addiction and Compulsivity* 7 (2000): 249–78.

Jennifer Schneider and Robert Weiss, *Cybersex Exposed: Simple Fantasy or Obsession?* (Center City, Minn.: Hazelden, 2001).

Dolf Zillmann, and Jennings Bryant, "Effects of Prolonged Consumption of Pornography on Family Values," in *Journal of Family Issues* 9, no. 4 (December 1988): 518–44.

———, *Pornography: Research Advances and Policy Considerations* (Hillsdale, N. J.: L. Erlbaum and Associates, 1989), 387–482.

———, "Pornography's Impact on Sexual Satisfaction," in *Journal of Applied Social Psychology* 18, no. 5 (1988): 438–53.

Notes

1. Albert Cooper, quoted in Jane E. Brody, "Cybersex Gives Birth to a Psychological Disorder," *New York Times,* May 16, 2000, F7.
2. Mark Schwartz, quoted in Brody, "Cybersex Gives Birth to a Psychological Disorder," F7.
3. Jennifer Schneider, quoted in Brody, "Cybersex Gives Birth to a Psychological Disorder," F7.
4. Quoted in Brody, "Cybersex Gives Birth to a Psychological Disorder," F7.
5. Jennings Bryant, Attorney General's Commission on Pornography, www.afo.net/statistics.htm (accessed April 28, 2005).
6. Jennings Bryant, Attorney General's Commission on Pornography, unpublished, 1986.

CHAPTER TWO

How Our Sex-Saturated Media Destroys Our Ability to Love

LaNae Valentine

The ideal of most people is to find love, companionship, and fulfillment in an enduring romantic relationship. Learning to give and receive love is a fundamental aspect of being human and is central to one's sense of well-being. Since marital and familial relationships are so important to our eternal progression and happiness, it makes sense that Satan, who seeks "the misery of all mankind" (2 Nephi 2:18), would attack, distort, and assault our capacity to connect with others in genuinely loving ways.

The consumption of sexualized media compromises our ability to truly love. Such damage is done not only by content that is blatantly pornographic, but also by messages that are subtle and generally accepted. What was once relegated to back rooms and adult theaters has now become prime-time television entertainment, particularly in homes where premium cable networks are available. This pervasive soft-core pornography may be more insidious than traditional pornography because it has become so common that it is no longer recognized as pornography.

The media has become more pervasive and powerful than at

any other time in history. From the moment we wake up in the morning until we fall asleep each night, we are exposed to hundreds, even thousands of images and ideas from television, newspaper headlines, magazine covers, movies, websites, photos, video games, and billboards, each influencing us to believe a certain idea, act in a certain way, or buy a certain product. Many of us live in such media-centered communities that we may know more about characters in the media than we do about our own neighbors. The many facets of the media no longer simply influence our culture: they *are* our culture.

Most of us don't think much about the effects of this media exposure. We may even think that we don't pay much attention to it or that we tune it out. It's true that, unless we view them with a critical eye, messages about gender, sexuality, and violence often go unnoticed; however, the fact that we don't consciously recognize these messages does not diminish their effect on us. In fact, part of the power of advertising comes from the belief that we're not being affected by it. Like carbon monoxide, the pollution in our media does its work silently, gradually overcoming victims who remain unaware. Thus the media constantly influences our conception of reality and shapes our perspective on love, success, and what is normal. We are being blinded and affected in ways we don't fully understand.

In order to protect ourselves from the influence of these images and ideas, we need to understand how the media industries work. What are they telling us to want, and what reasons are they giving us? What are they influencing us to believe? What role is the adversary playing? Only if we recognize Satan's tactics for what they are can we protect and empower ourselves against these corrosive images and challenge the faulty ideologies they proliferate.

THE EFFECTS OF OUR SEXUALIZED MEDIA

The way sex is portrayed and the fact that sexual messages dominate the media lead to the following identifiable effects:

We Are Conditioned to Objectify People

Television, movies, music lyrics, videos, and advertisements send messages daily that it's normal to treat people as objects. Women, and less frequently men, are depersonalized, sexualized, and exploited in order to sell anything from computers to chewing gum. Objects are inanimate; they aren't alive. They are simply there to please us. Objects don't speak up, they don't disagree, they don't have opinions, they don't challenge us, and they don't walk away. We can control objects. If they do not satisfy us, we can get rid of them.

The danger in objectifying people is that we begin to believe that people are there to please and gratify us. They are not to challenge or disagree with us. This is in sharp contrast to the Lord's plan for us. Our interactions with real, moving, living people with unique personalities, talents, quirks, and traits are designed to help us develop godly attributes, including love.

The ability to see another's humanity is essential to our ability to love. When we view people as objects, we cease to see their humanness, identity, and uniqueness. We lose our ability to empathize with them, to notice and respect their needs and feelings. The media constantly portrays images where a person's facial features are hidden so that instead of seeing a whole person, we see legs, breasts, midriffs, and derrieres. Women are airbrushed, digitally altered, cropped, and perfected to an unattainable standard of beauty. We forget that there are real women behind this façade. Reducing a woman to an object strips her of her dignity, intelligence, personality, gifts, and wisdom, emphasizing that her only value is to satisfy and to please, and that this is done through her body. Men and women alike are affected by these images.

Once human beings are objectified, it's not a stretch to see them as objects of consumption. Commercialism strengthens the appetite for buying and consuming and the idea of a mutually favorable exchange. The messages and images in the media often collapse consumerism and sex, erasing the boundaries between appetite and love and confusing our feelings regarding objects and real people. We are being conditioned to think of falling in love as finding the most attractive "package" available on the "market."

We Overemphasize the Visual

Throughout our culture—in movies, on television, in magazines, in public meeting places, on billboards, and on the Internet—men are continually assailed with images of naked and seminaked women who are thin and physically attractive. Women's bodies have become objects to be looked at, lined up, compared, and rated. Objective measures such as size, shape, and harmony of body parts become more important than human qualities. This glorification of the physical dimension trivializes other features of women and other aspects of a healthy relationship. This exaggeration of visual stimulation exploits, distorts, and compromises viewers' emotional and sexual health and creates dysfunction in the way males relate to women's bodies.

When women are presented as visually perfect, compliant sex objects, real women with real personalities become less appealing. Men rarely see images of women's bodies valued for their strength, their productive or reproductive capacity, or their general state of health. In fact, the bodies of women who contribute most to society, mothers, are noticeably absent in the media. Motherhood typically leaves women with stretch marks, enlarged hips and thighs, rounder buttocks, sagging breasts, cellulite-marked legs, thinned hair, and larger, flatter feet. The "battle scars" that should earn them respect for their devotion to their parental responsibilities may be viewed as ugly or repugnant by men who are so used to seeing women as objects.

The media's idealized images seduce men into having a false sense of entitlement and expectation regarding how all women *should* be. Rather than relate to real women, many men find it appealing to frequent a fantasy life dominated by visual images of idealized body types. Such fantasizing renders these men emotionally absent or unavailable for real encounters with real people, including their own wives and children.

We Develop Distorted Perceptions of Gender Roles

The pornographic images that surround us become encoded into the ways men and women think about themselves as male and female, masculine and feminine. Women are often portrayed in advertising with their heads cropped off, their eyes shaded, their mouths covered. They appear disoriented, ambivalent, childish, unnaturally thin, and sexy. These portrayals convey the message that women are barely there, they are not to make a sound, take up space, or be powerful in any way. The ultimate message that many women receive is that to be female is to be a sex object: their worth is associated with their ability to please and satisfy.

Historically, ads portray masculinity as muscular, strong, rebellious, forceful, and often violent. Men are portrayed as being powerful and in control. They are the conquerors, gladiators, and warriors. These images and ideas not only affect how men feel about women but also how men feel about the traditionally feminine traits within themselves, such as patience, gentleness, sensitivity, and kindness. These traits are needed in both genders in order to have satisfying relationships. When we label them feminine or masculine, we preclude the other gender from having them. Images that polarize masculinity and femininity are power-ful forces that keep us trapped in these dysfunctional roles and ideas about who we are.

We all notice these messages. Women understand that they are valued for beauty, passivity, and sex appeal, and that they will be left behind if they do not comply. They understand very well that the way to exert power is through their bodies, not their brains, and the way to communicate their value is through their physical appearance, their decorativeness, not through their voices, intel-lect, or talents. This is demonstrated by women's willingness to objectify themselves with immodest dress and behaviors.

We Come to Overemphasize Sex

Popular culture defines human connection almost entirely in terms of sex, exaggerating its relative importance in our lives and underemphasizing such other important things as friendship, loy-alty, fun, children, and community.

The Savior taught, "Whosoever looketh on a woman to lust after her hath committed adultery . . . in his heart" (Matthew 5:28). Lust is defined in the dictionary as the strong physical desire to have sex with somebody, usually *without associated feelings of love or affec-tion.*[1] It is not possible to view pornography and experience emo-tions of love, delight, generosity, consideration, sympathy, and kindness. We attempt to extract sex and experience it in isolation from the other aspects of genuine love. From every angle, when we are indulging in pornography, we are violating God's laws of love. Whenever we violate his laws of love we are separating ourselves from him, from his Spirit, and from one another. The end result is a state of numbness, isolation, and loneliness.

When sex is the overriding pattern in relationships, we don't develop other ways of relating. Although there are multiple ways that women could conceivably validate a man's masculinity, the media programs men to believe that the most critical is sexually. Gary Brooks explains, "Women's bodies . . . are objectified and treated as potential trophies—living testaments to a man's prowess as a financial success, skillful sexual performer, or fearless warrior."[2] When erotic contact is the prime objective, we become narrowly skilled. Men and women lose their ability to simply share their thoughts and feelings and to creatively think of ways to validate and please each other. They learn to sexualize all feelings of emotional and physical closeness, which cripples their ability to experience nonsexual intimacy. Basic skills such as showing respect are neglected. It is not possible to respect others without knowing them. Knowing others is not possible without talking, observing, and allowing them to be who they are. The blatant sexual images that surround us actually lead to disconnection rather than to connection. Our culture glamorizes the sexual adventurer, portraying him or her as sophisticated and powerful when in reality he or she may really be a frightened, inadequate person hiding from the complexity of full human relationships.

Sex in advertising, television, movies, and especially pornography is about a state of desire and arousal—never about real intimacy, fidelity, or commitment. Real love is more the result of choices and actions than feelings. Love works and lasts when those involved are committed to their relationship regardless of how they are feeling at the time. The addictive pursuit of passion or feeling without the work, effort, and behaviors involved in relationships actually leads to the erosion of real feeling and desire. By overemphasizing sex, the media actually trivializes it.

We Expect Instant Solutions and Instant Gratification

Perhaps the most insidious message of the media is the compelling myth of convenience—the illusion that it's possible to get from A to Z—desire to fulfillment—without having to do any work in between. Rarely do television, movies, magazines, and advertisers show us images of the work and effort required in maintaining relationships—or for the successful completion of any worthwhile project. What we see are images of ease and instant gratification.

We are bombarded on a daily basis with the idea that love should come easily and quickly, with little challenge or effort. We are flooded with messages that relationships should produce a constant state of exhilaration, comfort, and gratification. If by chance our relationships don't satisfy us, we can always turn to products to fill our needs. Rarely do we encounter the idea that love has more to do with what we bring to a relationship than what we get from it, or the idea that to make the most of a relationship, love must be patiently cultivated, along with such personal attributes as humility, courage, faith, discipline, and the capacity to love one's neighbor.

Consumers of media are conditioned to believe that they are entitled to sexual gratification at the drop of a hat, rather than understanding that the best sexual relationship is the result of a loving, respectful relationship carried out in the many aspects of everyday life.

These ideas run counter to our Heavenly Father's plan of happiness for us. Much of our mortal experience does indeed consist of studying, building, working, learning, making, planting, watering, waiting, waiting, and more waiting. Not to mention feeling, suffering, growing, repenting—all the verbs that enable us to acquire the attributes of kindness, patience, tolerance, and love.

WHAT WE CAN DO

What can we do to resist these destructive media messages and safely navigate our course through modern-day life?

Take Action

President Ezra Taft Benson noted that too many of us are complacent—willing to co-exist with evil so long as it does not touch us personally. We all need to wake up from this cultural trance. We are commanded in the scriptures to awake and arise from the dust (see Moroni 10:31), to awake to righteousness and sin no more (see 1 Corinthians 15:34). "*Awakening* means rousing one-self or being aroused in order to take action. Such calls to action are usually accompanied by urgency and intensity. It suggests an arousal from the passivity and vulnerability of sleep in order to seize the initiative, to take aggressive action."[3]

There is much need for a cultural revolution, for parents, educators, physicians, lawyers, and businesspeople to speak out and say enough is enough! Elder M. Russell Ballard stated, "The time has come when members of the Church need to speak out and join with the many other concerned people in opposition to the offensive, destructive, and mean-spirited media influence that is sweeping over the earth."[4] Each of us must get involved at the grass-roots community or national level, organize ourselves, and let our voices be heard.

Become Wise and Discriminating Consumers of Media

We must become more literate consumers of all forms of media and raise questions about what we are watching, reading, or listening to. At the heart of media literacy is the principle of inquiry. Huge and powerful corporate industries—alcohol, tobacco, junk food, diet, pornography—depend upon a media-illiterate population. Indeed, they depend upon a population that is gullible, lazy, oblivious, nonchalant, ambivalent, disempowered, and addicted.

Media researchers now say that television and the mass media have become so ingrained in our culture that we should no longer view the task of media education as providing "protection" against unwanted messages. Instead, our goal is to become competent, critical, and literate in all media forms so that we can control the interpretation of what we see and hear rather than letting the interpretation control us—so that we are the consumers instead of the consumed. We must help our children and ourselves to be more critical viewers and listeners. We must be mindful of the kind of music we listen to, the kinds of movies we're going to, and the kinds of TV shows we watch. What attitudes do they portray? Are they respectful toward all groups of people? We must be honest about how we are interpreting and being affected by these messages. Below are some questions we might consider and discuss with family members:

Who created this message and why are they sending it?

What techniques are being used to attract my attention?

What is omitted from the message?

What lifestyles, values, and points of view are represented in the message? Are they respectful toward girls and women, to all groups of people? Do they support the values that are important to me?

Do the lives portrayed in my favorite TV shows contribute anything positive to my life?

Does repeated exposure to crime and violence contribute to my peace of mind?

Does engaging in these media forms invite the Spirit?

Are the images I'm exposing myself to inviting me to be a more sensitive, loving person?

Simplify Our Lives

Voluntary simplicity is a movement of many diverse groups and organizations who are trying to reduce consumption and consumerism. We can limit our consumption not only of goods, but also of television watching, Internet surfing, radio, CDs, and movies. We can encourage and engage in such other activities as reading, sports, drama, volunteerism, and environmentalism. Here are some suggestions:

Turn off the TV for a month. Many who have taken on this challenge report their homes are more peaceful and more joyful. They have more time for conversations with one another, more time to do things they've always wanted to. And family members get along better.

Have a buy-nothing day or week. Once people in our society shopped to buy what we needed, period. Now that we don't need much, we shop for other reasons: to impress each other, to fill a void, to kill time. Take a break from shopping and see what happens.

Cancel magazine subscriptions. Research shows that women feel guilty and inadequate after viewing magazines for three minutes.

Practice Delaying Gratification

Rather than expecting quick fixes, we must be willing to face problems and do the work required to find solutions. It is in this process of meeting and solving problems that we grow spiritually and find meaning in life. Elder Boyd K. Packer reminds us: "We live in a day when the adversary stresses on every hand the philosophy of instant gratification. . . . We are indoctrinated that somehow we should always be instantly emotionally comfortable. When that is not so, some become anxious—and all too frequently seek relief. . . . It was meant to be that life would be a challenge. To suffer some anxiety, some depression, some disappointment, even some failure is normal. Teach your members that if they have a good, miserable day once in a while, or several in a row, to stand steady and face them. Things will straighten out. There is a great purpose in our struggle in life."[5]

Work on Relationships and Real Connections

We must be willing to do the work required to nurture and foster relationships. The real work on relationship begins when the infatuation ends and when things get hard. Erich Fromm suggests that loving is an art and like any other art it requires a great deal of discipline, concentration, and patience to master. He stresses that the ability to love depends on one's capacity to emerge from narcissism; it requires the development of humility and the ability to accept what is instead of distorting it with one's self-interest, needs, and fears. We must be humble and courageous as we strive to know and be known by others. It might take a whole lifetime to master the art of relationships and the art of loving.

In *Bonds That Make Us Free*, C. Terry Warner refers to an idea that made an impression on him as a young boy: "To the immature, other people are not real."[6] When other people are not real to us, their feelings and desires do not matter as much as our own—if at all. They are a mere "It" whose inner life is unimportant. In contrast is what Martin Buber calls an I-You or I-Thou way of being, in which we regard others as having their own inward lives and when we respect their hopes and needs as we do our own.

Personification is the process of reversing the effects of objectification. Since objectification strips people of all their human qualities and turns them into an unreal fantasy, personification reattaches the humanness and reality of them. It requires that we develop respect for other people's unique individuality. To Erich Fromm, "Respect means . . . I want the loved person to grow and unfold for his own sake, and in his own ways, and not for the purpose of serving me."[7] The following questions might help us personify the human beings we see in the media:

Who is the person in this image? Does he or she have a name? Whose wife, daughter, sister, mother, or friend might she be? Whose husband, son, brother, or father?

In real life, if I were to meet them at a social function, how would I approach them?

What would I find interesting about this person as I get to know him/her?

What would I like to know about him/her?

What might they find interesting about me?

In addition to seeing others as real, we have the opportunity to express who we really are more fully as well. However, it's difficult to be close to and truly known by another. Many of us experience the fear of not being enough and the associated feelings of inadequacy. The reason we're frightened of intimacy is probably because at some time in our lives our intimate experiences were frightening. Risking being close to another throws us back to that time when we decided that being close was too scary and when, as a result, we decided that we were not lovable or acceptable. Intimacy is showing another person the parts of ourselves that we believe to be unworthy and thereby risking that they might turn from us. As we risk speaking truthfully and exposing our real selves, we come to understand when and why we learned to hide.

Basically, we learned to hide because being ourselves wasn't validated. We learned instead to be the person we thought would please the people around us. We learned to hide our real self and developed a self that we thought would be more acceptable to others. We must turn around this process of hiding. How can we be in a relationship if our real self is missing? Being in a relationship requires a willingness to stop defending ourselves against pain and discomfort, because turning this process around will be uncomfortable.

Relationships require us to face, then strip away, the layers we have constructed between us and allowing someone to make a difference to us. Addictive behaviors are a convenient way to avoid the closeness and growth of relationships as they deaden us to the valuable feelings that reveal who we are. In order to achieve intimacy, we must be willing to show our feelings and talk honestly about ourselves. It's the only way to be close and to feel truly alive.

In order to express our true selves, we must be able to experience and express a wide range of feelings. The real self does not block feelings or deaden the impact of emotions but provides a sense of what is appropriate to express. This is a delicate process. We cannot deaden ourselves to our feelings or to ourselves if we want to have intimate relationships with others. Addictions deaden us, intimate relationships invite us to awaken and live. The following are some suggestions to help in this process:

• Admit to human failings.

• Recognize the need for other people.

• See the emptiness of a life compulsively controlled by the need for admiration and achievement.

• Discover the ability to lead an ordinary life—one with real joys, sorrows, successes, and disappointments.

• Rid yourself of the desire for immediate perfection in yourself and others.

• Encourage connection, expansion, and playfulness. It's more rewarding than being private and secretive.

Coming to more fully know others and be more fully known ourselves requires a lot of work over a long time. Genuine love and its full expression in marriage and family life are not for the faint of heart. But, as Elder Boyd K. Packer notes: "Marriage is not without trials of many kinds. These tests forge virtue and strength. The tempering that comes in marriage and family life produces men and women who will someday be exalted."[8] Catherine Thomas calls marriage "a tutorial in love. Each [spouse] has something to teach the other, and the learning is usually not easy. . . . And so marriage, perhaps more than any other relationship . . . is our greatest spiritual challenge and has the greatest potential, along with parenthood, to make godly beings of us."[9]

SUGGESTED READINGS

M. Russell Ballard, "Let Our Voices Be Heard," *Ensign,* November 2003, 16–18.

Gary R. Brooks, *The Centerfold Syndrome* (San Francisco: Jossey Bass, 1995).

Erich Fromm, *The Art of Loving* (New York: Harper and Row, 1956).

Jean Kilbourne, *Deadly Persuasion* (New York: The Free Press, 1999).

Boyd K. Packer, "Marriage," *Ensign,* May 1981, 13–16.

————, "Obedience," *BYU Speeches of the Year* (1971).

————, "Solving Emotional Problems the Lord's Own Way," *Ensign,* May 1978, 91–93.

M. Catherine Thomas, *Spiritual Lightening* (Salt Lake City: Bookcraft, 1996).

Michael Ventura, "Beauty Resurrected," *Family Therapy Networker* 25 (January/February 2001).

Joseph Walker, "Reel Life vs. Real Life," *Ensign,* June 1993, 15–20.

C. Terry Warner, *Bonds That Make Us Free: Healing Our Relationships, Coming to Ourselves* (Salt Lake City: Shadow Mountain, 2001).

M. S. Wylie, "Our Trip to Bountiful," *Family Therapy Networker* 21 (May/June 1997): 28.

NOTES

1. *Encarta World English Dictionary,* s.v. "Lust" (New York: St. Martin's Press, 1999), 1074.

2. Gary R. Brooks, *The Centerfold Syndrome* (San Francisco: Jossey Bass, 1995), 7.

3. *Dictionary of Biblical Imagery,* Leland Ryken, James C. Wilhoit, Tremper Longman III, eds. (Downers Grove, Ill.: InterVarsity Press, 1998), 64.

4. M. Russell Ballard, "Let Our Voices Be Heard," *Ensign,* November 2003, 17.

5. Boyd K. Packer, "Solving Emotional Problems the Lord's Own Way," *Ensign,* May 1978, 93.

6. C. Terry Warner, *Bonds That Make Us Free: Healing Our Relationships, Coming to Ourselves* (Salt Lake City: Shadow Mountain, 2001), 41.

7. Erich Fromm, *The Art of Loving* (New York: Harper and Row, 1956), 23–24.

8. Boyd K. Packer, "Marriage," *Ensign,* May 1981, 15.

9. M. Catherine Thomas, *Spiritual Lightening* (Salt Lake City: Bookcraft, 1996), 62.

CHAPTER THREE

Pornography and the Loss of Liberty

John L. Harmer

M y first courtroom appearance with regard to a pornographic publication was in 1964 in the Superior Court of Los Angeles. From that time until now I have observed with great anxiety the ever-increasing presence of pornography in our society, along with the ever-increased degree of degenerate carnality, vileness, and perversion contained within the various forms of pornographic materials now awash in the American culture. For many years I asked myself the question, "Where will it all end?" The answer is now all too clear that if the present trend continues the "end" will soon come, and it will be defined by the ultimate loss of our freedoms and liberties as endowed to us by the nation's founding fathers. I am convinced that such loss of our freedom will be the direct result of the inundation of our society with pornography.

As individuals consume pornography and then become consumed by it, they descend into darkness, and the "light of Christ" is driven out of their souls. The prisoner of pornography loses the capacity to exercise agency. They become as those Nephites that Mormon described to his son Moroni as having become "past feeling" (Moroni 9:20). At that point neither law nor conscience are capable of imposing any restraint upon their actions. Their addiction has enslaved their body, mind, and spirit.

As an individual becomes addicted to pornography, the capacity for self-restraint is eroded away. The greater the degree of perversion in the materials the pornography addict consumes, the less capacity there is for self-discipline under the influence of the Spirit and the written law. Husbands become abusive of wives and children. Women who have become corrupted by pornography become contemptuous of those attributes of true femininity that are the nature of a virtuous woman. Young people of both sexes abandon restraint in language and behavior. They become coarse and rude.

When a sufficiently large segment of the population becomes thus estranged from the virtues and the norms that are the legacy of our nation's founding fathers, we will actually be in danger of losing our constitutional freedoms. Perhaps that seems like a strong statement, but the Constitution of the United States was based on the premise that the individual citizens were possessed of virtues that enabled them to be self-governing under law. Americans have remained free of tyrannical despots because they were willing to honor the laws of the land and capable of the self-restraint that such freedom under law required.

The darkness of pornography results in the loss of respect for dignity, virtue, and the rights of others. Thus, the protection of our individual rights, both legal and spiritual, requires that we do all in our power to protect ourselves and our loved ones from being seduced by pornography.

There have been many voices of warning regarding the ultimate loss of our political freedom if decadence (which is so pervasive in pornography) becomes accepted in our society. From scripture, from the writings of the founding fathers, and from the pens of honorable men and women of our own day have come ample testimony of the terrible fate that awaits us if we do not awaken to the awful situation that now confronts us.

Secret Combinations

In completing his father's work on the history of the ancient inhabitants of the American continents, Moroni came to the task of editing the twenty-four gold plates that comprised the record of the Jaredites. Having seen with his own eyes the destruction of the Nephite nation by secret combinations, he is amazed to learn from the Jaredite record that that nation was also destroyed by the emergence and the dominance of such secret combinations. Then, having received a direct commandment to do so (Ether 8:26), Moroni issued a prophetic warning to us, who he knew would one day receive his record, regarding such secret combinations. In that warning he clearly and explicitly prophesied of the loss of our freedom if we allowed this secret combination to prevail. Please carefully consider his somber warning:

"And whatever nation shall uphold such secret combinations, to get power and gain, until they shall spread over the nation, behold, they shall be destroyed; for the Lord will not suffer that the blood of his saints, which shall be shed by them, shall always cry unto him from the ground for vengeance upon them and yet he avenge them not.

"Wherefore, O ye Gentiles, it is wisdom in God that these things should be shown unto you, that thereby ye may repent of your sins, and suffer not that these murderous combinations shall get above you, . . .

"For it cometh to pass that whoso buildeth it up seeketh to overthrow the freedom of all lands, nations, and countries; and it bringeth to pass the destruction of all people, for it is built up by the devil" (Ether 8:22–23, 25).

After forty years of personal experience in confronting the pornography industry, I can state with absolute certainty that there does exist a very real secret combination of powerful forces that are determined to see among the American people the same change in attitude toward pornography as they have experienced toward homosexuality. This secret combination includes a variety of huge corporations, such as AT&T, Time Warner Corporation, EchoStar Communications, many of the major hotel chains, and above all, the entertainment industry.[1] It is international in scope and utilizes billions of dollars as it seeks to create a broad acceptance of pornography. Using the approach followed by those who created a broad acceptance of homosexuality, they propagandize that pornography is innocent private entertainment that in many instances is therapeutic for otherwise lonely or dispirited men and women.

More and more we see that big lie being accepted and repeated by presumably responsible medical and educational authorities.

Attacking the Youth

It will only be a few years until the present-day youth of twelve to eighteen years of age are adults. Consistent with the total lack of conscience that permeates the pornography industry, leaders of the industry have embarked on an extensive campaign to seduce these youth into an addiction to pornography. One way that campaign is being orchestrated is through music. One of the nation's most powerful and well-financed pornographers, Larry Flynt, has entered into contractual relationships with a variety of performers in the rap and hard-rock music industry. The youth who are the principal audience for these individuals are now being brainwashed into accepting pornography through recorded lyrics and live performances.

Thus, it may only be a few years until we have a large group of adult citizens who have been so desensitized by the pornographer's message that they will have no ability to identify with the standards of decency and self-restraint that are essential for a society that is to be ruled by law and not by force. The rap music industry features porn stars on their national tours, where thousands of young fans become acquainted with the top names in pornographic motion pictures and videocassettes. These national tours generate millions of dollars in profits when they sell out stadiums and concert halls all around the country. There is no age limit on these shows. The porn producers are supplying autograph and merchandise booths to cater to the thousands of young fans who attend these live rap shows. An immense amount of money changes hands at such venues. When a major porn producer like Flynt is able to team up with an industry that sells millions of albums to children as young as thirteen (which are also listened to by younger children), the porn industry gains a new market among the vast number of early teenagers.

Wall Street and Porn "Terrorists"

Such venal and corrupt individuals as Larry Flynt are not the only ones engaged in the conspiracy to destroy our liberties by destroying the moral foundation of our society. In testimony given before the United States Federal Communication Commission (FCC), Janet LaRue, Chief Legal Counsel for Concerned Women of America, made the following statement:

"Some mainstream corporate giants, allured by immense profits, have reached a new low trying to reach a new high on Wall Street. Profiting from porn-peddling is a dirty ring around the white collars at AT&T, MCI, Time Warner, Comcast, EchoStar Communications, GM's DirecTV, Hilton, Marriott, Sheraton, Radisson, VISA, MasterCard, and American Express. The corporate prospectus and reports to shareholders of these 'Porn-Wallers' will never mention [the disgusting pornographic titles that] are revenue producers. It is no surprise that most corporate leaders are unwilling 'to speak publicly about the sex side of their business.' "[2]

Continuing her testimony, Ms. LaRue quoted one major Wall Street investment house executive, who in a response to a request as to how he could justify the initial public offering of the shares of stock of a firm that produced and distributed hard-core pornography, said: "I'm not a weirdo or a pervert, it's not my deal. I've got kids and a family. But if I can see as an underwriter going out and making bucks on people being weird, hey, dollars are dollars. I'm not selling drugs. It's Wall Street."[3]

Few events in our history have awakened the American people to an awareness of the threat to their freedom as did the terrorist attacks of September 11, 2001. In this instance, the threat originated with a worldwide conspiracy of terrorists who are determined to destroy governments based upon democracy. Because of the subtlety and ease with which pornography enters the lives and homes of its victims, we see no corresponding awakening to the danger to our freedom and liberty from the secret combinations extracting billions of dollars per year in profits from pornography. Those who have attempted to awaken the nation to an understanding of this peril are universally derided as "eccentric religious fundamentalists." In an insightful response to the question as to why government should concern itself with the danger of pornography, a British jurist, Lord Patrick Devlin, as chairman of a royal commission on the issue of pornography in the United Kingdom wrote:

"An established morality is as necessary as good government to the welfare of society. Societies disintegrate from within more frequently than they are broken up by external pressures. There is disintegration when no common morality is observed, and history shows that the loosening of moral bonds is often the first stage of disintegration, so that society is justified in taking the same steps to preserve its moral code as it does to preserve its government and other essential institutions. The suppression of vice is as much the law's business as the suppression of subversive activities."[4]

Wise Counsel from the Past

The founding fathers of this nation gave us counsel that clearly confirms what their attitude would have been toward pornography. If they were among us today, they would warn that if the perversion of pornography is allowed to gain ascendancy in our society and its basic institutions (including the family, the school, and the church), it will ultimately destroy the republic. They understood that teaching moral values brought the assurance that the nation would be protected by those moral values. If we fail to teach and live such moral values, the tragedy of hedonism and the loss of our political freedom will inevitably result.

Consider the following comments from some of our founding fathers. First, from George Washington: "Of all the dispositions and habits which lead to political prosperity, Religion and morality are indispensable supports. In vain would that man claim the tribute of Patriotism who should labor to subvert these great Pillars of human happiness—these firmest props of the duties of Men and citizens."[5]

From Thomas Jefferson: "It is the manners and spirit of a people which preserve a republic in vigor. A degeneracy in these is a canker which soon eats to the heart of its laws and constitution."[6]

Finally, from John Adams: "Statesmen . . . may plan and speculate for Liberty, but it is Religion and Morality alone, which can establish the Principles upon which Freedom can securely stand."[7]

In a more recent time, President Theodore Roosevelt observed, "Freedom is a gift that cannot be enjoyed save by those who show themselves worthy of it."[8]

Showing ourselves "worthy of" freedom was the essence of the prophetic warning that came to us from Moroni, as quoted above. The rationale of our founding fathers, and many subsequent leaders such as Theodore Roosevelt, is very clear and concise. To be free of tyrannical government a people must be willing to be governed by the supremacy of law. The greater the commitment to the supremacy of law, the greater their ability to be self-governing under law.

Clearly the same rationale applies to individuals. Those who cannot conquer the appetites and passions of the flesh are destined to live as prisoners to those appetites and passions. The inevitable and inescapable effect of pornography in the life of any individual is the loss of the will and the self-discipline to govern one's appetites and passions. Those who become enslaved in this fashion are no longer capable or worthy of living in a society that is free.

Edmund Burke wrote a very insightful analysis that can be applied to our present problem. His words explain why the increased production and distribution of pornography in America looms as the most serious threat to our continued survival as a nation and the preservation of our freedoms under our Constitution. He wrote:

"Men are qualified for civil liberty in exact proportion to their disposition to put moral chains upon their own appetites—in proportion as their love of justice is above their rapacity; in proportion as their soundness and sobriety of understanding is above their vanity and presumption; in proportion as they are more disposed to listen to the counsel of the wise and good, in preference to the flattery of knaves. Society cannot exist unless a controlling power upon the will and appetite is placed somewhere; and the less of it there is within, the more there must be without. It is ordained in the eternal constitution of things, that men of intemperate minds cannot be free. Their passions forge their fetters."[9]

When I have been in the presence of those who produce, distribute, and defend pornography, I have invariably felt the powers of darkness and the fearful sensation of impending evil. When I have been in the presence of those whose lives have become enmeshed with the consumption of pornography, I have sensed the despair and bitter sorrow of one who has lost his or her personal freedom and is now bound in the chains of hell. There are communities in our land that have become so inundated with pornography that this same spirit of darkness and this same sensation of impending evil dominate the entire community. When the individuals and families in such a community have become so possessed, they and their community are destined to a tragic end.

A Timely Warning

I conclude by returning to the words of Moroni as found in the book of Ether. Notwithstanding his very specific warning of the consequences that will befall us if we do not heed his words, Moroni leaves us with an understanding that his words, combined with our works, may yet save the day.

"Wherefore, I, Moroni, am commanded to write these things that evil may be done away, and that the time may come that Satan may have no power upon the hearts of the children of men, but that they may be persuaded to do good continually, that they may come unto the fountain of all righteousness and be saved" (Ether 8:26).

As I have appeared before numerous audiences throughout the United States, I have concluded that "they that be with us are more than they that be with them" (2 Kings 6:16). We have every reason to be assured that virtue will triumph over vice, that light will dispel darkness. An intense combination of faith and works by the decent people of this nation will yet be able to push back the seemingly unstoppable tidal wave of degeneracy that is threatening us.

The Lord knows the desires of our hearts. He knows that many of us desire to retain the freedoms so honorably purchased for us by our founding fathers. I do not know how it will be done, but I am certain that Moroni was not commanded to write these things just to see it all end. Our society may have to be destroyed by the sweeping powers of divine justice when the cup of iniquity is full, but that will not be the end for the righteous.

I paraphrase the German poet philosopher Goethe, who wisely noted "that to truly possess anything inherited from the fathers we must earn it anew." The founding fathers cannot be asked to return and once again deliver us from political slavery. Under the leadership of the Latter-day Saints, the good and honorable people of this nation must arise and earn anew their legacy of freedom.

We learn from the book of Revelation that the war in heaven was won "by the blood of the Lamb, and by the word of their testimony" (Revelation 12:11). The war against pornography will be won by those who possess and express a testimony of the truth: that only by following the Son of God and obeying his commandments can we preserve and retain the liberties that allow us to enjoy the full potential of the gospel of Jesus Christ.

NOTES

1. www.cwfa.org/articledisplay.asp?id=2909&department=LEGAL& categoryid=pornography (accessed April 14, 2005).

2. www.cwfa.org/articledisplay.asp?id=2909&department=LEGAL& categoryid=pornography (accessed April 14, 2005). See also www.nytimes.com/2000/10/3/technology/23PORN.html

3. Brendan I. Koerner, "A Lust for Profits," *U.S. News & World Report*, March 27, 2000, 44.

4. Patrick Devlin, *The Enforcement of Morals* (Oxford: Oxford University Press, 1968), 13.

5. George Washington, in *The Founders' Almanac*, Matthew Spalding, ed. (Washington, D.C.: Heritage Foundation, 2002), 191.

6. Thomas Jefferson, in *The Founders' Almanac*, 134.

7. John Adams, in *The Founders' Almanac*, 190.

8. Theodore Roosevelt, quoted by George Mellon in *The Wall Street Journal*, 11 November 2003.

9. Edmund Burke, in *The Works of the Right Honorable Edmund Burke*, comp. Humphrey Milford (Oxford: Oxford University Press, 1907).

CHAPTER FOUR

Raising Decency Standards
in Our Communities

Shelley Y. DeVries

A statue of a young boy in Royalton, Vermont, honors Hannah Hendee, a Revolution-era American mother who rescued nine boys from certain death. In 1780 the British offered a bounty for every captured man and boy. The Hendee family was warned of the approaching raid. Mr. Hendee rushed to alert others, while Hannah escaped to the neighbors with their two children, a son and a daughter. Not far from home, an Indian party accosted Hannah and took seven-year-old Michael.

Alone but resolved, Hannah followed the Indian party down the river. Upon spotting the main group on the opposite bank, she crossed the treacherous and swift current. With firmness, Hannah demanded of a British officer, Captain Horton, that he see to the return of her son. He replied that the Indians were not in his control. Hannah importuned: "You are their commander and they must and will obey you."[1] Horton continued to resist, but finally, "intimidated by her determination, Captain Horton told her to take her son and leave. He could face an army of men but not a mother driven by the strongest of emotions."[2]

With difficulty, Captain Horton convinced the Indians to part with Hannah's son. Then he insisted her little family remain at camp until nightfall. As the day wore on, neighborhood boys arrived with succeeding Indian parties. Upon seeing Hannah, the boys desperately clung to her skirts. Emboldened by the rescue of her own son, Hannah entreated for and secured their release as well. No doubt with God's help, Hannah managed to cross the river with nine boys and her daughter. Hannah led the children three miles farther into the woods until the safety of morning.

Today, we face a foe equally willing to take our households captive. This enemy seeks to enslave society with inappropriate materials ranging from the salacious to hard-core pornography. The war it wages is backed by unlimited resources, greed, and a destructive agenda. During the past decade, pornography has spread freely with little opposition. Without hesitation, we must find Hannah's uncommon resolve and determination to protect our homes and communities from the plague of pornography.

Latter-day Saints are directed to make a difference by standing up for decency. President Gordon B. Hinckley counsels: "Billions of dollars are involved for those who pour out pornography, for those who peddle lasciviousness, for those who deal in perversion, in sex and violence. God give us the strength, the wisdom, the faith, the courage as citizens to stand in opposition to these and let our voices be heard in defense of those virtues which, when practiced in the past, made men and nations strong, and which, when neglected, brought them to decay."[3]

We are being recruited as foot soldiers—not just casual cheerleaders—in the fight between good and evil. However overwhelming the task may appear, God will direct our efforts to reclaim decency.

PROTECTING OUR HOMES

Pornography has gradually desensitized our culture. Some Latter-day Saints have come to accept suggestive materials. Some fool themselves into thinking they are sophisticated enough to handle the world's sexual messages. Others are simply apathetic. Comments like, "It doesn't bother me" or "There are just a few bad parts" are warning signs that our spirits are being desensitized and thus we are no longer shocked by something that once bothered us. Elder Bruce C. Hafen cautions, "Too many Latter-day Saints today somehow believe they can stand with one hand touching the walls of the temple while the other hand fondles the unclean things of the world."[4] In addition, Elder M. Russell Ballard warns:

"Often media's most devastating attacks on family are not direct or frontal or openly immoral. Intelligent evil is too cunning for that, knowing that most people still profess belief in family and in traditional values. Rather the attacks are subtle and amoral—issues of right and wrong don't even come up. Immorality and sexual innuendo are everywhere, causing some to believe that because everyone is doing it, it must be all right. This pernicious evil is not out in the street somewhere. It is coming right into our homes, right into the heart of our families."[5]

Today obscene materials are channeled into homes by network TV, subscription TV, broadcast radio, Internet, movies, printed materials, mail, phone lines, music, and gaming media. It is not enough to resist the saturated sexual media: we must actively avoid it. To actively avoid illicit images, LDS families will need to create their own systems for judging media, products, and public places we patronize. We must establish sure boundaries.

This work must start in the home. We must define our own decency standards and adhere to them in our homes before we can work on raising community standards. Ratings generated by outside associations such as the Motion Picture Association of

America, gaming and music labels, and television companies are rarely good indicators of decency; we simply cannot rely on these as gauges of appropriateness. Defining a family standard of decency is one way to protect our families from the false and explicit sexual messages modern media delivers into our homes. The following steps provide one example of how your family can create a decency standard.

Hold one or two family council meetings with family members ages ten and older.

Discuss and write down what is sacred to your family. This list may include such things as God, our bodies, marriage, physical intimacy in marriage, and human life.

Talk about specific influences your family encounters that do not meet your standards for decency. This discussion may include such things as excessive violence, lifestyles with no moral code, profanity, and portrayals of inappropriate sexual relations, explicit or implied.

Create a set of personal definitions by which to measure appropriate entertainment. Definitions may include:

"We will not watch or read content with explicit images, either violent or sexual, that offend our family's belief in the sanctity of life, marriage, and procreation."

"We will not watch or read thematic or interpretive indecency that presents evil as good and good as evil."

"We will not watch or read materials with excessive profanity or actions that undermine the sacredness of Deity."

Family decency definitions should apply to printed materials, games, movies, television shows, Internet, and music. In order to implement the decisions of your family council, you should examine all entertainment and Internet sites used in your home to make sure they comply with your family's new standard.[6] Then educate yourself about any new media choices by using such resources as moviemom.com, screenit.com, www.parentstv.org, anysonglyrics.com, and www.mediafamily.org. These and other sources provide information to help you assess whether entertainment meets your family's decency standard.

In addition to creating a decency standard, we can use available technology to insulate our homes and reduce the risk of accidental exposure to inappropriate materials. These products include V-chip, Weemote Control, TVGuardian, video and DVD players with built-in TVGuardian, Time-Scout, video clubs with edited movies, TVBlanket, TiVo, and computer filters. The following websites offer more information as to the price and effectiveness of these resources: www.thefamily.com, www.tvblanket.com, and www.internetfilterreview.com.

Many families are hesitant to try computer filters because they are uncertain about what a good filter can do. Computer filters are the most valuable technology parents can use to protect children at home. Just as seat belts provide safety and control over a child's activities in the car, computer filters can provide protection and parental monitoring against pornography and harmful materials on the Internet. While technology solutions are not a replacement for parental guidance, they offer useful assistance in protecting families.

Generating a decency-driven society begins with actively creating standards at home. Citizens can then educate, patronize, and effect change in businesses, libraries, schools, and public places in their communities.

PROTECTING OUR COMMUNITIES

Hannah Hendee is a good example of someone who didn't stop with preserving her own son. As she looked at that band of Indians, Hannah probably wished somebody could help her. What would have happened to those nine children without her willingness to confront the enemy alone? The question Hannah might have asked herself—"If not me, then who?"—also applies to rescuing today's neighborhoods from pornography's grip. President Gordon B. Hinckley has counseled, "We can and must maintain the standards for which this Church has stood since it was organized. There is a better way than the way of the world. If it means standing alone, we must do it."[7]

Resolving Questions

Many concerned citizens wonder how and where they can begin raising decency standards in the community. Valid questions include "What about the First Amendment and censorship?" "How do I approach a store manager about materials he or she has chosen to display in his or her store?" and "What difference will it make if I voice my opinion?" Such questions often arise as individuals begin the process of working with businesses and elected officials.

How and where do I begin to make changes in my community? Citizens should be aware that distribution channels for hard- and soft-core pornography in their communities can include retail outlets, billboard and in-store advertising, libraries, hotels with "adult entertainment," movie theaters, and sexually oriented businesses. Alone or with a group, you can begin making changes by requesting that inappropriate materials be removed from view at stores or public places frequented by your family.

What about the First Amendment and censorship? "The U.S. Supreme Court has never held that pornography is protected by the First Amendment. Slander, conspiracy, false advertising, libel, and certain other kinds of speech are not protected by the First Amendment either."[8] The First Amendment does guarantee individuals the right to speak up and request changes in their communities. Some business owners, however, believe that because soft-core pornography is legal, removing it is considered censorship. Actually, censorship in this setting applies to having an unauthorized group remove or cover materials without the consent of the owner. Just as individuals can decide what products come into their own homes, privately owned businesses have a First Amendment right to decide what is available in their stores. If the issue of censorship comes up, citizens can introduce the idea of "responsible ownership." Responsible ownership is what companies do to be good neighbors to local residents and other businesses. Community businesses have a responsibility to pay attention to the citizens' attitudes toward soft-core pornography because it is a safety issue for children, women, and families. Pornography never addresses the harmful consequences of its use, such as AIDS, rape, relationships without commitment, objectification of women, and unrealistic sexual expectations. Citizens have the right and responsibility to send a message about what kind of materials are and are not acceptable in their community.

At a lunch meeting with a local store, I asked that they cover certain offensive merchandise or not carry it at all. This business leader was very supportive and shared my concerns. I was informed that the store had in fact previously covered the questionable materials but decided to reverse its policy after several customers made accusations of censorship. Upon hearing the difference between censorship and responsible ownership, this executive felt empowered to make decisions based on the company's values instead of on inaccurate accusations.

How do I approach a business if I have concerns? Effective communication requires that individuals be firm without using emotional tirades and threats. Anger may temporarily intimidate store managers into removing merchandise, but businesses are less apt to listen to irate customers and often return to former practices. Bryan Youd, a business consultant and author, said, "We must not become shrill or act contrary to that which makes us Christian. We must act within appropriate bounds of kindness, respect, patience and love unfeigned."[9] The Golden Rule applies: you can correctly presume managers want for their children, grandchildren, nieces, and nephews what you want for yours. A successful approach includes the assumption that store personnel will help you, along with the use of polite but firm communication, a sincere compliment, sticking to the issue, and patience.

Recently, I found an offensive men's magazine on the regular rack of a department store. I expressed my concerns to the stationery department manager, who adamantly argued with my polite request to cover or remove the offensive magazine. Despite my best efforts to remain calm and logical, the store clerk became more and more angry. It occurred to me that this woman had no authority to make changes but constantly took backlash from customers. I felt prompted to change my approach and commented, "I can see you are doing your best to keep the stationery department in order, and I appreciate your time in listening to my concerns. Can you direct me to a manager or corporate buyer in charge of purchasing magazines for your store?"

An instant change came over the stationery department manager, who now solicited my help: "I am tired of awful magazine covers. Can you talk with the manager? No one listens to me."

Eventually I spoke with the head manager, who not only removed the magazine but committed to review magazine shipments each week. Even if my request had been denied, the Spirit had given me the answer on how to leave the door open for further dialogue with the manager. Remaining calm on the outside, despite the boiling emotion inside, will bring us much success in the struggle to regain lost community standards.

Taking Action

The future safety of our families depends on what we do now. Bishop H. David Burton warns, "Satan is the commander in chief of deception. He is not satisfied with just taking prisoners; he wants the souls of men."[10] Members of society can work on raising community standards today by doing the following six things:

1. Join with like-minded citizens. While one person fighting pornography can produce amazing results, a very vocal 5 percent appears to be a majority. Citizens can begin by joining a local decency group. If no local group exists, invite several friends to discuss pornography issues in your community. Assign a member to search the Internet for educational materials, ideas, and existing decency organizations. It is important that neighborhood groups exercise patience and focus on one project at a time. A Utah group called Communities for Decency spent three years working with local libraries and elected officials to finally get Internet filters on library computers. Because the opposition has so much money and power, community groups must remember this effort will be about small victories and big celebrations.

Because of the salacious nature of materials involved, your group will need to develop guidelines to limit exposure to indecent materials. For instance, if in the process of fighting pornography you ask men to view obscenity, you are placing undue risk on those involved. Women need to take the lead where pornography is perceptible. President Boyd K. Packer reminds us, "Men and women have complementary, not competing, responsibilities."[11] Remember that during the Indian raid of 1780, Mr. Hendee warned the neighbors while Hannah confronted the captain. Together they saved many lives. Equally important is the role men and women can play today in safeguarding the home and community from pornography.

2. Work with elected officials to create a safer moral atmosphere in your community. An important step in the antipornography effort is to be aware of local ordinances and state laws that regulate indecent and obscene materials. To find out what these are in your area, request information from your city council and state representatives. Constituents can write letters articulating their opposition to pornography and encouraging elected officials to enforce current laws and ordinances. Bruce Taylor from the United States Justice Department urges citizens to insist that district and county attorneys take on those who make and sell pornography. "You've got to come up with an answer when your grandkids say, 'Grandma, Grandpa, what did you do in the war?' . . . For those who say prosecutors have better things to do, 'There's nothing more important than protecting women who are getting abused and children who are corrupted' by the influence of pornography."[12]

All cities, regardless of size, should have an ordinance regulating sexually oriented businesses. Sexually oriented businesses (SOBs) such as adult bookstores, adult theaters, strip clubs, and escort services contribute to increased crime and decreased property values. Local governments may not be able to ban some of these types of businesses, but they can regulate hours of operation, licensing, structural configuration, and proximity to protected areas such as schools, churches, and residences.[13] Dan Panetti, vice president of the National Coalition for the Protection of Children and Families' legal department, suggests citizens urge elected officials to update their ordinances regulating SOBs every two to five years. Ordinances older than five years are less effective at protecting communities against new SOBs.[14] The best cure for sexually oriented businesses is prevention. Potential owners are aware of city codes and will look for unsuspecting areas in which to establish themselves. For more information about possible regulations for sexually oriented businesses, see www.ccv.org, www.planning.org, or www.nationalcoalition.org.

Elected officials are often aware that pornography in all its forms is affecting the community; and they typically appreciate hearing citizens' suggestions for making their city more family oriented. One idea is to attend a city council meeting and request that a city resolution be passed promoting child-appropriate standards in all businesses, schools, and public institutions.[15] This resolution sends the message to business leaders and citizens that elected officials oppose materials deemed unsuitable for children and families.

It is important to have and enforce decency laws and ordinances, but citizens should not rely on the current laws as the only solution to indecency. The Miller Test is the legal standard for obscenity and is often effective in court only against the most vile pornograpy. Most communities sanction a higher decency standard. If we want high community standards, we will have to speak up to elected officials and business leaders.

3. Rid your community of indecent displays at retail media outlets. To create family-friendly retail outlets, citizens will have to address such issues as suggestive and soft-porn materials that are inappropriately displayed. The following ideas may provide help in encouraging businesses to become family-friendly.

Voice your concerns with phone calls and letters, seeking to alter store policies. Letters are a valuable tool because companies often keep written correspondence for reference. Citizens can S.P.E.A.K. up for decency by writing letters that include an introduction with a Sincere compliment, a statement of the Problem, Education on the issue, requested Action, and Kudos for their time in considering your request. Here is an example of one such letter:

> Dear Video Store Manager,
>
> My name is Joe and I rent videos at *Movies Tonight* because I enjoy the large selection your store offers customers. I often bring my four children (ages five to thirteen) to rent movies at the Cambridge store located on 5th Avenue. *(Sincere compliment)*
>
> I am concerned about the number of *Playboy* videos placed in the new release section at the eye level of children. The suggestive and soft pornography covers on the *Playboy* videos are highly offensive to myself and my family. *(State the problem)*
>
> Because you do business in our city, I am sure you care

about our children, youth, and families. Videos like *"Hollywood Sex Lives"* promote the degradation and abuse of women. As a responsible owner, I am sure you will agree soft-core pornography fails to show the negative consequences such as AIDS, rape, relationships without commitment, and unrealistic sexual expectations. *(Education)*

For the safety of women, children, and families, I am requesting that *Movies Tonight* discontinue the rental of all *Playboy*-type movies. I look forward to your response and will call back on February first to discuss this issue with management. *(Action)*

Thank you for your time and consideration in reviewing my request. *(Kudos)*

Sincerely,
Joe Q. Public

Collect and send petitions. Petitions must include printed names, full addresses, and signatures. You can save time by circulating a general citizen's petition in support of raising community standards and protecting children and families from harmful material. This petition can be used to address a wide range of community decency issues.

Share information with businesses and government officials about the harms and safety issues associated with pornography.

Arrange for a group of like-minded citizens to meet with store management. Appoint a composed spokesperson to present group requests and suggestions.

Arrange to meet with the presidents of state associations, such as the food industry association or the retailers association, to articulate your concerns on a state level. Provide these organizations with information on community standards, responsible ownership, suggested solutions, copies of state and federal law, petitions, and letters.

Compile a list of family-friendly businesses and urge friends to send thank-you notes and to patronize these businesses.

Create a family-friendly plaque or certificate for local businesses that are dedicated to raising community standards. Gather a group of neighborhood friends to write thank-you notes and meet with the manager to present the family-friendly award.

Send an article to local newspapers about the family-friendly awards given to businesses in your area.

Host a web site with a list of family-friendly retail outlets in your area. Advertise on a local radio station or TV consumer show.

Solicit pro-bono work from a marketing consultant or university management school to conduct market research. Survey local families to determine if their shopping habits are influenced by the family-friendly policies of retail outlets. Use this information to educate business owners, assist companies offering products like edited videos, and show the demand for "family-friendly" packages from subscription TV services. A sample conversation might be, *"We have just concluded some market research. A statistical sampling in your community indicates that 67% of respondents are 'highly influenced' or 'influenced' in choosing a grocery store if magazines are covered near the checkstand. Here's a list of suggestions to get customers back in your store."*[16]

Antipornography advocates will find long-term benefits by working with businesses to create family-friendly places to shop. Managers who invest time and effort in dealing with customers' concerns will remain more earnestly committed to maintaining high decency standards.

4. Take a stand on indecent advertising. In addition to working with retail outlets, citizens can take a stand with advertisers who are constantly pushing the envelope on TV, radio, billboards, and store fronts. Advertisements are well calculated to entice a certain demographic group and acquire new customers in a very competitive market. Antipornography efforts can counter the barrage of unacceptable advertising with a letter-writing or phone campaign. If your efforts do not result in immediate change, know that companies will likely consider your feedback for future ad campaigns. After seeing a very offensive shoe ad on TV, I contacted the corporate headquarters and spoke with an executive who validated my phone call: "This ad does not offend me, but I can assure you the best thing you can do is pick up the phone and call us. Your concerns have been heard by the board of directors."

Citizens can also be part of a successful crusade against illicit TV shows and advertisers. One Million Moms and Parents Television Council have convinced many sponsors to stop spending their advertising dollars on revolting TV shows and have pressured companies to drop repulsive advertisements. One Million Moms uses email software on their web site that makes it easy for citizens across the country to send messages to erring sponsors. From the web site, you can instantly send a customized or a prewritten email to the sponsors of inappropriate media. To join these effective grassroots movements, add your name to the email lists at www.onemillionmoms.com and www.parentstv.org.

Advertisers may also display offensive ads on billboards. The American Family Association has outlined the following way to take action on inappropriate billboards:

Contact the company that owns the billboard and make a respectful request to remove the advertising.

If your request goes unheard, take two pictures of the billboard. Keep one for yourself and send the other picture with the name, address, and phone number of the billboard owner and the exact address location of the billboard to Outdoor Advertising Association of America (OAAA), 1859 M Street NW, Suite 1040, Washington, DC 20036 for a determination whether the billboard owner is violating the OAAA code of ethical conduct.

If the billboard violates the OAAA code of ethical conduct, OAAA will contact the owner directly.[17]

5. Make libraries a safe place. Libraries are considered one of the greatest customs in civilized society. Sadly, many libraries are also providers of Internet pornography and other offensive materials. The American Library Association (ALA) Bill of Rights states that all patrons, regardless of age, should have equal access to all videotapes, printed materials, or information offered on the web.[18] The philosophy of ALA raises valid safety concerns. While the ALA promotes reading, book awards, and programs for children, it often refuses to protect patrons from Internet pornography. With the availability of the Internet, libraries are now reporting incidents of pedophiles approaching children, a hostile work environment for librarians,[19] exposure to hard-core materials for adults and children, and an increase in lewd behavior.[20]

In addition, libraries without computer-filtering technology open the community door to pornographers. In a recent obscenity court case in Texas, defense attorneys for a pornographer used availability of pornography at the library as evidence that the community accepted pornographic materials. The court ultimately decided in favor of the pornographer.[21] Unfiltered and unrestricted access to sexual materials at libraries contributes to lower decency standards. Taxpayers fund libraries and therefore have a voice in determining what happens at these public places.

On June 23, 2003, the United States Supreme Court upheld the Children's Internet Protection Act (CIPA), requiring libraries to install antipornography filters to protect children from pornography in order to receive federal funding. The United States Supreme Court's ruling sends a clear message that filtering library computers is a valuable step in protecting children. Ironically, some libraries are choosing to forgo federal funding in order to avoid filtering computers. Citizens can call their local library to determine when and if antipornography filters are scheduled to be installed.

In addition, the Supreme Court's CIPA decision empowers local elected officials to pass similar measures in your area. Dan Panetti, vice president of legal and public policy for the National Coalition for the Protection of Children and Families, "agreed that this ruling was a tremendous victory for the family, but added that there is much work to be done."[22] Library patrons should become knowledgeable on this issue and attend city or county council meetings to request a CIPA ordinance requiring antipornography filters in city or county libraries. Constituents can also work with elected officials to enact a statewide CIPA law requiring filtering technology in libraries prior to receiving state funds. With the help of citizens and legislators, Utah became the first state to enact a statewide CIPA law.[23] Contact the National Coalition for the Protection of Children and Families for suggestions on how to develop CIPA in your area.

The following ideas and resources may help when working on library issues:

Order and view the "Excess Access" video, which documents the dangers of the American Library Association's Bill of Rights and the growing power of the ALA. Order it online at www.afa.net.

Review the article "Library Protection Plan" at www.nationalcoalition.org under the Resources heading.

Ask to look at the public complaint file at your local library. Check for red flags that suggest a problem (patrons viewing pornography, children accessing inappropriate material, and so forth). What was the library's response to the complaints?

Attend a library board meeting to request stricter policies, enforcement, and filtering. Most library boards are more responsive to requests by a large group of citizens with letters or petitions.

Invite representatives from a local filtering company to explain how their product could be used in libraries to protect children.

Suggest that your library board offer a juvenile library card, which restricts children under eighteen from checking out videos, CDs, and materials that have an R rating.

Write a series of letters to the editor articulating citizens' concerns at libraries.

It's time for citizens to join hands with library boards and government officials to restore the safe haven once provided at this noblest of institutions.

6. Ask hotels to remove adult entertainment. Among the largest purveyors of pornography are mainstream hotels distributing adult entertainment, which generates $175 million per year.[24] One may ask why so-called adult entertainment is such a concern. In August 2003 the American Family Association posted an article on its web site claiming that a New York mother and her two children, ages eight and five, were watching a family movie at a Marriott hotel when it switched "to a full-blown sex movie."[25] This distressing incident and others like it make it imperative for citizens to take action. A grassroots effort in Cincinnati was successful in ridding communities of hotel adult entertainment after local hotels received warning letters from local prosecutors.[26]

Mainstream corporations profiting from pornography hope members of the community will be uninformed, turn their heads, or tire of making complaints.

Here are some additional ideas for changing hotel X-rated pay-for-view fare:

• Make phone calls to hotels in your area. Ask whether these hotels offer adult entertainment in rooms. Send a letter or an email to local owners as well as corporate headquarters asking corporations to remove adult entertainment.

• Check www.cleanhotels.com prior to traveling to use your vacation dollars in support of hotels like Omni that no longer carry adult entertainment.

• Send a thank-you letter to Omni, Best Western, and other hotels that are making financial sacrifices to stand on moral principles.

Meaningful change comes from the collective force of small actions. Individuals and grassroots organizations must realize that establishing decency standards takes patience and focus. After two years of diligently sending letters, making phone calls, and speaking with managers of a local grocery chain about covering illicit magazines, I received a phone call from the corporate vice president inviting me to a lunch meeting to discuss my concerns and solutions.

Remember, we will make greater progress if we do not attempt to focus on all fronts simultaneously. The most important difference we make in raising community standards is to continually voice our opinion regarding indecent displays and materials at retail outlets, libraries, and places highly frequented by families.

PURPOSE AND PERSEVERANCE

Hannah engaged in a bitter fight to save the children she loved. We must be just as willing to fight to preserve our families. Our children are exposed at an early age to an unbelievable amount of pornographic images. A worried stake president shared his concern over the youth in his care. He had interviewed one hundred young men regarding pornography use. Ninety-four out of a hundred young men admitted to viewing pornography occasionally or regularly.[27] The threat is real, and the danger is imminent. So much sexual stimuli has taken a toll on relationships, families, children, and crime.

Today, if parents and leaders are not part of the solution, we are part of the problem. The problem is we are losing too many sons and daughters, too many spouses, siblings, and leaders to pornography. The solution is active involvement, first in protecting our families and second in cleaning up our communities. The children and teenagers in our homes are being targeted as never before.

President Hinckley counsels us: "No one need tell you that we are living in a very difficult season in the history of the world. Standards are dropping everywhere. Nothing seems to be sacred anymore. The traditional family is under heavy attack. In the

Church we are working very hard to stem the tide of this evil. But it is an uphill battle. And we sometimes wonder whether we are making any headway. But we are succeeding in a substantial way. We see so many of our youth who are faithful and true and who look to us for encouragement and direction."[28]

One way to provide direction and encouragement for youth is by helping them create a personal decency standard. We cannot just *hope* that our youth will be able to resist pornography; we must empower them with strategies to actively avoid and defeat it.

Protecting our communities means being willing to take a stand against destructive forces like pornography. In "The Family: A Proclamation to the World" we read, "We call upon responsible citizens and officers of government everywhere to promote those measures designed to maintain and strengthen the family as the fundamental unit of society."[29] Just as Hannah maintained her resolve until her purposes were accomplished, we must never give up importuning elected officials, prosecutors, business leaders, and library boards to do their part in strengthening families by maintaining high decency standards.

As Latter-day Saints we know the end from the beginning—that good will ultimately triumph. From Elder Neal A. Maxwell we find the valiancy to endure to that end:

"Even then, time and the tides are against us, so that courage will be a key ingredient. It will take the same kind of spunk the Spartans displayed at Thermopylae when they tenaciously held a small mountain pass against overwhelming numbers of Persians. The Persians could not dislodge the Spartans and sent emissaries forward to threaten what would happen if the Spartans did not surrender. The Spartans were told that if they did not give up, the Persians had so many archers in their army that they would darken the skies with their arrows. The Spartans said simply: 'So much the better, we will fight in the shade!'"[30]

Pornography has darkened the skies, but there is a growing

bright spot on the horizon. It is God's foot soldiers willing to defend the sanctity of marriage and family no matter the price. In Royalton, Vermont, a statue of a young child is the fitting tribute to a mother with insurmountable courage. At the end of the day Hannah had successfully rescued nine boys. At the end of our lives, if each of us has such a prize, our efforts will not have been in vain.

NOTES

1. Evelyn Wood Lovejoy, *History of Royalton, Vermont; with Family Genealogies 1769–1911* (Burlington: Free Press, 1911), 133.
2. Lovejoy, *History of Royalton, Vermont*, 131–35; quoted and paraphrased in Boyd K. Packer, *Let Not Your Heart Be Troubled* (Salt Lake City: Bookcraft, 1991), 58–60.
3. Gordon B. Hinckley, "In Opposition to Evil," *Ensign*, September 2004, 6.
4. Bruce C. Hafen, "Your Longing for Family Joy," *Ensign*, October 2003, 28.
5. M. Russell Ballard, "Let Our Voices Be Heard," *Ensign*, November 2003, 16.
6. Bryan Youd, "A New Front in the War against Pornography: An Application of the Disciplines of Business Strategy to Advance the War against Pornography," February 1, 2003, xii-xiv, unpublished paper in author's possession.
7. Gordon B. Hinckley, "We Must Not Give Up, Stand Immovable," *Church News*, January 19, 2004, 3.
8. Victor B. Cline, in "A Conversation on Things of the Spirit, Pornography, and Certain Kinds of Movies, Books, and Magazines," *New Era*, May 1971, 8.
9. Youd, "A New Front in the War against Pornography," xxiv.
10. H. David Burton, "Heroes," *Ensign*, May 1993, 46.
11. Boyd K. Packer, "A Tribute to Women," *Ensign*, July 1989, 72.
12. Bruce Taylor, quoted in Linda Thomson, "Utahns urged to wage war on pornography," *Deseret News*, November 2, 2003, B05.
13. National Coalition for the Protection of Children and Families, "Zoning and Regulation," www.nationalcoalition.org/zoning.html (accessed February 1, 2004).
14. Dan Panetti, interview with Shelley Y. DeVries, 9 February 2004.

15. JoAnn Hamilton, "How to Begin Helping Our Community Become a Model City," www.strengthenthefamily.net (accessed October 12, 2004).

16. Youd, "A New Front in the War against Pornography," xix.

17. American Family Association, *A Guide to What One Person Can Do About Pornography* (Tupelo, Miss.: American Family Association), 17.

18. American Library Association, "Bill of Rights," www.la.org/ala/oif/statementspols/statementsif/librarybillrights.htm (accessed January 29, 2004).

19. John Harmer, "Newsletter," Lighted Candle Society, January 2003.

20. Family Research Council, "Dangerous Access, 2002 Edition: Uncovering Internet Pornography in American's Libraries" (Washington, D.C.: Family Research Council, 2000), 1–19.

21. Marsha Crosby, "Trial Shows Apathy toward Obscenity," *American Family Association Journal*, May 1999.

22. National Coalition for the Protection of Children and Families, "U.S. Supreme Court Ruling in Favor of Internet Filters in Libraries Is a Victory for Families," press release, June 23, 2003, www.nationalcoalition.org/pr062303.html (accessed February 9, 2004).

23. Shelley Y. DeVries, "Utah Legislature Passes Utah Children's Internet Protection Act," http://www.communitiesfordecency.org/CFDNews/successstories.html (accessed October 12, 2004).

24. Don Wildman, "Omni Hotels Drop In-Room Porn," *American Family Association Journal* 24, no. 1 (January 2000).

25. Tad Walch, "Porn battle jams Y. e-mail," *Deseret News*, September 23, 2003.

26. Candi Cushman, "Why the Wait," *Citizen*, December 2003.

27. Stake president on the Wasatch Front who wishes to remain anonymous.

28. Hinckley, "We Must Not Give Up, Stand Immovable," 3.

29. "The Family: A Proclamation to the World," *Ensign*, November 1995, 102.

30. Neal A. Maxwell, "The Prohibitive Costs of a Value-free Society," *Ensign*, October 1978, 52.

CHAPTER FIVE

Pornography: Satan's Counterfeit

Brad Wilcox

Can you tell the difference between a real $20 bill and a counterfeit one? In 1996, the United States Treasury issued a new design of the United States currency to make it easier to tell the difference. I remember the first time I saw the new $20 bill and saying to the teller, "I feel like we're starting this big monopoly game. This is like play money." She said, "No, it's real." I asked, "Why did they change it?" She said, "It's because our society has become so high-tech that it became too easy to counterfeit the older bills with scanners and computers and copy machines. So they had to produce a new bill that had security features built in that would help us distinguish between something real and something counterfeit."

I remember an article about a man who got a job to clean out a big semi-truck. The truck driver hired him to clean out the whole truck, inside and out, and then reload the entire truck. The truck driver paid him. The man thought the truck driver was paying him very generously and profusely thanked him. He just felt really lucky until he tried to spend the money. The cashier looked at the money and then called the manager over. He looked at it and said,

"I'm sorry, this won't be acceptable because it's counterfeit." He no longer felt so grateful. Instead, he felt ripped off, bitter and angry and discouraged because he had nothing to show for his time and work. All he had was a handful of worthless counterfeit bills.

Unfortunately, too many people, young and old, are settling for a different kind of counterfeit, Satan's counterfeit: pornography. And often they don't recognize it as a counterfeit until it is too late.

What is more beautiful than the human body? What is more wonderful and pure than true love between husband and wife? These sacred things have incredible eternal value. No wonder Satan tries to counterfeit them. So we need to ask if we are going to let him rip us off. Are we going to settle for his cheap imitation?

One LDS young man named Matt became involved in pornography when he was visiting at a friend's house. His friend showed him some magazine pictures. Matt thought, "I have always heard pornography described as dirty, smutty, filthy, ugly. But what I saw in those pictures didn't look all that ugly to me. It looked pretty appealing."

Matt began to allow himself to be fooled. He found himself tempted to view pornography more and more. He started to buy magazines, rent videos, look up pornographic sites on the Internet. He said, "It wasn't hard to find once I started looking." In the months that followed, Matt found himself less and less satisfied with what he viewed but sought pictures that were more graphic and extreme. He soon found that his unworthy thoughts led to unworthy acts, one after the other after the other. He said, "I let my hormones override all of my better judgment. Guilt, fear, and depression became my constant companions. Guilt because I knew what I was doing was wrong. Fear because I was terrified that my secret indulgences would be found out. And depression because I could no longer feel the Spirit and I began to hate myself."

Matt was caught in a very dangerous downward cycle. In an effort to ease his depression he would view pornography. Then he would feel bad about what he'd done and he'd feel depressed. Then in an effort to ease his depression he would turn again to pornography. And this cycle continued and continued until he found himself just as addicted to pornography as other people find themselves addicted to alcohol or to drugs. He acknowledged, "I first started viewing pornography because it was exciting, and it gave me a rush. Later I no longer turned to pornography to feel good, but to stop from feeling bad."

That sounds like an addiction. He was hooked.

"Over and over," he said, "I'd tell myself that I would never view pornography again, and then I'd go right ahead and do it." He was like the man who received counterfeit bills from the truck driver. He put all this effort into his addiction and received nothing real in return.

Matt realized that what he originally thought was good was just a fake. Matt felt embarrassed, frustrated, and angry. He said, "I think of the time and money that I spent on that stuff and I feel sick. It affected my relationships with others. It affected my Church activity. It affected my grades in school. It consumed my life, and I feel angry about that. But I know I have no one to blame but myself." Empty-handed and broken-hearted, this young man finally found the courage to approach his bishop. With the help of a priesthood leader, he began the long process of repenting and breaking unworthy habits.

Matt asserted, "Turning away from pornography has been one of the most difficult things I have ever done. Sometimes it is such a battle to control my thoughts that by the end of the day I feel physically, emotionally, and spiritually drained. I would give anything to have never started in the first place."

I admire Matt's determination to make positive changes and his determination to repent. I also admire him for letting me share his story with you because he says, "Perhaps it can help others be smarter than I was. Maybe it can help them avoid my struggles."

So how do we avoid getting sucked in? How do we avoid repeating Matt's struggles in our lives? How do we keep ourselves from getting fooled? The new $20 bills have security features. Each one of those security features can help us. They remind us of things we can do to detect and reject Satan's counterfeit of pornography.

Getting a Bigger Picture

The first security feature on the bill is an enlarged portrait. The portraits have more detail so they are more difficult to counterfeit. We need to keep a bigger picture in our mind. Consider our bodies. Satan will never have one. No wonder he would want us to devalue our bodies, to disrespect them. Consider the sacred nature of sex in marriage. Consider the bonding that takes place between a husband and a wife, and consider the wonderful opportunity to be able to bring children into this world and have a family. No wonder Satan would want us to degrade that. No wonder he would want us to look at that in a negative way. But if we can keep a big picture in mind of what our bodies are for, of what a marriage is for, and the role of sex in a marriage, it can help us reject the counterfeit. The bigger picture is who we are, not just right now, but eternally. Keeping that in mind is important because it is information that will really make a difference when it comes to resisting temptation.

Pornography can distort the picture of who we really are and what we are really here for.

I once spoke to a young woman. She wanted to be sure that no one else was around before she blurted out, "I'm just sick of it." I asked, "What? What are you sick of?" And she said, "I'm sick of it, okay? Sick of it!" I asked again, "What?" She said, "Okay, I am sick of never getting asked out, all right? All of my friends get asked out. I never get asked out. I'm sick of never getting asked to the dances. All of my friends get asked to the dances. I never get asked to the dances." She went on, "I'm sick of being stupid. I'm sick of being unpopular." She went through a list of at least fifty items. "I'm sick of my eyebrows because they don't quite match right here and I'm sick of my nose because it looks just like my mother's and I'm sick . . . " When she finally finished, I said, "Honey, you're looking in the wrong mirror."

Stephen R. Covey compares our view of ourselves to the images we see in circus mirrors. How many of you have ever been to a carnival? You've seen the circus mirrors. You walk in front of one mirror and all of a sudden your head disappears and you go in front of the next one and your hips are huge. You see a reflection of yourself but you're not fooled. You don't exclaim, "Oh my gosh, I'd better go buy new pants." You recognize yourself, but you know that what you're seeing is a distorted image. It's an exaggeration of who you are.

I said to this young woman, "As you look in the eyes of those around you, as you look in the eyes of your peers, you are only seeing a distorted image of who you are. Don't buy that as reality. Recognize it is a distorted image. You have the anti-drug speaker who comes to your school screaming, 'You're awesome.' And you walk out thinking, 'Man, I'm awesome, I'm awesome.' And you go into your English class and your teacher says, 'You are challenged. You are definitely challenged.' And then you go home and your mother says, 'You're so special. You're so special.' So as people try to tell you what and who you are, whom do you believe?"

We need to recognize that all of those images are distorted, and pornography distorts them even more. We are looking in circus mirrors if we trust the eyes of those who surround us. And we're looking into a darkened mirror if we trust pornography. We must lift our gaze and look in the eyes of a Heavenly Father who knows us, not just for who we are right now but for who we are eternally. In his eyes, we begin to see a reflection we can count on. We see the negative as clearly as we see the positive, but we will see an image that we can believe in because we will see an image that is not distorted. That is something you can count on, and that is something you can believe in.

Keep an enlarged portrait in mind. Remember who you are, who you are eternally.

Finding a New Background

The next security feature on the $20 bill is a new background. The new background has many lines and details that make it harder to counterfeit.

Sometimes when we're trying to make changes in our behavior we need to find a new background. When we are fighting the counterfeit of pornography, we may have to consider some stores off-limits. There may be some friends' homes you simply cannot visit. You need to pull that computer out of your bedroom and put it into a public place and install protection software that is controlled by your parents with a password you do not know. You're going to have to make an effort to change your background. To quit drinking, you will not get much help around the bar. To lose weight, you cannot hang around the bakery or refrigerator. We have to have the courage to change our backgrounds.

The new background on the $20 bill is filled with little lines. Stopping a bad habit is not just a matter of saying, "These things I won't do." It is more effective to say, "Here are some positive, productive, building, uplifting things that I am going to fill my life with." That's one way that we can combat the pornography counterfeit. We can reject it because we will be engaged in more positive activities that are truly meeting our needs.

The Little Things

The third security feature is called micro-printing. If you look at the $20 bill you will see the little letters right at the very bottom of the portrait. If you look closely at the $50 bill, Ulysses S. Grant's collar has scrolled on it little tiny letters that actually are words. If you scan a counterfeit bill into a computer, those words will not appear, and you will know it's a counterfeit. The micro-printing gives us the security of knowing what is real.

It's the same way in our lives. It's the little things that start adding up to make a huge difference in our lives. In Alma 37:6, we read about how small and simple things allow great things to come to pass. When my daughter was in second grade, we were having family home evening. I asked her, "Honey, what do we need to do to be happy?" And she said, "Just, just do all that stuff." At first I thought she was being a little flippant, but then I realized that she was right—just do all that stuff. By "all that stuff" she means say your prayers, read your scriptures, go to church, talk to your priesthood leaders, read the *Ensign* and *New Era*. These things will give you the help you need to keep going and to be able to make correct decisions. Just do all that stuff.

Creating a Glowing Thread

The fourth security feature is a glowing thread. We can't actually see it as we hold up a bill, but if the bill is placed under ultraviolet light, you can see a vertical, glowing thread that has been embedded in the mesh of the bill.

We can know what's real in our lives by the glow. A marriage that is filled with love, trust, faithfulness, and fidelity is a marriage that glows. It glows with love. There is no love in pornography, only lust. With pornography, there is no concern for another, only concern for self. There is no relationship to be strengthened, only nameless bodies, dehumanized sexual objects.

Victor B. Cline has stated that most pornography presents highly inaccurate, unscientific, and distorted information about human sexuality. It is sex *mis*-education—sex mis-education marketed for financial gain. Where there is no love, there is no glow. Where there is no glow, then Satan's counterfeit can be seen for the dull, dark, lifeless forgery that it is.

Perhaps you have heard bragging stories and inappropriate jokes. Perhaps you have seen sexually suggestive scenes in movies and on TV. Perhaps inside your head you've thought for just a second, "Am I missing something? Everybody else in the whole world is getting something and I'm not getting it."

It worries me to know some might wish they were not Latter-day Saints and could experiment. I'm worried not only because of the consequences that follow such behavior, but also because it tells me that in their minds they think they're the ones getting ripped off. They look at their friends who are making wrong choices, and they think those friends are getting something of value and that people who are living God's standards are getting ripped off.

The truth is that those who live God's standards are the ones who are going to get it. You're the one who will have what other people want. They are the ones who are getting ripped off. Sex and making love are two completely different things. If just having sex was so satisfying, and as great as they pretend, why are they always looking? Why are they continually searching? Why do they jump from Internet site to Internet site, from magazine to magazine, from bed to bed, from partner to partner? Why are they always searching if what they're getting is so great?

Those married in the temple and keeping their covenants are not looking and searching. They have what they're looking for because in their marriage, sex is combined with love, trust, and fidelity. In their marriage, they have something that those caught up in carnality could never even dream of. While people in the world have had sexual experiences, physical experiences, they don't know anything about the emotional and spiritual experiences that can be associated with those sexual feelings. The people in the world are missing the fireworks show that comes from the intimacy coupled with spirituality that can be found in a righteous marriage.

If you can enter your marriage without carrying a lot of sexual baggage, you are setting yourself up for success. If your spouse does not have to compete with pornographic images in your mind, you are going to be much better off. If you can enter a marriage with the attitude that sex is something you give and not something you get, then you will be setting yourself up for something that your friends will never have. You're not the one getting ripped off; they're the ones getting ripped off because they are settling for something that is so unsatisfying. By living the law of chastity and keeping our standards, we are preparing for sex at its best. We are preparing for something that is truly satisfying. We will have something that glows.

Shifting Colors

The next security feature that a $20 bill has is color shifting. If you look at the bill from one angle, the number in the lower right corner appears green, but from another angle it is black. The world would try to convince us that there are no absolutes when it comes to good or bad, that right and wrong exist only in our minds. The world teaches that what is moral or immoral depends completely on the angle from which it is viewed. Do not be fooled. The shifting colors on the new bill provide security, but the shifting values of the world do not.

From any angle, pornography is wrong and it is sinful. President Spencer W. Kimball has stated, "Pornography pollutes the mind. The stench of obscenity and vulgarity reaches and offends the heavens. It putrefies all it touches. . . . Pornography and erotic stories and pictures are worse than polluted food. Shun them. The body has power to rid itself of sickening food. That person who entertains filthy stories or pornographic pictures and literature records them in his marvelous human computer, the brain, which can't forget this filth."[1]

Once while attending a youth conference, the stake leader who hosted me in his home warned me about his son's bedroom, where I would be sleeping. "Brother Wilcox, I need to warn you that my son has a very interesting taste in posters in his room. You may be a little bit shocked by some of the things he's chosen to put up on his wall. We've talked to him. We've told him we don't agree. But he says he has his free agency, and he says that it's not bugging him and all of his friends do it and it's no big deal and to lay off. I just want to warn you that you may not like everything that you see in the bedroom."

The entire room was covered with beautiful women who were not wearing much more than smiles. I thought, "This young priesthood holder has no idea what he's doing." No, they weren't naked, but he was crossing lines that he really shouldn't cross.

I thought I would be creative and put paper clothes on all the girls, until I realized that would take me all night. So I decided to cut out little cartoon bubbles that showed what these girls might say. I wrote in the bubbles such messages as, "I am a daughter of Heavenly Father. I love him and He loves me." In the next bubble I wrote, "I'm a child of God." And then, "I am only going to marry a returned missionary." And in another, "I love to see the temple. I'm going there some day." I put one by the mouth of every girl in that room.

As I did this, I hoped that this young man would remember what Elder Richard G. Scott said: "Do you thirst after righteousness? Or are there times when the allure of stimulating images is allowed to temporarily fill your mind because, after all, they are not really that bad? Do your actions focus on entertainment, immediate satisfaction, self-interests, or personal gratification even though your goals are elsewhere?"[2]

That young man later wrote me in a letter, "At first, I took what you did in my room as a big joke. I even invited a bunch of kids from youth conference to come and see your masterpieces. Everyone thought they were pretty funny. But then I started to really think about what you'd written on those papers. It's true. Those girls are daughters of Heavenly Father, and I certainly hadn't been looking at them that way. To see words about temple marriage on those kinds of posters seemed so inconsistent. Suddenly it hit me that by having those pictures up on my walls I was being inconsistent too. Needless to say, the posters came down."

Holding Our Actions to the Light

The last security feature in the $20 bill is called a watermark. It's made visible as you hold the bill to the light. If you hold the bill a certain way you can't see a thing. But if you hold the bill to the light, then you see some watermarks, such as a portrait and some words.

It is the same way in our lives. We must hold our actions and behavior to light. We must be willing to have the courage to talk about our struggles with a bishop. We have the responsibility to bring our choices to light.

We may start an exercise program with much enthusiasm, only to quit after a couple of days. But if you start with a friend, somebody who's going to help you out and who's going to encourage you, you stand a much better chance of actually reaching your goal even when it gets hard.

Your bishop can offer that kind of support system. If you know he's going to ask you on Sunday morning what you did on Saturday night, it may help you to keep your Saturday nights wholesome. A bishop is not just a friend, and he is not just a support system. He is one who holds priesthood keys that he can use in your behalf. He is one who can give blessings and inspired counsel. He is one who can help you set a positive plan of action and help you follow through on your commitments and goals.

A commitment to ourselves is easily overlooked. Even a commitment to God is easy to postpone. But when we make a commitment to another person it puts us in a very strong and positive position. The bishop is a person who can help you, and he can guide you to other professionals who can help as well. Parents can help. As we bring our actions to light, we put ourselves in the position of getting the help we need.

Those who are blinded by the counterfeit of pornography can get help and change. Positive changes are possible through the atonement of Jesus Christ.

The next time you see a $20 bill, remember that it has security features to thwart counterfeiting. Then remember that there are security features in our lives that can protect us from falling for Satan's counterfeits and being ripped off. I testify that it's worth it. We are not on a treadmill but actually a journey to eternity. It is a real goal that is possible, and each step we make, however private, moves us toward that goal. Do not be fooled by the counterfeits of the world. Keep working to stay on the right path. Your efforts are not in vain. God will reward you, and you will be blessed for living according to that which is real—and for not accepting the counterfeit.

NOTES

1. Spencer W. Kimball, *Teachings of Spencer W. Kimball*, ed. Edward L. Kimball (Salt Lake City: Bookcraft, 1982), 282–83.
2. Richard G. Scott, "Finding Happiness," *Brigham Young University 1996–97 Speeches* (Provo, Utah: Brigham Young University, 1997), 360.

CHAPTER SIX

We Can Bond to Pornography the Way We Were Meant to Bond to a Spouse

Mark B. Kastleman

Why are so many people—including otherwise valiant and devoted Church members—becoming caught in the trap of a pornography habit? What makes smut addictive? One reason pornography becomes compelling and difficult to give up is that it hijacks the physical and psychological processes designed to bind husband and wife together powerfully and permanently. In this chapter, I will show how the marital bonding mechanisms become perverted by pornography.

Can you imagine if every time you got into your car, you had to consciously refigure out how everything works? Fortunately, such is not the case. When we first buy a car, we may have to spend time studying the operator's manual to figure out how everything works. However, after a few weeks, we don't need to "think" about how to increase the volume on the CD player or how to turn on the rear defrost. Performing these functions just comes naturally.

Our nervous systems have exquisitely organized networks of cells, all waiting for our intention or instructions. Once our minds "lock onto" a goal, these networks act in harmony to bring it about. The human nervous system organizes incoming data so that it can function on autopilot. The brain naturally sets up automatic responses to familiar experiences and events so that we don't have to take the time to "think" every time we respond. The formation of habits frees up our attention so we can focus on other, more pertinent things. When we do something once, the nervous system initiates the processes that will enable it to be repeated more easily in the future.

Habits are the natural goal of your nervous system. Our very personalities, "who we are," are in part made up of the habits we've allowed our nervous systems to develop. While habits increase the efficiency of our responses, they also decrease their flexibility. Therefore, we should never do once what we don't want to do again in the future.

The development of habits is facilitated when a pattern of behavior is followed by a reward. The more potent the payoff, the more deeply ingrained becomes the habit.

One of life's most powerful and enjoyable experiences is sexual climax. This is no accident. The natural outcome of sexual union is sexual climax. It is a wonderful "high." When experienced between two marriage partners, it helps cement and enhance their love in unique and profound ways. The power of romantic attraction and sexual intimacy is a big part of what drives a man and woman to accept and carry out the responsibilities of marriage and parenthood. Coupled with love, compassion, and selflessness, sexual attraction can be a vital binding force for good.

Pornographers fully understand the power of sexual climax as a peak experience, and they seek to use this strong attraction for their own greedy purposes. Before considering how this bonding process can lead to an unhealthy and misguided attachment to pornography consumption, let's explore in more detail the way it operates within a marriage relationship, the realm for which it was designed by a loving Heavenly Father. (Note: The use of a *funnel* and the *narrowing process* to describe this process are based on the work of neuropsychologist Page Bailey.)

THE FUNNEL IN A HEALTHY MARRIAGE RELATIONSHIP

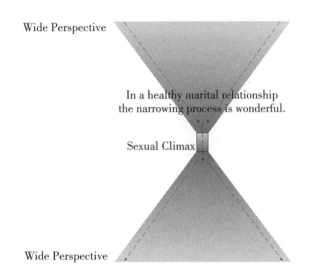

Wide Perspective

In a healthy marital relationship
the narrowing process is wonderful.

Sexual Climax

Wide Perspective

In a healthy marital relationship, physical intimacy creates a powerful change in the brain and body as follows:

At the top of the funnel, as the individual goes about day-to-day life, he has a wide perspective of the world and people around him. Then, as he and his wife become physically intimate, his brain begins to narrow its focus. As Dr. Bailey notes, "Sexual climax can only take place on a very narrow landing strip." In order to reach this place, the brain must narrow its focus and begin to block out all distractions.

In this narrowing process, the brain begins releasing *endogenous chemicals,* which flood the brain and the body. These *natural drugs* trigger feelings of euphoria, relaxation, and excitement—in other words, they produce a kind of "high"; we feel wonderful. These natural brain and body chemicals can include adrenaline, epinephrine, noradrenaline, ACTH, testosterone, various hormones, and many others. The brain and body are flooded with these endogenous chemicals. In fact, science now suggests there is actually a *bonding chemical* known as *oxytocin* that is released, increasing the bond between husband and wife.

The experience is not limited to the physical. In a healthy marriage relationship, the release of these chemicals brings an increase in feelings and emotions of love, closeness, and appreciation—minds and spirits also join and become one. Elder Jeffrey R. Holland refers to this sacred experience as a type of *sacrament* and indicates that we will never be closer to God than when we are exercising this power in righteousness.[1] The experience indeed can be a very spiritual one.

The further down the funnel one travels, the more intense the release of bodily chemicals, reaching a crescendo with a tidal wave of natural drugs flooding the brain and body—a culmination of the physical, emotional, and spiritual.

When husband and wife emerge from the narrow part of the funnel, their wide perspective returns. The experience leaves them feeling closer, more fulfilled, more positive, and better able to work individually and together to succeed in their family and life in general.

What a magnificent gift God has given us! Within a healthy marriage, this sacred power binds a husband and wife together in every way and becomes a beautiful and fulfilling part of their relationship. However, when this sacred power is exercised outside the bonds of marriage, through illicit sexual relationships or the viewing of pornography, a radically different outcome—another type of "bonding"—results.

THE FUNNEL AND PORNOGRAPHY

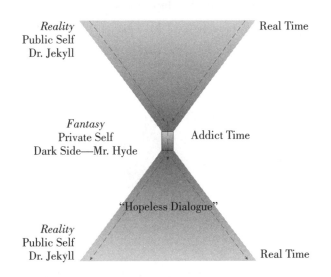

At the top of the funnel, the individual has a wide perspective: he can see reality; he can perceive real time; he presents his *public self* to others. In a sense he is like *Dr. Jekyll.* However, once he begins a pornography viewing session, his focus and capacities immediately begin to narrow.

In a process like that of physical sexual intimacy in marriage, the porn viewer's brain begins releasing chemicals. The viewer feels euphoric and excited. All of the stress, pressures, anxieties, and pains of life begin fading away as his brain and body are flooded with bodily chemicals that can have a drug-like effect. The pornography consumer is able to self-medicate and escape the reality of life.

In addition to all of the chemicals released during healthy intimacy, the porn viewer's brain may be flooded by additional chemicals. Feelings stirred by pornography consumption, such as guilt, shame, fear (of getting caught), shock (at the graphic images) may each trigger a corresponding chemical response. This crossfire of confusing and conflicting messages and the resulting cocktail of brain chemicals may help account for the potent "rush" associated with pornography use. The human system is not designed to deal with this level of overwhelming and conflicting stimulation. The resulting drug-like high can be compared to the state produced by powerful illicit street drugs.[2] The same physiological and psychological process that bonds a husband to his wife has now been activated to solidify and intensify the consumer's desire for pornography.

In this narrowly focused state, the pornography consumer's brain cannot process thoughts of God, family, marriage, covenants, or consequences. Rational thought is suspended and fantasy replaces reality. The viewer's brain and body respond as if he is actually having a real physical sexual encounter. Real time disappears—the viewer can spend many hours in this narrowed state and have no idea "where the time went." This is where the porn viewer's *private* or *dark side* is manifest—the *Mr. Hyde* he keeps secret from his wife, family, and the rest of the world.

At climax, the brain chemical rush crescendos and the porn viewer emerges from the narrowest part of the funnel back to a wide perspective. Suddenly, the capacity to think rationally returns, and thoughts of hopelessness often emerge: "What have I done? What was I thinking? What about my wife, my children, my covenants, my priesthood?" Intense feelings of guilt, shame, and regret flood in. These feelings can produce such an intense state of despair and hopelessness that the individual may go back into the funnel to escape the pain, starting the cycle all over again. Or he may pound his fist and declare "This is the last time this will ever happen!" He then may attempt to rigidly control every part of his life— especially the moral and spiritual aspects—so that he never looks at porn again. However, when the stress and anxiety of life become too much or a negative event takes place, he will once again find himself going right back to the funnel to self-medicate. The vicious cycle goes around and around, often for many years.

Once anyone begins using pornography as the means to reach sexual excitement or climax, his or her nervous system rallies all its resources to make this an automatic response—a habit. And tragically, for that individual, the pornography, instead of a loving and committed spouse, becomes the focal point of the "binding" process that has been initiated. The individual's nervous system organizes all aspects of this process so that the experience can be duplicated over and over in the future with very little conscious effort. All he need do is experience the desire for this type of stim-ulation, and his entire neurological habit networks kick into gear.

Unfortunately, such desire itself can become a potent habit. In the future, his nervous system turns on the pornography-seeking network automatically. There is no need for conscious intention. And the process can be triggered at any time or place. The next time a pornography viewer sees a fully clothed woman, a teenage girl, or even a child walking on the street, his neural networks may initiate sexual feelings and behaviors, just as readily as they would enable him to drive his car to a familiar destination.

When we received a mortal body, we also received a beautiful and glorious gift—the gift of procreation. Within each one of us are the sacred seeds of life. As part of his marvelous plan, our Father created within us powerful feelings, emotions, and attractions con-nected to this sacred gift. This was done to motivate each of us to join together as husband and wife and become "one" in every way. Our Heavenly Father commands that this power be used only within the bounds he has set. The use of this power triggers such a potent response in the brain and body that the only "safe" and sanctioned setting for its exercise is within marriage.

Many recovery tools, such as surrendering prayers, journaling, and communicating with others, can help someone who is addicted break out of the funnel, the perceptual narrowing I have described in this chapter. See part 3 of this book for information on recovery tools such as these.

THERE IS GREAT HOPE!

With an understanding of just how overwhelmingly powerful and addictive pornography and the funnel experience are, you may feel a sense of hopelessness. If you are struggling against the temptation of pornography and/or other sexual behaviors and find yourself giving in—occasionally, constantly, or somewhere in between—*do not despair, there is great hope!* Just as *many* have done before you, you can escape the awful grasp of pornography and move forward to attain all of the happiness and success that a loving Heavenly Father has waiting for you. While this chapter is not intended to fully explore the recovery process (this will be done later in the book), the following may help.

The latest brain science is demonstrating that existing brain structure and circuitry is changeable, alterable, and malleable. World-renowned neurophysiologist Dr. Jeffrey Schwartz states: "It is the brain's astonishing power to learn and unlearn, to adapt and change, to carry with it the inscriptions of our experiences. . . . The life we lead, in other words, leaves a mark in the form of enduring changes in the complex circuitry of the brain—footprints of the experiences we have had, the actions we have taken. . . . Contrary to Cajal and virtually every neuroscientist since, the adult brain can change. It can grow new cells. It can change the function of old ones. It can rezone an area that originally executed one function and assign it another."[3]

Despite the effects of our past choices, what we think about and do today makes a real difference, even a physical difference. Through making simple, consistent choices, you help generate small changes in brain structure which can, over time, help you become more and more free from the grasp of pornography.

Each time you exercise your will and turn away from pornography, you will find the next choice easier. You have been doing this since the day you were born. The fact that you can walk, talk, tie your shoes, ride a bicycle, and drive a car are just a few of thousands of examples of just how efficient and successful you are at this wondrous process. The more you make the right choice, the more you can. Shakespeare's Hamlet stated it this way: "Refrain tonight and thou shalt lend a kind of easiness to the next abstinence, the next more easy. For use almost always can change the stamp of nature, and either master the Devil, or throw him out with wondrous potency."[2]

You have probably heard the phrase, "Use it or lose it." Remember, your brain is efficient. Just as it immediately begins building habitual circuitry for a new behavior, it also begins *shrinking* circuitry that is no longer being used. Brain circuitry is not unlike muscles in the body: if you stop using them, they shrivel and atrophy. If you exercise them, they expand and strengthen. This reminds me of the story of an old Indian teaching his grandson about the battle between healthy and destructive habits that rages within each one of us. He said, "My son, this battle is between two wolves that live inside us." The eager boy inquired, "Grandfather, which wolf wins?' To which the old sage replied simply, "The one you feed."

Just as Joseph of old fled from Potiphar's wife, so we should continually develop and strengthen the habit of avoiding inappropriate situations, places, media, and people. However, in today's sexualized society, there are times when avoidance isn't possible. We can be unintentionally exposed to pornography on the Internet, catch sight of a racy magazine cover in the grocery store check-out line, encounter inappropriately dressed people in public, or be confronted by a provocative billboard while driving on the freeway. When an individual is trying to break free from pornography addiction, he often develops an intense *fear* of these and many other influences. The instant these images, or even inappropriate thoughts, enter his mind he fights to keep them out: "I can't think about that; I can't, I can't!"

The more he fights it, the more intense the images and thoughts become. He wages war until he is completely worn out and finally gives in and looks at pornography. Instantly he feels *temporary* relief from the battle: "Finally I don't have to fight these thoughts anymore." His fear has created an *obsessive-compulsive* cycle, not unlike the OCD sufferer who, upon touching a doorknob, fights to keep the thought of *germs* out of his mind, only to eventually give in and wash his hands for the forty-seventh time that day. Fearing the inadvertent sexual images and thoughts we encounter each day only increases their power over us.

We must learn to *confront and answer* temptations as the Master did. In Luke we read about the devil tempting Jesus face-to-face. The Savior didn't run, avoid, or tremble in fear. The account reads, "And the devil said unto him," "And Jesus answered him" (Luke 4:3, 4, 6, 8). The Savior simply *confronted* him and *answered* him with *the truth.*

Fear and intimidation are at the core of Satan's power. In the past you may have allowed fear to overtake you—fear that you will fail; fear that you will succumb; fear that you are unworthy or inadequate; fear that God will not stand by you and sustain you; fear that you are lost forever; fear that God no longer loves or accepts you; fear that you are not strong enough or cannot do it. When you feel gripped by temptation's icy-cold fingers, follow your Savior's pattern—face it squarely and answer it with power, confidence, resolve, and truth—"Satan, you say, '_____.' Well, I answer you with '_____.'"

Jesus countered Satan's temptation with a statement of truth: "And the devil said unto him, If thou be the Son of God, command this stone that it be made bread. And Jesus answered him, saying,

It is written, That man shall not live by bread alone, but by every word of God" (Luke 4:3–4).

When you are faced with a lustful or pornographic thought, urge, image, or the like, counter the "lie," the "deception," with a statement of the truth. Below are some examples of statements of truth created by recovering addicts working with psychologist Randy Hyde, Ph.D. When you are tempted, I recommend you engage in a dialogue: "Satan, you say, '_____' ["This will be pleasurable, you can't resist, you need this to cope, it's no big deal," and so forth], but I say '_____' [counter him with the truth and the real outcome and consequences, using one of the statements below or one of your own creation]." You can do this in writing, or, if you are by yourself, I suggest you do it boldly and *out loud*. Have fun with it. Feel the spirit, courage, resolution, and power fill your heart and mind as you confront, answer, and *"send the devil packin'."* In James 4:7 we read, "Submit yourselves therefore to God. Resist the devil and he will flee from you."

Statements of Truth

I feel the spirit and influence of my Savior with me in great power and strength when I am following his example by confronting and answering temptation with truth.

These sexual urges are a sacred gift from God that I choose to express with my beloved companion, where together we can receive the full joy of uniting spiritually, emotionally, and physically. Why would I give all of that up for a few moments of selfish indulgence? It's not worth it.

What would my beloved wife do if she were in my place? Can I show any less love, devotion, and loyalty? I appreciate all she does for me and I always show her my appreciation by making a righteous choice right now.

I see women through the eyes of my Savior, and I strive to protect, serve, and love them as he does. I do not fear being around women, regardless of how physically attractive they are, because "perfect love casteth out fear" (1 John 4:18). "Unto the pure all things are pure" (Titus 1:15). "The Lord seeth not as a man seeth; for man looketh on the outward appearance, but the Lord looketh on the heart" (1 Samuel 16:7), and so do I.

The body is one of God's greatest gifts. I look upon it the way he does—as a sacred temple for my spirit. To objectify and use the body of another for my own selfish desires is to dishonor a child of God and mock him who "bought us with a price." This I never do.

When I see an attractive woman, I acknowledge her beauty as I would any of God's wondrous creations, without lusting after her.

That which I persist in doing becomes easier, not that the nature of the thing has changed, but that my power to do has increased. As I continue to practice answering temptation, it will become easier until it is automatic.

The power of statements like these is clear: They invite the Spirit of God to be with you and activate different circuitry within the brain. As you use them, you are channeling and redirecting your attention, instead of gritting your teeth and fighting the urge, which often only serves to entangle you further in habitual thought patterns. Each time you activate an alternate nervous system response, it grows stronger and more dominant and is activated more readily.

By persisting in your efforts, you *can* change the negative effects of your past. You *can* break free of old, dominant habits and addictions and move forward to become all that you desire. You *can* embrace and enjoy all of the love, peace, success, and happiness God has waiting for you. You can do it by relying on the miraculous healing and transforming grace of your Lord and Savior Jesus Christ and by cultivating the power for change that is built in to the very structure of your brain.

NOTES

1. See Jeffrey R. Holland, *Of Souls, Symbols, and Sacraments* (Salt Lake City: Deseret Book, 2001).
2. See Judith Reisman, *The Psychopharmacology of Pictorial Pornography,* The Institute for Media Education, July 2003.
3. Dr. Jeffrey Schwartz, *The Mind and The Brain* (New York: Harper Collins, 2002), 373, 366, 130.
4. William Shakespeare, *Hamlet,* Act 3, scene iv.

CHAPTER SEVEN

Talking to Our Youth about Pornography: Guidelines for Parents and Leaders

Dan Gray

D ue to the complexity and delicate nature of the topic, many parents and leaders are reluctant or embarrassed to openly discuss sexual issues. As a result, many children are schooled by misguided friends in locker rooms or corrupt media in darkened theaters, often developing inaccurate conclusions and views of sexuality that may lead to inappropriate behaviors.

As parents, we want to teach our children the law of chastity and help them to avoid the pain of immorality. If, however, we teach only the negative side of sexuality and don't help them feel positive about their identity as a sexual being, they can become insecure and uncertain. We may inadvertently convey the confusing message, "Sexual thoughts and feelings are bad, sinful, and wrong—save them for someone you love."

To add to the confusion, children and adolescents who receive only the message about the sinful nature of sexuality may conclude, "Since sexual feelings or urges are bad, and I feel them very strongly, I, too, must be bad." This kind of thinking can result in feelings of low self-worth, unworthiness, and shame.

THE NEED FOR OPEN COMMUNICATION

To alleviate confusion, we need to openly discuss sexual matters with our youth so that they might learn (1) the sacred nature of these feelings, (2) the importance of managing and bridling them, and (3) the ways to cope with these strong drives and urges when they inevitably feel them.

The effectiveness of families in addressing these sensitive issues is determined by how comfortable the children feel in discussing their questions and concerns with parents. Every family has a system by which it operates and contributes to the development of its members. Though family systems are very complex, most family interactions can be broken down into two distinct styles: open and closed. It is important to note that few families fall exclusively on only one side of the scale. Also, the system may fluctuate between open and closed at different periods in the family's history, depending on the circumstances the family is facing at the time. The following chart illustrates the characteristics of these two kinds of family systems.

OPEN AND CLOSED FAMILY SYSTEMS

OPEN	CLOSED
1. The family is open and expanding, and change is welcomed.	1. The system is closed, rigid, and secretive.
2. Feelings are allowed and shared.	2. The family controls which feelings are allowed.
3. Individual differences are allowed and encouraged.	3. Individual identity is lost in the family identity.
4. Mistakes are disciplined and forgiven.	4. Mistakes are punished, judged, and "shamed."
5. Family and life-roles are chosen by the individual.	5. Family roles are assigned by the family.
6. The family supports and develops the individual.	6. The family is more important than the individual.
7. Expression of individual needs is encouraged.	7. Individual needs are rarely addressed.

I have found in my practice that most people who struggle with sexual addictions come from closed family systems, where there were rigid rules and a lack of open expression of feelings and information, creating secrets and a sense of isolation. This system creates "taboos" around sexual issues, which can lead to a mystical intrigue and inordinate curiosity for the "forbidden." Feelings of unworthiness and inadequacy many times ensue, soon leading to sexual "acting out," which is used as a temporary escape from emotional stress and feelings of alienation.

Conversely, an open family system provides a safe environment where expression of feelings and questions regarding sexuality are invited and encouraged. As a result, the child is more apt to develop a healthy view of his or her own sexuality. Also, in the event that the child experiments with inappropriate sexual activity, an open family system invites discussion where the child is more likely to ask for help and work through the issues before the behaviors become unmanageable.

The remainder of this chapter discusses specific topics that may be helpful for parents and leaders as we openly discuss these sensitive issues with our youth.

OUR BODY: ITS SACRED NATURE

As indicated earlier, too often in discussing sexual matters with our youth we use only negative references and warnings. It is important that they also hear a positive message regarding their bodies and the natural drives and urges with which they have been blessed. Today's media portrays an unrealistic view of how our bodies should look and what they represent. People of all ages are buying into these views and making them their own personal standard, which often leads to objectification (seeing the body as an object rather than part of a real person) and idolization (seeing the body as an object to worship). Many internalize the media's version of the "perfect body," setting the stage for self-loathing and low self-worth when they are unable to meet these unrealistic expectations.

The first thing we can teach our children is that our bodies, in all their variety, shapes, and sizes, are wonderful, God-given gifts, created to provide joy and fulfillment. In 1913, apostle James E. Talmage stated, "We have been taught . . . to look upon these bodies of ours as gifts from God. We Latter-day Saints do not regard the body as something to be condemned, something to be abhorred. . . . We regard [the body] as the sign of our royal birthright. . . . It is peculiar to the theology of Latter-day Saints that we regard the body as an essential part of the soul."[1] This understanding can help children look upon their own bodies and the bodies of others with the deep respect they deserve.

Elder Jeffrey R. Holland further articulates the sacred nature of our bodies: "We simply must understand the revealed, restored Latter-day Saint doctrine of the soul, and the high and inextricable part the body plays in that doctrine. One of the 'plain and precious' truths restored to this dispensation is that 'the spirit *and* the body are the soul of man' (D&C 88:15; emphasis added). . . . Exploitation of the body (please include the word *soul* there) is, in the last analysis, an exploitation of Him who is the Light and the Life of the world. Perhaps here Paul's warning to the Corinthians takes on newer, higher meaning: 'Now the body is not for fornication, but for the Lord; and the Lord for the body. . . . Know ye not that your bodies are the members of Christ? shall I then take the members of Christ, and make them the members of an harlot? God forbid. . . . Flee fornication. . . . He that committeth fornication sinneth against his own body. . . . Know ye not that your body is the temple of the Holy Ghost which is in you, which ye have of God, and ye are not your own? For ye are bought with a price: therefore glorify God in your body, and in your spirit, *which are God's*" (1 Corinthians 6:13–20).[2]

OUR SEXUALITY: A SACRED GIFT

We are all created as sexual beings. Our sexual drives—and the appropriate expression of them—should be seen as wonderful, sacred gifts. Hugh B. Brown said, "The powerful sex drives are instinctive, which is to say, God-given, and therefore are not evil."[3] Speaking to the youth of the Church, Elder Boyd K. Packer said, "There was provided in our bodies—and this is sacred—a power of creation, a light, so to speak, that has the power to kindle other lights. This gift was to be used only within the sacred bonds of marriage. Through the exercise of this power of creation, the mortal body may be conceived, a spirit enter into it, and a new soul born into this life. *This power is good.* It can create and sustain family life, and it is in family life that we find the fountains of happiness. It is given to virtually every individual who is born into mortality. It is a sacred and significant power, and I repeat, my young friends, that *this power is good.* . . . Much of the happiness that may come to you in this life will depend on how you use this sacred power of creation. . . . It is a gift from God our Father. In the righteous exercise of it as in nothing else, we may come close to him."[4]

Elder Jeffrey R. Holland states in addressing this issue, "Sexual intimacy is not only a symbolic union between a man and a woman—the uniting of their very souls—but it is also symbolic of a union between mortals and deity, between otherwise ordinary and fallible humans uniting for a rare and special moment with God Himself and all the powers by which He gives life in this wide universe of ours. In this latter sense, human intimacy is a kind of sacrament, a very special symbol." Elder Holland describes the nature of this sacred, symbolic union. "Human intimacy, that sacred, physical union ordained of God for a married couple, deals with a symbol that demands special sanctity. Such an act of love between a man and a woman is—or certainly was ordained to be— a symbol of total union: union of their hearts, their hopes, their lives, their love, their family, their future, their everything. It is a symbol that we try to suggest in the temple with a word like *seal*. The Prophet Joseph Smith once said we perhaps could render such a sacred bond as *welding*—that those united in matrimony and eternal families are *welded* together, inseparable if you will, to withstand the temptations of the adversary and the afflictions of mortality (see D&C 128:18). But such a total, virtually unbreakable union, such an unyielding commitment between a man and a woman, can come only with the proximity and permanence afforded in a marriage covenant, with the union of all that they possess— their very hearts and minds, all their days and all their dreams."[5]

President Spencer W. Kimball also spoke concerning the important dual role our sexual drives play in marriage: "In the context of lawful marriage, the intimacy of sexual relations is right and divinely approved. There is nothing unholy or degrading about sexuality in itself, for by that means men and women join in a process of creation and in an expression of love."[6]

THE HARMFUL EFFECTS OF PORNOGRAPHY

The Lord has taught us through his prophets and apostles that the viewing of pornography will lead to negative spiritual consequences. President Gordon B. Hinckley has told us that through its use "the minds of youth become warped with false concepts. Continued exposure leads to addiction that is almost impossible to break. Men, so very many, find they cannot leave it alone. Their energies and their interests are consumed in their dead-end pursuit of this raw and sleazy fare."[7]

Many individuals, even some in the professional community, excuse or even condone the viewing of pornography as harmless behavior. They rationalize that it is "normal behavior" that causes no harm when done in seclusion and privacy. This same rationale is used in excusing the practice of masturbation that usually accompanies pornography use. How do we respond when an adolescent asks, "What is really wrong with pornography and masturbation?" The following thoughts may be helpful in addressing this question.

As was mentioned earlier, the body is part of the soul of man (and woman). Therefore, when we look upon the body of another person to satisfy our own lustful desires, we are disrespecting and defiling the very soul of that person. Elder Jeffrey Holland, in warning us of the consequences of rationalizing or taking these things lightly states, "So partly in answer to *why* such seriousness, we answer that one toys with the God-given—and satanically coveted—body of another, he or she toys with the very soul of that individual, toys with the central purpose and product of life, 'the very key' to life, as Elder Boyd K. Packer once called it. In trivializing the soul of another (please include the word *body* there) we trivialize the atonement, which saved that soul and guaranteed its continued existence. And when one toys with the Son of Righteousness, the Day Star Himself, one toys with white heat and a flame hotter and holier than the noonday sun. You cannot do so and not be burned."[8]

In addressing the practice of masturbation, President Spencer W. Kimball stated, "Masturbation, a rather common indiscretion, is not approved of the Lord nor of his church, regardless of what may have been said by others whose 'norms' are lower. Latter-day Saints are urged to avoid this practice. Anyone fettered by this weakness should abandon the habit before he goes on a mission or receives the holy priesthood or goes in the temple for his blessings."[9]

The following metaphor may help to illustrate the importance of following this counsel of our modern-day prophets. When a person wants to know how to take care of his car, to know what type of fuel to use, how much air pressure to put in the tires, or how often to perform certain maintenance tasks, he will refer to the owner's manual. The owner's manual is written by the manufacturer of the vehicle, who knows what is required to make it run properly. It would be foolish not to adhere to the directives given by the car's "creator."

In like fashion, our Heavenly Father has created our souls: our bodies and our spirits. He has written the owner's manual through the scriptures and the words of the prophets. He knows how our body and spirit work together. He knows what we should put in them and what we should leave out. If we follow his directives we will be able to experience the fullest potential of our soul. We are told that putting pornographic material into our minds is detrimental to our spirits and that in so doing we jeopardize our ability to have the fullest extent of happiness and joy, physically and spiritually.

Another response to the question "What is wrong with viewing pornography?" is that this repeated behavior, coupled with masturbation, can become habitual, even addictive in nature. An addictive pattern can be established when a person becomes dependent upon the "rush" of the sexual arousal, enhanced by the body's production of adrenalin, endorphins, and other internally induced chemicals. He or she learns to depend upon this activity to escape or self-medicate in order to cope with life's challenges, difficulties, and emotional stressors (such as anger, boredom, loneliness, stress, or fatigue). This dependency becomes very difficult to break and sometimes escalates to inappropriate sexual encounters and possibly illegal behaviors.

Elder M. Russell Ballard has said, "Some become so addicted to viewing Internet pornography and participating in dangerous online chat rooms that they ignore their marriage covenants and family obligations and often put their employment at risk. Many run afoul of the law. Others develop a tolerance to their perverted behavior, taking ever more risks to feed their immoral addiction.

Marriages crumble and relationships fail, as addicts often lose everything of real, eternal value."[10]

It is important to note that when a person views pornography and becomes sexually aroused, the body does not differentiate between fantasy and reality. It experiences the same arousal patterns that occur in a real sexual encounter. It produces the same chemical reactions internally, and when coupled with masturbation, the body's sexual response is exactly the same as if it were having an actual sexual experience with another person. When this behavior is repeated frequently, the body and the mind become conditioned to certain sexual images and behavior, which can create unrealistic and many times unhealthy expectations of what a sexual relationship should or will be. It actually creates a counterfeit of what the "real thing" is intended to be. These expectations can be carried into marriage creating confusion, pain, and conflict in the relationship.

A FATHER'S COUNSEL

In Alma, chapters 36 through 41, Alma the Younger gave valuable counsel to his three sons. Here is a prophet who, in his earlier years, went about to destroy the Church and was known as "a very wicked and an idolatrous man" (Mosiah 27:8). He obviously knew that the powerful temptations of the adversary, when heeded, can destroy one's soul. In Alma 38:12, he counseled his son Shiblon by saying, "And also see that ye bridle all your passions, that ye may be filled with love." Notice that Alma does not counsel his son to ignore or destroy his passions, but to bridle them. Those who have ridden a spirited horse know how exciting and exhilarating the experience can be, but also how dangerous it is if there is no bridle. With the bridle, the animal can be controlled, can be reined in when necessary, but can also be given permission to run and express its spirited nature when appropriate and safe. However, if the bridle is removed, that same wonderful animal can become dangerous, even lethal. Children need to learn that those who ride the unbridled stallion of sexual passion will ride off into dangerous, even deadly, pastures. But when those same passions are bridled, guided, and directed, they will ride in the pastures of fulfillment and joy.

OUR HEAVENLY FATHER'S COUNSEL

In Doctrine and Covenants 121:45–46 the Lord offers tremendous blessings to those who have clean and virtuous thoughts, coupled with charity. He states, "Let virtue garnish thy thoughts unceasingly; then shall thy confidence wax strong in the presence of God; and the doctrine of the priesthood shall distil upon thy soul as the dews from heaven. The Holy Ghost shall be thy constant companion, and thy scepter an unchanging scepter of righteousness and truth; and thy dominion shall be an everlasting dominion, and without compulsory means it shall flow unto thee forever and ever."

How does one maintain virtuous thoughts "unceasingly"? Clients I see who are successful in overcoming compulsive sexual behaviors and thoughts are those who learn to engage in virtuous daily rituals and routines. They call them "dailies." These activities include listening to uplifting music, reading good literature, and participating in conversation that is not demeaning or lewd in nature. It can also include the enjoyment of God's creations in nature—the beautiful sky, a rainbow, the smell of pine or sage, the sight, sound, and smell of the ocean, the enjoyment of conversation and laughter with good friends, or a prayer of gratitude. Dailies can include surrounding ourselves with virtuous things in our homes and offices, including pictures, paintings, gifts from loved ones, items that make us laugh, or things that help us recall exciting or meaningful memories. These can become "symbols of virtue," which can keep our minds focused and less susceptible to the cravings of the natural man.

I know several men whose main struggle with pornography occurs when they travel on business, spending many hours alone in hotels viewing adult materials available on TV or online. They have learned to maintain virtue by saying a prayer when they first enter the hotel room, asking the Lord to help them make it a sanctuary where virtuous thoughts and actions will govern. They place pictures of their wife, their children, and the Savior around the room, including on top of the television. These activities, coupled with listening to enjoyable music, reading uplifting materials, journal writing, and phone calls to family and friends, change the meaning and purpose of that hotel room, creating an environment of virtue.

If children can learn and implement these same strategies in their lives, they will begin to experience the incredible blessings of Doctrine and Covenants 121. They will feel strength and confidence to resist external pressure from peers and media, because their source of confidence waxes strong "in the presence of God," and in no one else. Their minds, in a steady process of time, will be opened to insight and truth as the doctrine of the priesthood "[distills] upon [their] soul as the dews from heaven," and important decisions are more easily made because the Holy Ghost becomes their "constant companion."

It is also important for children and adolescents to understand that we all have weaknesses to overcome, of which "unbridled passions" may be one. Weaknesses do not make us unworthy of God's love. In fact, the process of feeling and acknowledging our weaknesses and overcoming them is actually part of the Lord's plan for us. In Ether 12:27 the Lord has given us a specific formula for this process: "And if men come unto me I will show unto them their weakness. I give unto men weakness that they may be humble; and my grace is sufficient for all men that humble themselves before me; for if they humble themselves before me, and have faith in me, then will I make weak things become strong unto them." Thus, when the Lord makes us aware of our weaknesses, and we follow the directive to first become humble (not distressed and wrought with hopelessness), wonderful things begin to happen. Through this humility, we can turn ourselves over to the Lord and yield our hearts to him in faith. In the twelve steps of Alcoholics Anonymous this is called "surrendering to our higher power." Through the Lord's grace and power, our weaknesses become "strong unto [us]." We do not become strong through our own willpower and strength. It is the Lord who brings this miracle about in our lives.

It is important to note here that we are not told that he will take weaknesses away from us, but rather he will "make weak things become strong unto [us]." We may continue to be troubled and tempted by our weaknesses; but as we are humbled and maintain faith, the Lord will help us to be strong in resisting temptations and having power over them. This can free us from the bondage of sin.

CONCLUSION

It is imperative that we as parents and teachers be involved in our children's lives and strive to create an environment where there is an abundance of communication regarding these important issues. We need to be aware and monitor their activities, including their Internet use, and openly discuss sexual matters by listening and giving sound direction and guidance. More important, we must set an example for our youth. They are watching how we as parents and leaders are coping with these same negative influences. We can also help those that are now struggling with these issues and teach them how to overcome. President Hinckley, in speaking to those who "are involved in such behavior," said, "now is the time to change. Let this be our hour of resolution. Let us turn about to a better way."[11]

We are currently on a battlefield. The adversary is using all of his forces to influence children and adults through the current media and other forms of information access. We cannot be passive in our efforts to combat these forces. Elder M. Russell Ballard has issued this challenge: "The time has come when members of the Church need to speak out and join with the many other concerned people in opposition to the offensive, destructive, and mean-spirited media influence that is sweeping over the earth."[12]

We need to be bold in our communications with our youth, encouraging them to stay close to the principles of the gospel and to fortify themselves against these powers of the adversary. They need to know of our knowledge and confidence that the influence of the adversary is no match for the divine power and influence of the Spirit of the Lord.

NOTES

1. James E. Talmage, in Conference Report, October 1913, 117.
2. Jeffrey R. Holland, *Of Souls, Symbols, and Sacraments* (Salt Lake City: Deseret Book, 2001), 11, 13–14; emphasis added.
3. Hugh B. Brown, *You and Your Marriage* (Salt Lake City: Bookcraft, 1960), 83.
4. Boyd K. Packer, "Why Stay Morally Clean," *Ensign*, July 1972, 111, 112; emphasis added.
5. Holland, *Of Souls, Symbols, and Sacraments*, 27, 17; emphasis in original.
6. Spencer W. Kimball, *Teachings of Spencer W. Kimball*, ed. Edward L. Kimball (Salt Lake City: Deseret Book, 1982), 311.
7. Gordon B. Hinckley, "A Tragic Evil among Us," *Ensign*, November 2004, 61.
8. Holland, *Of Souls, Symbols, and Sacraments*, 13.
9. Spencer W. Kimball, "President Kimball Speaks Out on Morality," *Ensign*, November 1980, 97.
10. M. Russell Ballard, "Let Our Voices Be Heard," *Ensign*, November 2003, 18.
11. Hinckley, "A Tragic Evil among Us," 62.
12. Ballard, "Let Our Voices Be Heard," 17.

CHAPTER EIGHT

The Role of Shame in Pornography Problems

James M. Harper

John (not his real name) found himself increasingly drawn to pornography. He couldn't resist going to those sites when he sat down at the computer. It happened at work and at home. He succeeded in keeping it a secret from his wife, his children, and his employer, but the complexity of trying to hide such a secret was slowly eating away at him.

His behavior was creating more distance in his relationship with people. He noticed that in his interactions with his wife, he was constantly monitoring whether she was catching on to the secret of his pornography involvement. He felt like their love-making had become more of a chore for him. He would rather spend time with pornography.

He felt terribly ashamed. At church he felt like an impostor. He often silently asked, "What would happen to me if others really knew who I am and what I am involved with?" The incongruence between holding an important position in his church and being involved in pornography was taking its toll. He seldom felt the Spirit, and he believed he didn't deserve to feel the Spirit. He wondered why he couldn't control the constant drive inside himself toward pornography. Was he defective somehow? Was he doomed to live a dual life forever? The shame he felt became more than he could bear.

What role does shame play in the lives of men and women who frequently become involved with pornography? When individuals who have pornography habits fail to understand how they operate emotionally, they often face multiple failures in their attempts to abandon pornography. Sometimes the emotion of shame precedes a pornography problem, and the pornography involvement is an attempt to escape from the shame. Other times, shame is a consequence of chronic involvement with pornography. The purpose of this chapter is to explain what shame is, to consider how it is associated with pornography use, and to suggest possible helps to heal the shame associated with pornography.

WHAT IS SHAME?

Shame is often confused with guilt, since the words are frequently used synonymously. Both shame and guilt need to be dealt with in order to overcome a pornography problem, and seeing them as different from each other ensures that both will get addressed. When working with members of their congregations, ecclesiastical leaders usually address guilt, but shame is often passed by because individuals seek to hide their shame from others.

Guilt is a recognition that our behavior has violated a standard or value that is important to us or significant others, such as parents, spouses, and friends. It involves recognizing that others or ourselves may have been hurt by our choices (particularly when we have violated standards), and it usually motivates us to change behavior either by not doing it again or by doing something else that is acceptable under the standard and that doesn't hurt others. In a sense, then, guilt is a healthy response to mistakes we have made. It motivates us to engage in a process that leads to increasing integrity, where what we believe matches what we do. It motivates us to be more congruent between our beliefs and our actions. It also helps us to recognize that our behavior can hurt others, as well as ourselves, so that we seek greater harmony and unity in relationships important to us.[1]

In contrast, *shame* is an emotion that involves negative feelings about ourselves and a deep desire to keep others from discovering what we think are the negative aspects of self. It can be intertwined with guilt, since we are often ashamed of ways we have behaved and subsequently seek to hide our actions from being known to others. The emotion of shame can help motivate us to desire to live according to socially and doctrinally acceptable standards.

We have all felt humiliated or ashamed at times, but when individuals have chronic shame experiences, they develop what is called *internalized shame*. People who experience strong internalized shame view the world through negative, shame-tinted glasses. Every incident in their lives is seen as validation of how worthless they are, how unlovable they are, how incapable they are of making relationships with others really work. People with internalized shame experience a lot of guilt, but the guilt is rarely healthy. Instead it is excessive, intense, and rarely produces behavior change. Rather than changing behavior and restoring themselves to a personally accepted standard, shame-prone persons just keep feeling guilty.

These people assume they are the way they are because they are bad or flawed inside. They hide this reasoning from others, and the act of hiding makes the guilt even worse. In their own internal world, they see themselves as unable to change the negative emotion. From their view, simply changing their behavior doesn't make a difference. In fact, they may hold to a higher standard of behavior for years and yet still be unable to feel better about themselves.

It is the nature of people to hide their feelings of shame, especially when it has become a chronic way of being. Feelings are seen as bad, not something to be faced or explored; they are internalized experiences to be avoided. They experience feelings as bad parts of themselves. They seek to escape their uncomfortable feelings, which never ultimately works because human beings naturally feel emotions. Emotions in and of themselves are part of living, but our response to feelings and our actions associated with feelings can be problematic if we are frequently trying to escape or avoid unwanted feelings. Rarely do such strategies produce lasting solutions that lead to spiritual and emotional well-being.

Internalized shame is an enemy to our belief that all of us are spiritual children of God, and it leads to a loss of hope that behavior change can make a difference. It is an inwardly focused experience that often has little awareness of others. In contrast, healthy guilt is what children of God, with the seeds of godliness and goodness in them, experience when they violate a standard given them by a loving Heavenly Father. In a healthy view of the world, good people make mistakes, and it is precisely their goodness and their dependence on Christ that allows them to change their behavior through repentance. In contrast to shame's inward focus, guilt's focus is more outward in that we are concerned about our relationship with Heavenly Father and how our actions have affected others.

The following table summarizes different aspects of peoples' experience along a continuum, with little internalized shame on the left side and severe internalized shame on the right.

WHAT LEADS TO DEVELOPMENT OF INTERNALIZED SHAME?

Internalized shame can develop in a number of different ways. Frequent trauma or humiliation and chronic bullying from one's peer group can lead to shame. Family dynamics that include substance use and/or verbal, physical, and emotional abuse can lead

TABLE 1. CHARACTERISTICS OF PEOPLE SUFFERING FROM INTERNALIZED SHAME[2]

1 . . . . . 2 . . . . . 3 . . . . . 4 . . . . . 5 6

Low Internalized Shame   High Internalized Shame

INTERNAL EXPERIENCE	I am good at the core—a child of God. I accept boundaries and limits as helpful and have a set of internalized values.	In some situations, I feel flawed/broken/bad. In other situations, I feel I am a child of God—good at the core.	I am bad and disgusted at who I am; feelings that emanate inside of me are bad.
DEALING WITH FEELINGS	I experience a range of feelings; I view emotion as part of life. I deal with feelings rather than escaping from them. I experience shame as an emotion that can be dealt with.	At times I am either intensely emotional or totally blocked from emotion.	I am chronically either stuck in intense emotion or totally blocked to emotion.
BELIEFS	I am a good person inside. When I make mistakes, I can change because I am good.	I am bad, but maybe I can still change. Maybe others can really accept who I am.	If others discover how bad I am, they will abandon me. I cannot control my badness; it often just takes over.
BEHAVIOR IN RELATIONSHIPS	I am warm and self-disclosing; I can have friends.	I am cautious, but warm up after testing the waters. I often find it difficult to self-disclose.	I am very guarded and secretive. I am afraid to give out any personal information.
USE OF GUILT	I feel guilt, but it motivates a change in my behavior.	I often feel guilty; sometimes this leads to a change in my behavior.	I feel excessive, chronic guilt that doesn't lead to a change in my behavior.

to shame. Chronic failures in school, work, or relationships might intensify shame. Compulsive behavior that has negative consequences for relationships, such as chronic lying or drug use, also creates internalized shame.

Three specific processes can be antidotes to shame. They are accountability, dependency, and intimacy. *Accountability* is the process in which people in relationships such as marriage or family consider themselves obliged to account for their own behavior to themselves and others in the relationship according to a set of standards. *Dependency* is the process in relationships that allows one person to be dependent on another for physical sustenance, emotional needs, and a sense of order, values, and beliefs about the world. *Intimacy* is a feeling of emotional closeness between people in relationships; it involves time spent together sharing positive, mutually enjoyable, activities. When any one of these areas is chronically missing in marriages or in families, internalized shame can result.[3] The secrecy that goes along with failing to be accountable, for example, is part of the fire that feeds internalized shame.

Internalized shame impairs spirituality.[4] A person who experiences high internalized shame will have difficulty feeling loved, even by Heavenly Father. The ability to have confidence in feeling the Spirit is diminished when you believe your very being is bad or broken in some way. Because shame-prone people doubt emotions and feelings in general, they also doubt spiritual influence. To muster spiritual help to stop habitual pornography use, people must also deal with their shame. The two go hand in hand. If people can accept the belief that they are literally children of a Heavenly Father with godly capacities in embryo, and if they can *really* believe it, they will be more open to spiritual influence.

Because dependency in relationships has often been absent or violated, shame-prone people are reluctant to trust and have difficulty reaching for a higher power beyond themselves. When they learn to trust in God and be dependent on him rather than having to control everything themselves, shame-prone people can let go of their negative beliefs and feelings about the world.

Internalized shame can also develop as a consequence of habitual behavior, particularly when that behavior seems to be a driving force. Some habits seem beyond control, especially when the behavior violates the person's standards and would be looked down upon by others—and when the compulsive behavior would likely have negative consequences for important relationships such as in one's marriage or family.[5] The subsequent hiding and work to keep the behavior a secret, the distance created between one's private behavior and public self; and the accountability, dependency, and intimacy violations that might occur in relationships all become part of the pattern that feeds internalized shame.

HOW ARE SHAME AND PORNOGRAPHY RELATED?

Shame is associated with pornography use in at least two different ways. First, if a person has high internalized shame, he may get involved in pornography as a way of numbing or escaping the feelings of shame. This is not much different from engaging in any negative behavior that might alleviate tension and reduce anxiety, such as drinking alcohol.

Second, even a person with little internalized shame who gets frequently involved in pornography will experience shame as a consequence of doing something that is not acceptable to God, family, friends, and self. Pornography use frequently leads to attempts to keep the behavior a secret, coupled with the fear and worry of discovery. This process of hiding personal information from others and living an increasingly dual life will inevitably heighten the emotion of shame. Such a pattern, if engaged in for a sufficient time, will inevitably lead to internalized shame.

At that point the user will be filled with questions about why he is so driven toward pornography and why his attempts at controlling the habit have failed. He may become hopeless, assuming there is no solution for him, and he will wonder why other people seem to be able to have more control. He may be aware of his change in attitudes toward both men and women, and he will be shamed by the erotic lens through which he appreciates others only for their capacity to arouse. When this happens, he has become "me"-centered in his views of others.[6] He will begin to ask if he is flawed in some way, and these wonderings will, in turn, heighten the shame even further (James 1:8).

THE FUNCTION OF SHAME IN A PERSON'S INTERNAL WORLD VIEW

Internalized shame is associated with a particular view of the world and assumptions regarding how we relate to others. This view is permeated with beliefs that we must hide a part of self from others and that if others were to discover that part, they would immediately and vehemently reject and condemn us. In this world view, the person eventually learns to expect rejection from others and anticipates it before it really happens.

Shauna had been secretly involved in sultry chat relationships with men on the web for several years before her husband discovered what was really happening. The chats started out innocently, and Shauna appreciated the warm acceptance she found in her Internet relationships. The fact that she was involved in chatting regularly with a number of different men didn't seem to her to be a violation of the spirit of her marriage. She still loved her husband. He was just busy and unavailable. Because no sexual relationship had occurred with any of her "Internet men," Shauna rationalized that what she was doing was all right.

Over time, however, almost all of her frequent chat partners became sexual in their language with her. As she fell into these ever-increasing spirals of sexual chat, she became aroused. She began to yearn for times when her husband would go to sleep or leave the house so she could spend time on the Internet with these men. During one period she was chatting on the Internet as much as ten hours a day.

The hiding and secrecy, the lack of accountability to her marital relationship, the violation of dependency and intimacy dynamics in her marriage all left her feeling more and more empty, a signal that internalized shame had her in its ugly grasp. She became more self-centered, less likely to reach out to people in real relationships. This "me"-centeredness versus "we"-centeredness is typical of people with high internalized shame.

Eventually, she decided to meet one of these men when travel with work took her to the city in which he lived. Of course, the relationship quickly became sexual. She returned home devastated, but she continued to hide and keep her liaison a secret. Although she knew it was not in her best interest to continue chatting with men on the web, she felt driven to do so and soon succumbed.

Her seeming lack of control and her continued hiding began to affect every aspect of her life.

She felt disconnected spiritually. She felt isolated from people in her ward. She especially felt a distance in her marriage. She was consumed with guilt, but it did not motivate her to change her behavior. She was consumed with fear, anxiety, sadness, and a foreboding sense that this "awful, bad" part of her would never change. It was not until her husband finally discovered a sultry e-mail from one of her male chat friends that she confessed her behavior.

What started out as a short-term escape from feelings had become a long-term wallow in internalized shame. In her case, as in most cases of habitual pornography involvement, she experienced intense internalized shame as a consequence of hiding, secrecy, living like an impostor, failing to be accountable, violating trust of marital intimacy and dependency, separation from the Spirit, and isolation from God.

WILL SHAME EVER GO AWAY?

The good news is that internalized shame can change, but only when people pay attention to being accountable, creating intimacy in significant relationships, being appropriately dependent on others and on God, and developing integrity, so their private behavior matches public behavior. The result will be openness and transparency rather than hiding and secrecy. Continued involvement in pornography—which fosters independence rather than dependency on God and others, "me-ness" in relationships rather than "we-ness," hiding, and secrecy—will, of course, make it impossible to change one's insides and heal from the toxic shame.

Recovering from shame can occur at the same time a person works at freeing himself from the clutches of pornography. However, when a person works only on avoiding pornography and neglects to address issues with shame, he or she may impair full recovery.

Internalized shame also has spiritual solutions. Acquiring a true sense of being a child of God, with divine potential, is hard for people immersed in shame to connect to. Reaching out to others, especially to ecclesiastical leaders, helps because they can testify and affirm that one is a child of God, worthy of having the atonement of Jesus Christ applied to them. Church leaders help people turn to Christ and to become more attuned to the child of God within them. Reaching out to ecclesiastical leaders can eventually restore processes of accountability, intimacy (emotional closeness to others), and dependency on others and on God. Such an act breaks up secrecy and personal hiding and relieves one from feeling like an imposter. The first step, gaining a sense of being a "child of God," needs to take place in relationships with others, especially ecclesiastical leaders, who can affirm a person's eternal worth.

Rather than saying "I am bad because I desire pornography,"

people can say, "I am a child of God who has made mistakes. These mistakes have made it harder for me to connect with this godly sense within, but I am nonetheless a child of God with divine potential. I can change my behavior and heart and still live up to my divine potential."

Uncovering and overcoming internalized shame includes learning new ways to regulate and handle feelings. Stress, anxiety, fear, anger, hurt, and sadness are experiences everyone has. People who say to themselves, "I can feel pain and get through it without having to resort to escapes like pornography" have better emotional health than those who say, "I can't deal with these feelings." If a person is having trouble dealing with negative feelings and copes by trying to split them off as something that is not part of themselves or by trying to ignore the feelings, pornography use will only make all the feelings worse in the longer term. Pornography use is a fake fix that allows only temporary escape at best. Clearly it is more healthy to face feelings and get through them rather than escaping or avoiding them.

Since lack of emotional connection and dependency leads to shame, trying to become emotionally connected with others by reaching out to people and forming supportive relationships helps alleviate shame.[7] When one experiences intense internalized shame, it is natural to want to avoid people because of fears that they might discover the part of you that you despise. Fighting this tendency by being social, by being with other people, challenges the shame-prone person's internal representation of their world. Being with other people allows greater potential for acceptance, including our weaknesses. Reaching out socially also fights the tendency of a shame-prone person to be "me"-centered rather than "we"- (or relationship) centered.

Married people can overcome previous patterns of hiding, secrecy, and lack of self-disclosure by reaching out to their spouses through either talking or activities. Marriage is one of the best places to practice being who you are at all times and in all places. While using pornography can lead to hanging a "Do Not Disturb" sign out for one's spouse, reaching out with accountability and openness, trying to restore mutual dependency, is an invitation to a joyful relationship.

Stress reduction practices such as relaxation, deep breathing, prayer, and meditation also help people become less anxious about being with others. Always monitoring the environment and the people in it to protect oneself from being discovered is hard, tense work. Becoming honest rather than secretive, transparent rather than opaque, helps alleviate much stress, but other stress-reducing practices will also help.

For those healing from shame, it is important for them to identify and acknowledge things that trigger the pattern of shame. Steve learned that he would flip into what he called "a shaming period" any time he perceived that someone important to him discovered a mistake or some part of him that he didn't like. He felt unacceptable and bad even though the other person in the relationship probably wasn't seeing things that way at all. He became hopeless about his ability to have fun, loving relationships. The shame triggered by such circumstances often made him vulnerable to temptations of pornography. In his mind he had reached a state where relating to a screen or a piece of paper was easier and less threatening than relating to a real person.

With the help of a counselor, Steve eventually changed the way he responded in relationships. He learned to stop the negative shame cycle much earlier by questioning whether his assumptions about relationships were accurate. He questioned, "Has the other person discovered some negative aspect about me that she could not tolerate?" and "Even if she discovers this, will she really reject me?" Steve became much more aware of what triggered his entry into the world of shame, and this awareness allowed him to make different choices early in the shame cycle.

Other triggers for shame can include church meetings, hearing others talk about pornography, and hearing about others' successes. These are but a few of many possible triggers. Regardless of what the trigger is, it is important to be aware of it, choose how to respond to it before the trigger occurs again, and then implement that action when the trigger occurs. Practiced consistently over time, these strategies will take power away from triggers so that they no longer evoke great shame.

Two great antidotes to shame are integrity, meaning you do what you say you will do, and being the same person in all situations, including your private life with yourself. Of course, pornography involvement makes development of both of these conditions impossible. As one begins to loosen the bands of pornography, it is important that he also work on being totally accountable in all aspects of his life. He needs to work hard to have integrity. What he says is what he will do. Not having to worry that he is a different person in private than in public gives him a great sense of confidence in relationships.

Many who have suffered from the shame associated with pornography are free from both today. They did this by working on their spiritual connections with God, by trying to be accountable in all relationships, by reaching out to others to form appropriately dependent relationships that are also emotionally close, and by being the same person full of integrity in all situations. Although not easy, the path of freedom from shame and pornography is open to all who choose to take the journey.

SUGGESTED READINGS

Robert H. Albers, "Shame and the Conspiracy of Silence," in *Journal of Ministry in Addiction and Recovery* 7 (2000): 51–68.

A. J. Bridges, R. M. Bergner, M. Hesson-McInnis, "Romantic Partner's Use of Pornography: Its Significance for Women," in *Journal of Sex and Marital Therapy* 29 (2003): 1–14.

Ryan J. Burns, "Male Internet Pornography Consumers and Their Attitudes Toward Men and Women," in *Dissertation Abstracts International* 62, 5-A (2001): 1622.

Alice D. Domar, and Henry Dreher, *Self-Nurture: Learning to Care for Yourself As Effectively As You Care for Everyone Else,* New York: Viking, 2000.

James M. Harper and Margaret H. Hoopes, *Uncovering Shame: An Approach Integrating Individuals and Their Family Systems* (New York: W. W. Norton, 1990).

Elizabeth Oddone–Paolucci, Mark Genius, and Claudio Violato, "A Meta-Analysis of the Published Research on the Effects of Pornography," in Claudio Violato, Elizabeth Oddone-Paolucci, Mark Genius, eds., *The Changing Family and Child Development* (Burlington, Vt.: Ashgate, 2000), 48–59.

Notes

1. James M. Harper and Margaret H. Hoopes, *Uncovering Shame: An Approach Integrating Individuals and Their Family Systems* (New York: W. W. Norton, 1990).
2. Modified from Harper and Hoopes, *Uncovering Shame,* 10–11.
3. Harper and Hoopes, *Uncovering Shame.*
4. Robert H. Albers, "Shame and the Conspiracy of Silence," in *Journal of Ministry in Addiction and Recovery* 7 (2000).
5. Elizabeth Oddone–Paolucci, Mark Genius, and Claudio Violato, "A Meta-Analysis of the Published Research on the Effects of Pornography," in Claudio Violato, Elizabeth Oddone-Paolucci, Mark Genius, eds., *The Changing Family and Child Development* (Burlington, Vt.: Ashgate, 2000).
6. A. J. Bridges, R. M. Bergner, M. Hesson-McInnis, "Romantic Partner's Use of Pornography: Its Significance for Women," in *Journal of Sex and Marital Therapy* 29 (2003).
7. Alice D. Domar, and Henry Dreher, *Self-Nurture: Learning to Care for Yourself As Effectively As You Care for Everyone Else* (New York: Viking, 2000).

CHAPTER NINE

Confronting Pornography on the Internet

Rory C. Reid, Richard Crookston, and Evan Christensen

Pornography on the Internet is a problem that is growing at alarming rates. This chapter will address some of the tricks, traps, and tactics used by those who produce and distribute pornography on the Internet and provide information to help you know if your computer is being used inappropriately. It will also offer suggestions about how to minimize your risk of being exposed to pornography on the Internet.

The Internet itself is neither good nor bad. Brigham Young taught: "Every discovery in science and art, that is really true and useful to mankind, has been given by direct revelation from God. . . . We should take advantage of all these great discoveries . . . and give to our children the benefit of every branch of useful knowledge, to prepare them to step forward and efficiently do their part in the great work."[1]

NOTE: *Due to the rapidly changing technology of the Internet and the continuing research in the field of pornography problems, the authors of this chapter recommend www.confrontingpornography. com for additional information.*

President James E. Faust also spoke about the benefits of the web while warning about its dangers: "The miracles of modern technology have brought efficiency into our lives in ways not dreamed of a generation ago, yet with this new technology has come a deluge of new challenges to our morals and our values. Some tend to rely more on technology than on theology. I hasten to add that scientific knowledge, the marvels of communication, and the wonders of modern medicine have come from the Lord to enhance His work throughout the world. As an example, the Church's FamilySearch® Web site has more than seven million hits a day. But Satan, of course, is aware of this great progress in technology and likewise takes advantage of it for his purposes, which are to destroy and despoil. He delights in the pornography on the Internet and the sleaze in many of our movies and television shows."[2]

We encourage everyone to become familiar with the Internet and embrace every good thing it has to offer. Whether you're researching family history, keeping in touch with loved ones through email, or taking a virtual tour of the San Diego Zoo, the Internet has unlimited possibilities for learning and growth.

TRICKS, TRAPS, AND TACTICS USED BY PORNOGRAPHERS

Many tactics can be used by skillful web programmers to lure people to their Internet sites. Some of these tactics are legal; others are not. There have been some promising initiatives recently by different groups, including government entities, to curtail unethical and deceptive practices on the Internet. Unfortunately, purveyors of pornography also continue to become more skillful in finding ways around advancing technology and regulations.

The following are some of the more common tactics used:

1. Misspellings. Web site programmers can capitalize on

common spelling mistakes when they register their web site address by approximating web addresses that generate high traffic.

2. Registering Expired Domains when an owner neglects to reregister it. The expired domain's regular visitors will then be directed to the new site's content. Of course, this creates problems for the organization that owned the formerly legitimate website, its loyal visitors, unsuspecting organizations that continue to link to the site, and new visitors who find their way to the site by way of existing links.

3. Cybersquatting. With various extensions for domain name registrations such as *.net, .edu, .com, .org, .gov,* and others being added to the list, it is easy for pornographers to capitalize on the legitimate Internet address of another company, organization, or agency by simply registering the root name with a different extension. A good Internet filter can reduce the risk of being lured by those who cybersquat.

4. Page-Jacking. This tactic is employed when web programmers copy the content of a legitimate site, register their new site with search engines such as Yahoo, Lycos, or Alta Vista, and then subsequently redirect searchers for legitimate information to web pages containing pornography. A good Internet filter can reduce the possibility of exposure to page-jacking tactics.

5. Spam Email Unsubscribe. Those who promote pornography send millions of unsolicited emails each week containing inappropriate pictures and content. Clicking on links to "unsubscribe" from the junk email list can actually validate your email address to the sender, and they in turn can sell a validated list of working emails to others. This increases the risk of being exposed to pornography. In order to avoid this, just delete unwanted emails, and avoid clicking on the "unsubscribe" link.

6. Mousetrapping or Looping. Many pornography web sites contain code in the web page that keeps you trapped. You close one window and another opens, until you're inadvertently exposed to a half dozen images in a matter of seconds. A variation of this trick disables your web browser "Back" button so you cannot exit the page. One way to avoid these problems is to use a browser or browser extension program that supports pop-up blocking, but this causes problems with some sites that legitimately use pop-up windows. Another method is to shut down the browser when pop-ups occur. This can be done by using a task or process manager to shut down the application. For example, on a Windows XP machine, this is accessed by pressing Ctrl-Alt-Delete, clicking on Task List, selecting your browser's file (iexplore.exe if you're using Internet Explorer), and clicking on the End Process button. Another method for doing this is to close the windows faster than they appear, by repeatedly pressing Alt-F4 (Windows or Linux), which is faster than using the Task Manager method.

7. *Doorway Scams* use Internet search engines to bring unsuspecting traffic to their site by creating web sites or pages with non-pornographic themes; these are indexed on search sites but have computer code that redirects users to sites containing pornography. Even good filters may not avoid the initial nonpornographic page; however, they should flag the subsequent page you're being redirected to.

8. *Stealth Mode Downloads.* Sometimes files can be downloaded from the Internet to your computer without your knowledge. These files can launch programs that have numerous possibilities, such as changing your dial-up or browser settings. They can also push pornography to the user or harvest personal information, such as financial data, from your computer. To avoid becoming a victim of these tactics, never download or execute popup windows that occur while you're surfing the net unless you know what the program is installing. You can also install a program like Adaware, which monitors stealth installations.[3]

CHECKING FOR EXISTING PROBLEMS

Many individuals who access pornography on the computer know how to cover their tracks. This is one reason people view pornography on the computer: they assume they can hide the evidence and keep it a secret. However, even if an individual is meticulous enough to cover all his or her tracks, there are other usage habits that indicate possible problems with pornography. In time, most pornography habits come to light.

Don't panic if you discover some pornographic pictures on your computer. Unfortunately, if you have an Internet connection, it is common to find a few inappropriate pictures, which could have arrived through an unsolicited email or some other way besides someone actively searching for pornography. There are other signs however, that may suggest someone has been using your computer to deliberately access sexual content on the Internet. The following list is not exhaustive, and some of the suggestions are specific to the Windows operating system:

The first and easiest thing to check on the computer is the browser history. The most common browsers (Internet Explorer and Netscape) keep a history of all the WebPages accessed from those browsers. By simply going to the history in the browser (in Internet Explorer, press *Control + H*), you can see what has been accessed on that computer. If you notice after a couple of times that the history is always erased (indicated by time gaps in the entries of when pages are accessed), then someone may be trying to hide their browsing habits.

Even if the browser history has been erased, browsers store the actual contents of the most recently visited websites in the cache of your computer. (In Internet Explorer, go to the *Tools* menu and click on *Internet Options*. From the Internet Options Box click on *Settings*, then on *View Files*.) Cached files can also be deleted, and you can set your computer to not store any cached files, so the absence of cached content on your computer might indicate that someone is trying to hide evidence of his or her viewing habits.

Cookies are another way you can discover what websites have been visited on your computer. Cookies are an electronic notation in your computer that shows whether you have visited a particular website. Cookies are stored in your web browser's cache files and are usually labeled with the web site's address name. By looking at the cookies in your cache, you can see what types of websites have been visited.

Web browsers are not the only programs that store histories of what has been done on the computer. The Windows operating system keeps track of all files that have been recently opened on the computer. By looking at the "My Recent Documents" list from your Windows start menu, you can see if anyone has recently opened pornographic files, even if they deleted the original file after opening it.

Many programs keep track of recent files that have been opened within them. Two programs in particular include Windows Media Player and RealPlayer. These are two of the most popular programs to view video files on a computer. If someone has been viewing pornographic video clips, then one of these players will most likely have a record of it in their recently opened document list.

Any of these recent documents lists can be erased or can be set so they don't record any of the recent files that have been opened. If you go into any of these programs and notice that there are not any records in the recent file lists, it may indicate that someone is trying to cover his or her tracks. There is typically no legitimate need to delete these lists, since they take up such a small amount of storage space.

Most pornography on the computer is in the form of image and video files. Each file on the computer has an extension that indicates what type of file it is. You can quickly do a search for these types of files to discover if any of them contain pornographic material. In Windows XP check the Pictures and Photos and Video boxes and leave the search field blank. In other versions of Windows do a search for *.jpg, *.mov, *.avi, *.mpg files.

While chat and file-sharing programs can be, and often are, used for harmless purposes, they are so often used for pornographic reasons that it is wise to be aware of them.

Chat programs are one form of interactive technology that has been plagued by pornography and sexual predators. Internet robots infiltrate chat rooms and send messages to people that can make the receiver think the robot is a "real" person. When links are clicked by the receiver, they are subsequently redirected to a porn site. Various chat programs include AOL Instant Messenger, MSN Messenger, Yahoo! Messenger, and more inclusive IRC chat programs and newsgroups (programs include newsgroups, IRC chats, web-based chats, or HTML-accessible chats, Java chats, and instant messenger chats: AOL, MSN, ICQ, and Yahoo.)

While many people think chat programs are only for text conversations, many chat programs are used to share graphics and video files. If you find a number of chat applications on a computer, or you know of someone who is constantly spending time in chat rooms, it's worth exploring the possibility of a pornography problem.

Special care should be exercised when teenagers are using chat programs to communicate with their friends. It is important to make sure they are not venturing into "public" chat rooms. Horrific stories have flooded the news media about adolescents and adults who have been sexually assaulted during offline encounters with adult predators who pretended in chats they were teenagers.

File-sharing programs or peer-to-peer applications enable an individual to share any files on their computer with anyone else in the world who has the same program. There are a number of file-sharing programs available to freely download. (Some of the most popular file-sharing programs include Kazaa, BearShare, Limewire, Audiogalaxy, iMesh, BadBlue, Filetopia, Grokster, Azureus, Shareaza, Bit Torrent tt, eDonkey2000, Smirk, and Slyck.) It is wise to be aware of what file-sharing programs are on your computer and to know what they are being used for. It is also very simple to go into most of these file-sharing programs and view what type of searches have been done and for what type of content.

One of the final ways to discover if there is pornography on your computer is by doing a search in the registry. The registry is a system file in the Windows operating system that keeps track of all the settings on your computer. (Get the Windows Registry Editor by clicking on the *start* menu and then clicking on the *run* menu. In the run dialog box, type *regedit* and click *ok*. WARNING: Any settings changed in the registry editor can cause unwanted effects in the Windows operating system.) By doing a search on key words within the registry, you will be able to see if any content related to your key-word search is on your computer.

As pointed out earlier, there are many ways to inadvertently come across pornographic material while surfing the web or using any of the above programs. In determining whether or not you have reason to be concerned, take into account patterns in both the amounts of material found on the computer and the frequency with which it has been accessed.

ESTABLISHING EFFECTIVE BOUNDARIES FOR INTERNET USE

If you have a computer, there's a potential for pornography to enter your home. It's like a box waiting to be opened. Measures must be taken to ensure that the box stays closed, just as we do with household bottles containing toxic chemicals. Because pornographers are aggressive, we must take extra care when our children are using the Internet so we can reduce the possibility of their exposure to sexually explicit material. Even though there is no way to eliminate *every* possibility of being exposed, computers are still worth having. After all, we wouldn't remove all of the phones in the house if one had been used or could be used by a family member to indulge in phone sex. We must be able to co-exist with computers while establishing reasonable boundaries to help keep everyone safe!

Monitoring and Filtering Software. These programs are not fool-proof, but they offer a certain amount of protection and they keep getting better. Sometimes they block access to legitimately desired information—they may block a search for information about "breast cancer," for example. Some also significantly diminish the performance of your computer. Programs that offer a trial download can help you determine what product best suits your needs.

Despite the limitations of Internet filters, we recommend some form of protection. In order to offer you the most up-to-date information about filtering software, we have created the website www.confrontingpornography.com. The site www.internetfilterreview.com also reviews and compares filtering software. At the time of this writing, the top four filtering programs in a comparison of features and functionality are: (1) ContentProtect (www.contentwatch.com), (2) CYBERSitter (www.cybersitter.com), (3) Net Nanny (www.netnanny.com), (4) CyberPatrol (www.cyberpatrol.com).

These software products can usually be purchased for approximately $50. Be cautious with free programs because generally they have strings attached such as popup ads, or the programs themselves are spyware intended to harvest personal information from your computer.

Options for software that filters pornography may be offered by your Internet Service Provider (ISP).

Some programs monitor computer activity by taking "snapshots" of the computer screen at periodic intervals. SpectorSoft software (www.spectorsoft.com) is a program that can be installed in stealth mode so that it is undetected. It monitors the screenshots, email, and keyboard logging and recalls them in a slide show to provide visual evidence of computer use. Many companies use this type of software to monitor employee use of Internet access at work.

The best filters, of course, are moral filters. As President James E. Faust observed: "As the traffic on the communications highway becomes a parking lot, we must depend more and more on our *own personal moral filters to separate the good from the bad*. Marvelous as it is in many ways, there is something hypnotic about using the Internet. I refer specifically to spending endless time in chat rooms or visiting the pornography sites."[4]

Spam Email. Spam email is unsolicited and undesirable email that clogs up our "Inbox" email software. Distributors of pornography often send spam emails to entice people to their web sites. Programs such as SpamAssassin allow some rules to be applied to how email is prioritized in your Inbox, tagging suspect emails in advance. SpamStop, SpamEater Pro, and Qurb are some of the available Spam protection software programs, sites, and services. Sites that review spam filters include www.spamreviews.com and www.spam-filter-review.toptenreviews.com.

Popup Banner Ads. Some Internet sites contain popup banner ads that are intended to entice you to take tangents to other sites. Although many of these ads redirect you to sites about low-interest mortgages, online credit cards, and such, some redirect you to harmful sites such as online gambling casinos and possibly pornography sites. Google, a prominent online search engine service, provides a free popup blocker that significantly reduces the occurrences of these ads (www.toolbar.google.com).

ONLINE SAFETY CONSIDERATIONS

1. Place your computer in an area of your home where there is lots of traffic. Many families use the family room or the kitchen. If computers must be in bedrooms or home offices, establish a policy that requires doors to be open when the computer is being used, with monitors always facing the direction of the door so people passing by can easily see what's on the computer screen.

2. Computers should be protected with some level of security and regulation. Internet access should be filtered through parents who log children on to the web with supervised and limited hours of use. Teenagers should be afforded more latitude, but there should still be a system of regulating computer access and types of use.

3. Avoid computer use late at night when people are tired and may be more vulnerable to exploring inappropriate content.

4. Establish a policy that requires anyone exposed to pornography on the Internet to shut the *monitor* off and get a parent (preferably mother) to come and reboot the computer. Some people advocate "crash and tell," suggesting kids turn the *computer* off and then get a parent. We discourage this approach because it can damage computers to be shut down improperly, and it also erases any clues that might help determine what led to the unwanted exposure. When these events occur, write down the date and time and use the experience as a teaching tool. Have the family talk about what happened and adjust your policies to accommodate the newly acquired information and to prevent any additional exposure of the same type. This family practice also teaches children they do not have to be ashamed or hide unwanted exposures on the Internet.

5. Discuss as a family what personal information will be given over the Internet. Children should never give out personal information such as their name, email address, or phone number. Ken Hansen, a law enforcement official who works with the Utah Internet Crimes Against Children's Task Force, recently

demonstrated how a predator could locate a child with as little as two identifying pieces of information, such as first name and school mascot. Before you ever transmit personal information, make sure the Internet site is being hosted on a web server that is secure. You can usually determine if a site is secure (your online banking for example) because the URL will be https:// instead of http://. There will also usually be a yellow padlock on the bottom right corner of your web browser that looks like this: 🔒 This indicates that the server is secured and a complex encryption system is being used to transmit data.

Three groups that offer information and games that promote child education about safe Internet use are Media Awareness Network (www.media-awareness.ca), Disney (disney.go.com/surfswell), and NetSmartz (www.netsmartz.org), which is sponsored by the United States National Center for Missing and Exploited Children and Boys and Girls Clubs of America.

6. Use the Internet with a purpose. Elder Dallin H. Oaks commented: "We also need focus to avoid what is harmful. The abundant information and images accessible on the Internet call for sharp focus and control to avoid accessing the pornography that is an increasing scourge in our society."[5]

7. Use chat rooms and other instant messenger services with caution. Many people misrepresent themselves (e.g., their weight, sex, income, or age). If you do use such a service and arrange to meet your cyberfriend offline, meet in a public place. Children and youth, of course, should meet such friends only with a parent present. Even better, follow the counsel President Gordon B. Hinckley gave to youth and BYU students: "Don't try to create associations through the Internet and chat rooms. They can lead you down into the very abyss of sorrow and bitterness."[6]

On the positive side, Internet chat allows families who live far from each other to stay in touch without expensive phone bills and allows discussions among students and faculty of online independent study courses.

8. Consider bookmarking search engines in your web browser that are child friendly such as Yahooligans (yahooligans.yahoo. com). Kids Click (www.kidsclick.org) is a database of over 6,400 sites compiled by librarians with child-friendly searches.

9. Regularly take the steps described in the "Checking for Existing Problems" section of this article to check for inappropriate usage.

10. Get educated about the Internet. Take a community college class or ask your teenagers for an education about the web. Ignorance will only keep you in the dark.

Pornography represents a small portion of all the content in cyberspace; take advantage of the good and do what you can do to avoid being exposed to the bad. When proper policies and boundaries are established for Internet use, the likelihood of being exposed to harmful material can be minimized.

Notes

1. Brigham Young, in *Deseret News*, October 22, 1862, 129.
2. James E. Faust, "Of Seeds and Soils," *Ensign*, November 1999, 47–48.
3. http://www.lavasoftusa.com/software/adaware/ (accessed April 26, 2005).
4. James E. Faust, "The Power of Self-Mastery," *Ensign*, May 2000, 44; emphasis added.
5. Dallin H. Oaks, "Focus and Priorities," *Ensign*, May 2001, 82.
6. Gordon B. Hinckley, "A Prophet's Counsel and Prayer for Youth," *New Era*, January 2001, 4.

CHAPTER TEN

The Making of an Addict

Todd A. Olson

Addiction. The very word conjures up grim reaper–like images—a cloaked specter lurking in the shadows just waiting to strike out and claim another victim—a terrifying phantom with so many different snares in his bag of tricks that one of them is bound to find its mark. If he can't get you through the old standbys of alcohol, tobacco, and drugs, there's always sex and pornography. Or if those don't work, what about food and eating disorders, or even exercise? And nowadays, there are even twelve-step groups to help workaholics, chocoholics, and even the organizationally impaired.

Unlike the grim reaper, however, some among us seem to escape addiction's clutches, which brings up the question: Why do some people seem so drawn to a substance or behavior that others are loath to even try? Is there such a thing as a predisposition or propensity toward addictive behaviors? What, if anything, can you do to protect yourself and your loved ones from being sucked into the murky darkness of addiction?

To an addict, sex is central to his or her life in spite of the consequences that may result. It becomes more important than family, friends, and work. To ascribe to this level of dependency may sound absurd to some. It has been argued that people cannot be addicted to sex, as they would be to substances like alcohol or drugs. However, in 1988, the First Presidency issued this statement:

"Because of the addictive influence of pornography, one at first may simply tolerate its existence, then unconsciously come to accept it until moral feelings become desensitized, no longer outraged at its content. Pornography is a poison to the mind and spirit, ruining the lives and homes of innocent men, women, and children."[1]

President Faust even stated that "pornography is as addictive as cocaine or any illegal drug."[2] Of course, an individual must have engaged in the sexual behavior in question repeatedly in order to become addicted, but are there also other factors that might play a role? Consider the following:

There may be a family history of addiction or compulsive behaviors. When parents or family members try to deal with life problems and stresses with such behaviors (by overeating, overspending, overworking, using drugs, drinking, or engaging in other excessive behaviors), the children in that home face an increased risk of becoming addicted themselves.

Childhood abuse (sexual, physical, emotional, or substance abuse) and neglect is a factor in many cases of sexual addiction.

Sex addicts tend to come from rigid and disengaged families. (These terms will be described in greater detail below.) An environment that does not support a healthy, open forum for discussion of sensitive matters, such as sex, often leads to obsessive thinking on the very issues that are being avoided.

Even when genetics and family history are not predisposing factors, addiction may manifest itself in adult life during times of stress due to the pressures of school, marriage, family life, work, health problems, and mental health problems.

Feelings of low self-worth are common in most addictions, but what causes those feelings? Let's take a look at how we develop our core beliefs and how they affect our feelings of self-worth and subsequent choices.

THE CORE BELIEFS OF AN ADDICT

I will use the term *core beliefs* to refer to the way we feel deep inside about ourselves and the world. They are the basic, implicit assumptions that guide our very approach to life. Your core belief system usually originates from experiences and pivotal events in your life, particularly the experiences you had in important relationships. If you have developed faulty beliefs and, hence, feelings of low self-worth, they may have come from early childhood experiences. Or you may have developed a faulty belief system as an adult through unhealthy relationships or sexual acting out.

Most sexual addicts have woven a complex set of faulty beliefs around four essential anchor points, which are:

Self-Image

How do you perceive yourself? Deep down, most addicts see themselves as bad or unworthy. When you act out in a sexually inappropriate way and are unable to stop or control it, these faulty beliefs are confirmed. You may spend an inordinate amount of time maintaining your image and overcompensating for your perceived deficiencies. Many sexual addicts are perfectionists who play the exhausting game of overachievement, with the debilitating fear that they will be found out.

Relationships

Does your spouse or partner complain that you seem aloof, unavailable, or unattached in the relationship? A faulty belief system often contributes to a lack of intimacy in sexual addicts' relationships. In fact, sexual addiction is often seen as an intimacy disorder—an inability to love or be loved. Since most addicts feel unlovable, they believe that no one could ever love them as they really are so they must hide their real self. These secrets are the lifeblood of addiction. The fear of being rejected by those closest to them can be so strong that addicts retreat into their own private worlds.

Needs

Are you generally very independent, preferring to do things yourself rather than asking for help? As a rule, addicts find it hard to trust and feel that no one else can be depended on. It's easier and safer not to rely on anybody else. Sex addicts commonly feel that they can heal themselves; they don't need a therapist. In their minds, they are certain that they can handle it on their own.

Sexuality

Could you survive without sex? Addicts often confuse sex with love and feel desperate to have it. Life becomes unmanageable when sex is more important than everything else, but to the addict, life without sex seems terrifying or impossible.

THE FAMILY SYSTEM

Since our core belief system usually originates from experiences and pivotal events in our family of origin, it is often valuable to take a closer look at how your experiences in your family may have contributed to the way you see yourself and feel about yourself. This is not about blaming the family, but about gaining insights that can help you in your efforts to change unwanted behaviors.

A well-respected method of analyzing the family's effect on an individual member was developed in the 1980s by David Olson,

Ph.D., and his colleagues. Their Circumplex Model examines two essential components of the family system: *adaptability* and *cohesion.* It provides a way to look at the family system and proposes that when there is moderation in both of these dimensions there is a greater chance that family members will develop and maintain a healthy self-image and a balanced lifestyle.

Family adaptability is measured by the ability of a family system to change its power structure, role relationships, and relationship rules in response to situational and developmental stress. The continuum used to analyze a family's adaptability fits on the following scale: (See Figure 1.)

Rigid: controlling and authoritarian leadership with strictly defined rules and roles

Structured: mix of authoritarian and egalitarian leadership, resulting in stable rules and roles

Flexible: egalitarian leadership, some shared decision-making, with easily changed rules and roles

Chaotic: erratic and ineffective leadership, inconsistent rules and roles

Figure 1

ADAPTABILTY

Extreme	Balanced	Extreme
(1) Rigid	(2) Structured	(3) Flexible	(4) Chaotic

Family cohesion is defined as a) the emotional bonding members have with one another and b) the degree of individual autonomy a person experiences in the family system. (Autonomy is a sense of independence and self-sufficiency.) Family cohesiveness also fits on a continuum of four levels as follows: (See Figure 2.)

Disengaged: creating emotional distance between family members

Separated: fostering a sense of self and individual autonomy outside family

Connected: emphasizing family togetherness and loyalty, working together to allow for some individual autonomy

Enmeshed: extreme closeness and fierce loyalty, allowing no individuality, and little sense of self

Figure 2

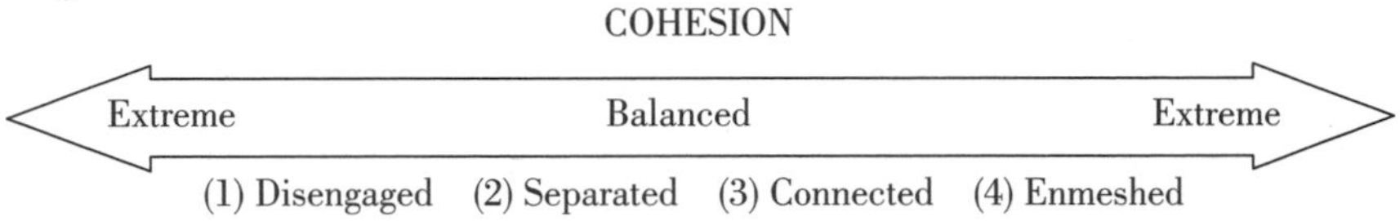

COHESION

(1) Disengaged   (2) Separated   (3) Connected   (4) Enmeshed

In terms of both adaptability and cohesion, the healthiest family styles fall within the center of the scales, often fluctuating between (2) and (3) on both dimensions. On the other hand, when family styles tend toward the extremes, (1) and (4), the probability of resulting addictive behaviors is much higher. The research I've done in my practice indicates that two-thirds of those who are being treated for addictive behaviors, come from families representing the extremes in both cohesion and adaptability, with the most common combination being *rigidly disengaged.*

When addicts and partners assessed their own marriages, the results often ended up being similar to their families of origin, with the majority being rigidly disengaged marriages.

These extremes—rigid, chaotic, disengaged, and enmeshed—do not allow for the development of high regard for self. In other words, healthy boundaries have not been developed. When a marriage falls in the same extremes as the family of origin, there will be a hard road to recovery if the current system does not change.

DEVELOPING HEALTHY BOUNDARIES

As infants we come into the world with no sense of boundaries or of being separate from others around us. Our caregivers set boundaries for us in order to keep us safe. If we are in a healthy environment, as we grow we become aware that we are separate beings with separate needs and emotions. We learn to express ourselves and to make our needs known. With this growth and autonomy comes the need to establish boundaries that define us as individuals. These boundaries become an imaginary perimeter that provide a secure sense of individuality.

Some children learn to set healthy, appropriate boundaries for themselves. These children usually come from homes where the parents and other members also have healthy boundaries; their family systems are flexible yet structured, connected but with room for separateness. Such family systems create the opportunity for family members to develop healthy boundaries, which translate into a healthy sense of autonomy.

Those who are not taught consistently how to set boundaries are left to figure out significant life experiences without proper guidance. Unable to define healthy boundaries, these children grow into adulthood without a clear sense of their own needs, wants, emotions, or beliefs.

If we have learned to develop healthy boundaries, we continue to develop new boundaries—or adjust our existing boundaries—as we grow into adulthood. But if we have not learned to define boundaries for ourselves, or if our boundaries have been consistently violated, we will adapt to surviving without defined boundaries, sometimes with disastrous results. Those struggling with sexual addictions may not have learned how to develop healthy boundaries during their childhood. They most likely grew up in a closed family system where childhood experiences fell into the extremes of:

Being sheltered from life experiences.

Being exposed to certain experiences at an inappropriate age.

Poor communication between parents and children.

Being raised by parents with unhealthy boundaries.

Not being taught properly about sex or maturation.

Being physically, sexually, or emotionally violated.

Being verbally abused.

Sometimes events happen outside of the family that contribute to a child's low self-regard. For example, if a child who does not fit in is taunted and bullied during his school experience, he may develop feelings of low self-worth, a poor self-concept, or a negative body image. These early feelings of self-doubt and insecurity, as well as diminished self-confidence, can potentially contribute to negative core beliefs later on as an adult. If such an individual comes from one of the extreme family styles mentioned above, his risk is enhanced further. Sometimes the traumatic events are such that even a child from the most functional family can have his or her coping capacities overwhelmed. In either case, the extra help of a therapist can benefit the family.

CONCLUSION

The complex issue of how present patterns are affected by one's childhood and family of origin should be handled with care and without looking to place blame. To explore these issues further, you may benefit from the help of a qualified, licensed therapist.

NOTES

1. Ezra Taft Benson, Gordon B. Hinckley, and Thomas S. Monson, in "Statements by Leaders of The Church of Jesus Christ of Latter-day Saints Concerning Pornography," June 1, 1988.
2. James E. Faust, "The Enemy Within," *Ensign*, November 2000, 45.

Supporting Those Who Struggle

CHAPTER ELEVEN

From One Wife to Another: Dealing with Your Husband's Pornography Addiction

Colleen C. Harrison

When you find out your husband has a sexual addiction, it may feel like the worst tragedy you could imagine. Maybe you had *no* idea, assuming his fidelity was as unwavering as your own. Or maybe you had some clue that he'd indulged just a little, experimented with pornography in earlier years, but he had *assured* you it wasn't an ongoing problem. Then the day comes when you learn there's a repetitive pattern already established in his life—the secret soul-sickness of pornography and masturbation. You confront him. You sob. You rage. You frantically try to police his life. Over and over again, he either pledges to reform with tears and sorrow or he responds with defensiveness. Bitterness begins to replace love in the heart and mind of each of you.

Or maybe, by the time you discover it, his addiction has escalated so that his heart and mind have been enslaved, his values twisted and perverted to the point he has actually acted out. He's had an affair or been with a prostitute. And all the while you were faithful, believing, trusting. Now your trust turns to humiliation and pain. Your own sanity feels like it's hanging by a thread. You walk through your days, dealing with the children, going about your routine like a zombie. Nothing seems real or tangible any longer. It feels like something in you has died, and so it has. In the Book of Mormon, the prophet Jacob speaks to the men who had violated their marriage covenants in those very terms:

"Behold, . . . ye have broken the hearts of your tender wives, and lost the confidence of your children, because of your bad examples before them; and the sobbings of their hearts ascend up to God against you. And because of the strictness of the word of God, which cometh down against you, *many hearts died, pierced with deep wounds*" (Jacob 2:35; emphasis added).

I have experienced this pain, anger, sorrow, and hurt. I have also experienced the miracle of being restored to life and emotional wholeness. I have lived to know that the power of the Lord Jesus Christ to resurrect a person from the dead applies just as surely to the things of the heart and spirit as it will someday apply to the physical body.

You may be at the beginning of your own "dark night of the soul" brought on by discovering your husband's illicit sexual behavior. Or you may have been aware of it and suffered from it for days, weeks, months, or maybe even years. You may still be living with him, trying desperately to control his agency. You may be separated from him, or even divorced. Wherever you are in your journey, hope and peace can truly come into your heart even after this devastating situation you now face. It may take some years and a lot of rethinking and redesigning of your life and priorities. However, I can promise you that your faith, hope, and trust in marriage and even in your husband, if he chooses to allow it, can be rebuilt.

You can *choose* to survive this and heal, whether your husband chooses to or not. It is a choice between living in denial—pretending it didn't happen and keeping it a secret—and facing this reality and reaching out for help to overcome it. Just like strenuous exercise causes temporary pain because of torn muscle fibers, which then heal by building new fiber, resulting in increased strength, this terrible pain and heartache can actually be left behind and make you a stronger person.

This season of your life is a time of intense exercise of all the principles of the gospel. First you must start seeking help by asking questions, reading literature, and talking to priesthood leaders, trusted family and friends, or professional counselors. Above all you must start seeking direct counsel and comfort from your Heavenly Father and from His beloved Son, Jesus Christ. Elder Richard G. Scott of the Quorum of the Twelve made this statement about seeking help to recover from a devastating life experience:

"No matter what the source of difficulty and no matter how you begin to obtain relief—through a qualified professional therapist, doctor, priesthood leader, friend, concerned parent, or loved one— no matter how you begin, those solutions will never provide a complete answer. The final healing comes through faith in Jesus Christ and His teachings, with a broken heart and a contrite spirit and obedience to His commandments."[1]

Mary is a young friend of mine. Our deep sense of friendship comes from an afternoon we spent together over two years ago when she came to my home to talk. She had heard about my husband, Phil's, successful recovery from pornography addiction. She wanted to know what I had done to help him. She was shocked at my answer, "As little as possible." She demanded an explanation. She went home incredulous that day, maybe even a little skeptical. However, she prayed and felt impressed to just believe and start experimenting in her life with the principles we had discussed. The alternative was to leave her husband and throw away their temple marriage, and she couldn't imagine doing that. She has thanked me over and over again in the years since. As I prayed about what I could share here, I gave Mary a call.

I was thrilled to hear that her husband, John, was still in

recovery from his addiction and, in fact, had just been called to the elder's quorum presidency. It had been over a year since he had acted out with pornography. I could hear the tears in her voice.

I asked Mary to remind me what we talked about so long ago that had proven most valuable to her. Without hesitation, she recited a list of suggestions I had given her, a list she had committed to memory from the notes she had taken that day. Below are those suggestions, in the form of a conversation like the one Mary and I had.

LIVE IN THE LIGHT OF TRUTH AND LET IT SET YOU FREE

Learning the truth about your husband's sexual addiction is so hard, but it is actually, for most wives, the *beginning* of sanity, not the end of it. Perhaps we had suspected something was wrong with our marriage, even assumed it was our fault. Often our spouse allowed us to take the blame to draw attention away from himself. Thus, a marriage becomes damaged and unhealthy in direct proportion to the secrets the partners keep from one another. This is actually Satan's goal when he entices a partner to secret sin: the soul-sickness of pretending and outright lying that begins to infect an entire family.

I had to learn that although honesty hurts, it is the only way to clean things up and begin to heal. I once heard someone say, "The truth will set you free, but first it will make you mad." I had to accept the unavoidable truth that if my husband and I weren't willing to bear the burden of each other's reality, we weren't really experiencing a true marriage but only playing house. I look back now and realize that the crisis of facing the reality of my husband's addiction to pornography was the crisis that demanded we finally start having a heart-deep, honest relationship based on the *whole* truth of both of our realities, weaknesses and all. I had to be willing to hear him talk about what was really going on with him, including how far his addiction had progressed.

I also had to be willing to tell my husband the truth about how I felt. I learned that it was absolutely essential that I tell him the truth about how his actions were affecting me and our family. At first, I was ashamed that I couldn't speak of these things calmly, without tears and terrible pain, but I came to realize they had to be said *honestly*, even if that meant I had to admit the heart-rending pain I was in. I came to realize that only the *truth*, even the painful part of the truth, could contribute to making the situation right. I had to be *plain* and I had to speak *truly* (see 2 Nephi 33:6).

You may be unable to avoid crying and expressing yourself with energy when you share your own pain and fear with your husband. People who feel like their whole world is collapsing aren't usually able to be totally unruffled or calm about it. For this reason, you may want to arrange to be away from the children when you tell him how you feel. Go for a drive, or, *better yet, make arrangements to include your bishop or a therapist if possible.* The one boundary for this hour of reckoning is this: Don't rage. Don't attack. Don't tell him your feelings in a spirit of vengeance or hatred. Believe me, he doesn't deserve your hatred as much as he does your pity. Do it in a spirit of someone who is hurting so badly they can't avoid crying out about it. Without raging or attacking him personally, explain the repercussions his behavior is having on you emotionally and physically. Tell him how close you are to having your own heart and the love in it die, pierced through, as Jacob put it, "with deep wounds."

But what if he just ignores my feelings? I've actually expressed my feelings before and he's gone right back to acting out.

Telling him the truth about how his addiction is affecting you can't be done as a front or guise to try to make him change. The harsh, cold truth is that his inability to change immediately is not an indication of whether he respects your feelings or not. He is *addicted.* No matter how much he may want to change, even motivated by a deep love for you and his children, he no longer has the power to stop. Addiction is not just a bad habit. One of the truths you must deal with is that during his recovery process, he probably isn't going to have perfect, "black-or-white" abstinence at first.

In the first year of my husband's recovery work, he had an occasional slip. Part of his recovery was to tell me when it happened, and part of my recovery was to let him tell me. Keeping a prayer in my heart, I would listen. I didn't ask for details.

But I feel desperate to know the details. How can you not want to know the details?

Because dwelling on details isn't helpful for anyone involved. Perhaps the *details* of our sins is what the prophets refer to when they say we should remember (ours and others) sins no more once we've repented. Obviously, they don't mean forget that the experience ever happened, because then we would learn nothing from our experience and would be setting ourselves up to have it happen again. But we need to stop obsessing about and rehearsing the particulars. Both of you will be tormented if you choose to replay the details.

As I enlarged my own understanding of prayer by studying the scriptures, especially the Book of Mormon, I learned that I could look unto the Lord in *every* thought (see D&C 6:36) and counsel with him continually in my heart and mind (see Alma 37:37; 3 Nephi 20:1). I began to pray in the midst of my conversations with my husband, seeking the Lord's Spirit to guide me and to give me the ability to react as he would react. Drawing on this power, I found myself able to hear my husband's truth and recognize it as the burden, the scourge, and the sorrow that it was to him. I learned to help him understand that his descent into addiction happened over time and that recovery would also take time. We would both have to be patient and long-suffering with the process of recovery, which for most people includes a few slips. If he's honest, expressing sorrow and remorse, you can both be reassured that he's on his way out of the abyss. Discouragement and panic need to be avoided if a slip occurs.

I began to realize that it took a lot of pressure off my husband when he knew I wouldn't go into hysterics if he shared his reality with me. This actually removed another excuse for him to lie—to protect me. Gradually, I came to genuinely value living in the light of truth. It helped to remember that Satan thrives and revels in secrecy. The truth could and did make me free. It made me free to live in reality and to make my decisions from a more informed position. It wasn't always what I wanted it to be, but the truth made us both become real to each other.

"DON'T TAKE HIS BEHAVIOR PERSONALLY"

How can you say, "Don't take it personally"?

Your husband's sexual addiction *is not about you.* Many boys have their first exposure to pornography when they're still prepubescent—before twelve years of age. And contrary to the expectations of most men with an addiction, getting married doesn't cure it.

It's not uncommon for a wife to believe that if she were more attractive, more alluring, if she were "enough for him," he wouldn't turn to these "perfect" images of other women. This belief is totally unjustified. If a man's satisfaction with his wife depended on physical attractiveness or sex appeal, we would expect men married to supermodels or movie stars to be the most faithful of husbands.

When my husband and I began to honestly face his addiction together, though it was hard for me to understand, he explained his involvement with pornography had *nothing* to do with him admiring the women in the pictures. He said they really weren't *people* but flat, two dimensional *images* that caused a certain reaction in his body, a reaction that he had become addicted to as a teenager.

As I listened, I thought of the books on sexual addiction that I had started reading. Hormones are the most powerful chemicals in the human body; they cause sexual arousal, which is extremely mood altering. Some experts have compared their power to heroin or cocaine.

But there must be something I can do to get him to quit!

As backwards as it may sound, the least you do to get him to change, the greater hope there is of him changing. It may help to picture what experts advise us to do if while we're on a camping trip in the mountains we wake up with a giant grizzly bear breathing in our face. *Lay very still.* This is probably the single most illogical and terrifying thing to do. Be still and pray.

Probably the single most powerful version of this counsel came in likening Doctrine and Covenants 123:17 to my own circumstances:

"Therefore, dearly beloved brethren, let us *cheerfully* do all things that lie in our power; and then [when we can not longer function with kindness and good humor] may we stand still, with the utmost assurance, to see the salvation of God, and for his arm to be revealed" (emphasis added).

But I'm terrified that if I quit trying to help him control this thing, he'll just get worse.

That is a real possibility, if he has either been (1) relying on your censure and blame to keep him from doing his addiction *or* (insane as it may sound) (2) using your censure and blame to *justify* doing his addiction. Your pulling out of the "game" may leave him without a conscience on the one hand or an excuse on the other. He will be left alone with his own choices as well as with the pain they cause. He will have to begin to face and decide what *he's* going to do about it.

While it may be good to monitor a child's behavior and teach them right from wrong, it is *not* healthy to treat a grown adult in the same fashion. When I tried to manage my husband's life, I treated him like a child and only contributed to his excuse to continue behaving in a childish way. I learned to get out of the way and let him come face to face with the truth of how addicted he really was and how deeply it was damaging his life. I had to have the humility to allow him to find answers on his own, through other means besides me. I had to learn not to panic about the amount of time he spent attending recovery meetings and studying recovery principles. I had to take my heart and mind off of him and turn to the Lord to develop my own parallel life—close to his, but only interweaving as two sovereign equal adults, not as someone playing the exhausting role of parent figure.

This will be one of the greatest challenges *you* will ever face in your own life. It will be just about as difficult for you to face as your husband's challenge is for him. This is what is meant when it is said that the spouse of an addict may be codependent and that this codependency is an addiction too.

The spouse is an addict too? What in the world do you mean? I don't understand this whole idea of codependency.

Codependency is a challenging concept because it can show up in two almost opposite forms. It can manifest as either fear *of* the addict or as fear *for* the addict. If your codependency takes the form of fear *of* your husband, then you fear his moods, such as anger or depression, and what he will do if he gets in that mood. You're terrified to say or do anything that will set him off. You're willing to put up with anything rather than upset him. In other words, you're about as dependent on him to make your life okay as he is on his addiction to make his life okay. On the other hand, if you fear *for* the addict, you're likely to take exactly the opposite attitude toward him, trying to control him and save him from his own choices, no matter what his reaction may be.

Either way, you are as caught up in the addict's life as he is trapped in his addiction. You are being robbed of a peaceful, happy life by his choices, *just like he is!* It's sort of like breathing secondhand smoke. You're not the smoker, but the quality of your life is being sacrificed to his addiction. You will be in recovery from codependency when you realize *you* must make choices for your own life, regardless of the choices he makes.

"REALIZE THAT ADDICTION IS NOT JUST A BAD HABIT"

Many people do not understand the dynamics of addiction. They think it is a habit that can be broken just by the exercise of more willpower. Your husband probably thought that in the early stages of his addiction. Then, when he tried to quit, he began to realize it was a *really bad* habit. When he tried to quit again and again, maybe dozens of times, and couldn't stay "quit," he began to despair. What had happened to his ability to choose?

Elder Russell M. Nelson taught that: "Agency, or the power to choose, was ours as spirit children of our Creator before the world was. (See Alma 13:3; Moses 4:4.) It is a gift from God, nearly as precious as life itself. Often, however, agency is misunderstood. While we are free to choose, once we have made those choices, we are tied to the consequences of those choices. We are free to take drugs or not. But once we choose to use a habit-forming drug, we are bound to the consequences of that choice. Addiction surrenders later freedom to choose. Through chemical means, one can literally become disconnected from his or her own will!"[2]

Elder Boyd K. Packer made this statement concerning the progressive slide into bondage addiction represents: "It begins as an innocent curiosity, Satan influences your thoughts, and it becomes a pattern, a habit, which may imprison you in an addiction . . . (see John 8:34; 2 Pet. 2:12–14, 18–19)."[3]

Addicts have forfeited their "response-ability" when they let their curiosity become a repeated choice, then a bad habit, and then, unbeknownst to them, an addiction. These progressive stages lead to the hell of addiction, and just as the Book of Mormon testifies, they start out as light as flaxen cords (see 2 Nephi 26:22) but end up being the very chains and shackles and *fetters of hell* (see D&C 123:8).

"THE LOSS OF AGENCY TO ADDICTION"

SINGLE ACT
(done in ignorance or foolish experimentation)
⇩

REPEATED ACT
(sought out deliberately in order to alter mood)
⇩

HABIT
⇩

ADDICTION OR COMPULSION
(loss of ability to resist doing it)

These steps will help you understand how your husband was (and still is) the really decent guy you originally thought him to be, but who has contracted a serious illness—*addiction*. To think addiction is the same as a habit could be compared to confusing a wart with skin cancer. As we all know, a wart can be taken care of with a quick, comparatively painless procedure. A skin cancer may go deep into the tissue beneath. Or worse yet, it may have metastasized and spread throughout the body of the victim.

An addictive behavior in its early stages is usually resorted to as an attempt to escape a bad mood. None of us likes to be in a bad or negative mood, whether it be fearful, anxious, sad, lonely, or even bored. These moods are uncomfortable, and we all look for some way to alter them or to escape them. People turn to a variety of things to ease the discomfort, such as food, cleaning, shopping, service, or working hard. And some turn to sexual stimulation. As mentioned earlier, the hormones that cause sexual arousal are extremely mood altering.

Addiction must be considered a multidimensional problem.

The actual act of unhealthy, undesirable behavior is just the obvious part—sort of like the bright yellow flowers on a dandelion. Below that are the emotional foliage that draws on the environment to keep the flowers alive. These could be compared to the current emotional climate of the addict. And finally, there are the extremely deep roots of the addiction that go deep into the *spiritual* dimension of its victim's life.

Remembering the stages of this progressive illness will help you understand why other people you love (including yourself) may continue eating or working or spending money or watching television or several dozen other things even when these behaviors are done in excess and hurt them and their loved ones.

Addiction *must* be treated on all three levels, *especially* on the spiritual level where the roots are. Stopping the behavior and even dealing with emotional factors are only like mowing the tops off a dandelion plant. As long as its spiritual roots are not dealt with, the addiction will constantly be reasserting itself.

"LET GO AND LET GOD WORK WITH HIM"

Remember that your husband's addiction is about him and his relationship with God and the Lord Jesus Christ. The question *he* needs to ask *himself* is, "What think ye of Christ?" Not, what think ye of your wife or children? No loyalty less than a love and devotion to God Himself is going to sustain your husband to face the deluge of sexual temptations he encounters. There is no other way to escape. We must all become immune to the world from the inside out, from the spiritual depths of our *living*, loving relationship with the Savior and Heavenly Father.

Until we allow the Savior's Spirit and his power to remit the effects of sin—whether our own or another person's—we will keep returning to the addictive cycle:

"And they all cried with one voice, saying: Yea, we believe all the words which thou hast spoken unto us; and also, we know of their surety and truth, *because of the Spirit of the Lord Omnipotent, which has wrought a mighty change in us, or in our hearts, that we have no more disposition to do evil, but to do good continually*" (Mosiah 5:2).

Note that it was *not* the people's exertion of their own will that wrought a mighty change in their hearts. Heart surgery is solely the province of the Lord. Once a person submits his heart to Him, He can literally change that disposition so he no longer desires wrongdoing.

"DON'T ISOLATE. FIND OTHERS WITH WHOM YOU CAN COUNSEL"

You need to separate your husband's challenge (the fact that he's developed a sexual addiction) from your problem (you're living with someone with a sexual addiction). You need to realize that you have your own bishop to whom you need to go for your own sake, not just to fix your husband. Go to your bishop in the same spirit in which you must approach the Lord—seeking counsel and guidance, strength and blessings for yourself. It's not tattling on your husband to go to your bishop for your own needs and for help in your decisions.

What if I've actually participated in unrighteous sexual behaviors myself in order to appease or try to stay close to my husband?

Sadly, others in close relationship with the addict may get pulled into participating. Far too many boys, for example, have been introduced to pornography by finding their father's or brother's stash. Don't think you're unique if, as a wife, you've been enticed to participate in some way. While there can be a great deal of overlap between men's and women's reasons for getting involved in sexual activity, a woman is usually motivated by a desire for emotional intimacy and a sense of connection with her partner. If this is your situation, it is even more reason to seek your bishop's help.

"TURN TO THE SAVIOR FOR YOUR OWN COMFORT AND STRENGTH"

Just as your husband must "come unto Christ," so must you in order to find his peace (see Omni 1:26; Philippians 4:7). "And moreover, I say unto you, that *there shall be no other name given nor any other way nor means whereby salvation can come unto the children of men,* only in and through the name of Christ, the Lord Omnipotent" (Mosiah 3:17; emphasis added).

Never did the following scripture mean more to me than when I was dealing with my husband's addiction: "Counsel with the Lord in all thy doings, and he will direct thee for good; yea, when thou liest down at night lie down unto the Lord, that he may watch over you in your sleep; and when thou risest in the morning let thy heart be full of thanks unto God; and if ye do these things, ye shall be lifted up at the last day" (Alma 37:37).

As you have to think through this terrible challenge, you must look to the Lord in as many thoughts as you can (see D&C 6:36). You must cultivate your own ability to perceive the whisperings of the Holy Spirit of Truth. Only by that source can you know what to do. More than just being active in your ward, you will need to have personal devotion, including sincere prayer and deep pondering of the scriptures. As you consult daily with the Lord (and sometimes each hour), he will lead you to know what you need to know in order to do what you need to do. You will be led to the right people to talk to. He will guide you to know what to say to your husband and when to say it. He will guide you to know when to show mercy and when to be firm.

The way you and your husband are going to get through this challenge (as well as the many others mortality will bring) is for both of you to put God first, come unto the Father through his Beloved Son, Jesus Christ, and seek the companionship of the Holy Ghost and the counsel of the Lord. *Then,* your love for each other will be grounded in his love, even charity. Charity is the pure love *of* Christ (for Christ as well as from him). When each of you comes to the Savior, you will come to each other in a way that you've never known before. The greatest love you will ever feel for each other is *his* love.

Please pray and ponder these words. I know that you can enter spiritually into the Savior's arms (see D&C 6:20–21) and find an immediate relief from your hopelessness and trauma. His promise of comfort and rest is not just for someday, but for right now—in the midst of your sorrow and pain.

"Wherefore, I would speak unto you that are of the church, that are the peaceable followers of Christ, and that have obtained a sufficient hope by which ye can enter into the rest of the Lord, from this time henceforth until ye shall rest with him in heaven" (Moroni 7:3).

It is my prayer that you will remain close to the Church and to your family, friends, and Church leaders. They will be the Savior's instruments in bringing you much of the fellowship you need. But always remember, no one else's help is equivalent to the Savior's. I pray that you can "enter into the rest of the Lord" and have him strengthen and inspire you, no matter what your husband's choices may be.

Notes

1. Richard G. Scott, "To Be Healed," *Ensign,* May 1994, 9.
2. Russell M. Nelson, "Addiction or Freedom," *Ensign,* November 1988, 7.
3. Boyd K. Packer, "Ye Are the Temple of God," *Ensign,* November 2000, 73.

CHAPTER TWELVE

Participating in the Work of Spiritual Redemption and Healing

Ruth Davidson and Tamara Davies

O nly those who have borne the heartaches, sorrows, and trials of working with people bound by pornography addictions can understand the depths of pain and grief that are a part of the process of moving toward recovery and healing. But the Lord, in his infinite wisdom and mercy, will often call upon those who are carrying these great burdens to help in the redemptive and healing process of transgressors, transgressors whose souls truly are of great worth in the sight of God (see D&C 18:10). It is often through loved ones and their efforts that transgressors come to feel the miraculous power of the Lord's saving atonement—the inward cleansing and the "mighty change" of heart that goes along with it. (see Mosiah 5:2) It is many times through these saving efforts that transgressors can come to taste of the Lord's everlasting patience for them in working out their salvation. Though it is not always easy, those who work hand in hand with the Lord through this redemptive process can come to taste of his everlasting mercy and become, as the scripture says, "saviours . . . on mount Zion" (Obadiah 1:21).

ALLEGORY OF THE OLIVE TREE

The allegory of the olive tree in the fifth chapter of Jacob in the Book of Mormon can be applied to the miracle of healing in the lives of couples or others who have had to struggle through pornography addictions and have overcome them together.

In the first place, transgressors have been planted "in a good spot of ground; yea, even that which was choice . . . above all other parts of the land of my vineyard" (v. 43). In other words, transgressors may have been planted in places where the gospel has been taught and the gospel light has been available to them. The Lord knows their "roots are good" (v. 36), that these souls have valiant spirits who have good desires and intentions.

But the "loftiness" of these transgressors—their pride and haughtiness—have "overcome the roots which are good" and they have become "corrupted" (v. 48). Their behaviors and actions have become wicked. The Lord says of these transgressors that they "[profit] me nothing, and the roots thereof profit me nothing so long as [they] shall bring forth evil fruit" (v. 35).

The Lord feels deep sorrow for their wicked actions and evil behaviors: "The Lord of the vineyard wept, and said unto the servant: What could I have done more for my vineyard? Behold, I knew that all the fruit of the vineyard, save it were these, had become corrupted. And now these which have once brought forth good fruit have also become corrupted; and now all the trees . . . are good for nothing save it be to be hewn down and cast into the fire" (vv. 41–42).

The Lord claims that these transgressors should be lost "except we should do something for [them] to preserve [them]" (v. 37).

Therefore, the Lord plants servants in their lives who will, along with the Lord, "labor with their mights" and who will "obey the commandments of the Lord of the vineyard in all things" (v. 72).

Together the Lord and his servants work hard and long in these efforts to cleanse. They "graft" (v. 54) and "pluck" (v. 52) that they may "preserve" the soul of the transgressor, "that when they shall be sufficiently strong perhaps they may bring forth good fruit unto [the Lord], and [he] may yet have glory in the fruit of [his] vineyard" (v. 54).

This is a slow, gradual, arduous process, done in a specific time frame for both the transgressor and those surrounding him. The Lord counsels His servants, "Ye shall not clear away the bad thereof all at once, lest the roots thereof should be too strong for the graft, and the graft thereof shall perish, and I lose the trees of my vineyard" (v. 65). The Lord continues, "Ye shall clear away the bad according as the good shall grow, that the root and the top may be equal in strength, until the good shall overcome the bad" (v. 66). In other words, the Lord waits until his servants have become sufficiently strong in testimony and inward steel before he calls them to this work of overcoming the bad.

He then asks his servants to continue to labor "with all diligence" (v. 74). They do such labor insomuch that "there began to be the natural fruit again in the vineyard; and the natural branches began to grow and thrive exceedingly; and the wild branches began to be plucked off and to be cast away" (v. 73). They continue even until "the bad had been cast away out of the vineyard, and the Lord had preserved unto himself . . . the natural fruit, which was most precious unto him from the beginning" (v. 74).

The Lord then calls his servants who have labored with him and commends them for their diligent work: "Blessed art thou; for because ye have been diligent in laboring with me in my vineyard, and have kept my commandments, . . . *behold ye shall have joy with me because of the fruit of my vineyard*" (v. 75; emphasis added). The Lord then promises that generations afterward will be blessed because of this great work. "For a long time will I lay up of the fruit of my vineyard unto mine own self," he claims (v. 76). This came about, in part, because of the diligent work of his faithful servants who labored with him in his vineyard.

The Lord can truly effect this miracle of healing in the lives of transgressors when righteous and faithful servants work hand in hand with him. "And then shall they rejoice; for they shall know that it is a blessing unto them from the hand of God; and their scales of darkness shall begin to fall from their eyes; and many generations shall not pass away among them, save they shall be a pure and a delightsome people" (2 Nephi 30:6). This blessed promise can apply to transgressors and their loved ones who cleanse lives and lineages through the redeeming power of our Lord and Savior, Jesus Christ.

"IN THE DAY OF MY WISDOM THEY SHALL RETURN"

The Lord, in working with transgressors, will in his mercy most often bring to light sins and transgressions when there is the greatest possibility of healing. It may not seem that the Lord has a hand in engineering events like this, but as he has said in the scriptures, he "knoweth all things from the beginning, wherefore, he prepareth a way to accomplish all his works among the children of men" (1 Nephi 9:6).

These times of darkness and trial will one day be turned into blessings. As C. Terry Warner said, "Heaven, once obtained, will work backward and turn even . . . agony into glory."[1] The scriptures say it this way: "Let your hearts be comforted; for all things shall work together for good to them that walk uprightly, and to the sanctification of the church" (D&C 100:15).

Transgressors can rest assured that although the Lord has "suffered . . . affliction[s] to come upon them, wherewith they have been afflicted, in consequence of their transgressions" that he "will own them, and they shall be [his] in that day when [he] shall come to make up [his] jewels" (D&C 101:2, 3).

Those willing to work with transgressors in overcoming sin can find comfort and strength from a special promise given by the Lord: "If it so be that you should labor all your days . . . and bring, save it be one soul unto me, how great shall be your joy with him in the kingdom of my Father!" (D&C 18:15). Notice the Lord puts an exclamation point at the end of the verse. This indicates the depth and magnitude of his promise. Many of those who do this come to realize that transgressors have often come on foreordained missions to cleanse lineages that have been plagued by sexual or other grievous sins. Like the Lamanites, "it is because of the traditions of their fathers that caused them to remain in their state of ignorance; therefore the Lord will be merciful unto them. . . . And at some period of time they will be brought to . . . know of the incorrectness of the traditions of their fathers; and many of them will be saved" (Alma 9:16–17).

Might not the Lord assign valiant spirits these missions of cleansing, perhaps blessing them with valiant, faithful partners or others who have been ordained to help and assist in this process? Perhaps he trusts that these great souls who have sinned would strive beyond the wickedness and damaging influence of intergenerational traits or other weaknesses to overcome them and finally begin a pure and chosen generation. He promises, "He that is weak among you hereafter shall be made strong" (D&C 50:16). The Lord truly loves his wandering souls with a depth and breadth one only begins to sense when working hand in hand with him in healing the life of a transgressor.

WORKING WITH TRANSGRESSORS IN THE HEALING PROCESS

It should be noted that not all relationships where pornography addictions have been present can and will move toward healing. Often a transgressor has become so entrenched in sin that he will not be able to make his way out in time to heal a marriage and family. Despite others' willingness to help, unless there is willingness on the part of transgressors to overcome sin and see where problems in relationships truly lie, healing will not occur.

Elder David E. Sorensen said it like this: "Forgiveness of sins should not be confused with tolerating evil. . . . The Savior asks us to forsake and combat evil in all its forms, and although we must forgive a neighbor who injures us, we should still work constructively to prevent that injury from being repeated. A woman who is abused should not seek revenge, but neither should she feel that she cannot take steps to prevent further abuse. . . . Forgiveness does not require us to accept or tolerate evil. It does not require us to ignore the wrong that we see in the world around us or in our lives. But as we fight against sin, we must not allow hatred or anger to control our thoughts and actions."[2]

The Prophet Joseph Smith said it this way: "You need not be teasing your husbands because of their deeds, but let the weight of your innocence, kindness and affection be felt, which is more mighty than a millstone hung about the neck."[3]

Throughout the process of working with transgressors, there will be a constant battle to handle circumstances either Satan's way or the Lord's way. Satan's paths will always cause worse and more extensive damage; the Lord's way will encompass moves toward healing, wholeness, and forgiveness.

Satan would have someone blame, manipulate, and control a partner; the Lord would have someone try to love, forgive, and help that person. Satan would plant seeds of disgust, repulsion, and bitterness for past mistakes and weaknesses; the Lord would cultivate compassion and forgiveness. Satan would continually bring past deeds forward, never letting them be forgotten; the Lord would ask that past misdeeds be given to him, letting him be the one who hands out judgment and retribution. Satan would have someone hold relentlessly to hurts and injuries; the Lord invites that person to come to him to have those wounds healed. Satan would make someone feel as if overcoming the transgression is impossible, that weaknesses will always prevail; the Lord would have someone believe "I am able to make you holy" (D&C 60:7) and that he "knoweth the weakness of man and how to succor them who are tempted" (D&C 62:1).

Fruits that come from Satan's tactics include despair, feelings of hopelessness, depression, bitterness, anger, rage, contention, and retribution. Fruits that come from the Savior include peace, inward calm, strength, comfort, wholeness, forgiveness, determination, and hope. Though there will always be a struggle between these two forces, more and more light and greater and greater peace will come into the lives of those who seek the Savior's way in the paths of healing. Satan would only create greater wounds, deeper darkness, and lasting misery. It is only the Savior's hand that can rebuild broken relationships and bring happiness back into a home or marriage.

One woman had some experiences that helped her gain insight into the patience she would need in helping her husband overcome his addictive tendencies. During the year before she found out about her husband's sinful behavior, she went through some tremendous physical trials that resulted in two surgeries and months and months of healing. During this time, she struggled with fatigue, depression, and pain. She could hardly function and felt emotionally drained and weary. Increased weight became the most troublesome issue for her, but she scarcely had the time to exercise and felt increasingly discouraged.

When the sinful actions of her husband came to light, she realized, through an impression, that the Lord gave her all the previous physical difficulties—especially the inability to lose weight—so she could relate, in a small way, to what it would be like for her husband to overcome his sins. She knew and sensed the hardship of it because she had tasted some of her own. This experience gave her added capacity to seek the patience she would need to deal with the difficulties in their marriage.

Those who need patience like this should pray like Alma: "O Lord, wilt thou grant unto me that I may have strength, *that I may suffer with patience these afflictions which shall come upon me,* because of the iniquity of this people" (Alma 31:31; emphasis added). By adopting this attitude, those working with transgressors can become instrumental in helping them discover needed keys and tools for overcoming sin. They can be messengers of the promise that the Lord "has all power to save *every man* that believeth on his name and bringeth forth fruit meet for repentance" (Alma 12:15; emphasis added).

COMPENSATING BLESSINGS

Those who take upon themselves the burdens of working with transgressors need to understand that one day the Lord will compensate them for every unjust burden placed upon their shoulders because of the unrighteous choices of others. Blessings will come abundantly to help through times of trial and challenge. The Lord will "impart unto [them] of [his] Spirit, which shall enlighten [their] mind[s], which shall fill [their] soul[s] with joy" (D&C 11:13). He will give "strength such as is not known among men" (D&C 24:12) to those attempting to do his work. He will also help them bear "with patience the persecution which [is] heaped upon them" (Alma 1:25), especially when these persecutions come from the very people they are attempting to help. The Lord will also give blessings of peace to those working with transgressors during times of oppressive darkness when they cannot overcome it on their own. Like the Lamanites converted by Nephi and Lehi, the "cloud of darkness" will be "removed from overshadowing" them when they call upon the Lord in faith (see Helaman 5:41).

Many testify of how the Lord will reach out in mercy and

tenderness during times of struggle and heartache. For one woman, priesthood blessings became a tremendous source of counsel, strength, and insight. She recalls one blessing where she was told to "cling to the iron rod with both hands for those who are clinging to you," knowing this meant she needed to stay spiritually strong for her children and her husband, who had been trying to overcome sin. Another woman recalled during a time of intense darkness and struggle that a beautiful hymn played over and over in her mind. She was not familiar with this hymn, but after a careful search through the hymnbook, she found that the music went to "Jesus, Lover of My Soul," which includes the plea, "Other refuge have I none, hangs my helpless soul on thee. . . . Cover my defenseless head with the shadow of thy wing."[4]

THE MIRACLE OF REDEMPTION

A man who struggled with sin in his life shared a dream that helped him overcome transgressions that had been a part of his past. In that dream, he entered a place where he saw, through an opened doorway, a darkened, hazy bar where people were laughing and enjoying worldly pleasures. They seemed to be having a good time. For a moment, he felt drawn to them and thought of joining them, participating in their indulgences. Then he quickly decided, "No. I've decided against doing those things. I don't want that to be a part of my life anymore."

As he turned away from the doorway, he noticed a stairwell nearby. The light on the stairs seemed to grow with each successive step upward. He became curious about these stairs and decidedly turned toward them to begin an ascent to the top. The higher he got, the more clearly he could hear music that was being sung by a choir. The music almost beckoned him because of its beauty. When he arrived at the top of the staircase, he could see a large crowd of spectators watching and listening to this choir sing.

Surprisingly, the choir was small; there were "few singers and a lot of empty seats." Still, choir members sang powerfully. These people were singing under the direction of the choirmaster, who he sensed innately was our Lord and Savior, Jesus Christ.

The music became so compelling it soon became apparent he didn't solely want to listen; he felt a deep desire to participate in the singing. In his longing to do this, he worked his way through the large crowd and finally approached the choir. He sat on the ground near them, listening intently to the music. He knew he couldn't join them because he "didn't know the words." So he sat on the ground and listened. Finally, there was a woman who glanced over at him and saw him sitting on the floor. With one hand, she beckoned him to join her, and he got up and sat beside her. She then showed him the words to the song they had been singing, pointing at them in the book she held. From this gesture, this man became able to participate in the choir and began to sing. He now knew the words.

This man found great spiritual significance in this dream. He came to believe that his wife, who had been a light and strength to him through times of sin and transgression because of her faith in the Savior, was the woman who shared her songbook with him and taught him to sing. He feels his desire to become sanctified and cleanse his life came from her sharing the music of her testimony and love of the Savior—that because of her prayers, the "prayers of the righteous," he was spared (see Alma 10:23).

"HOW GREAT SHALL BE THEIR JOY"

The miracle of healing has come to many couples who have struggled through the consequences of sin and transgression. Those who align their wills to the Savior's can begin to taste of his healing power. As President Howard W. Hunter once said, "If Jesus lays his hands upon a marriage, it lives."[5]

One woman described the miracle of healing this way: "The path was never easy, but it was worth it—to see what my husband is today. It's amazing to watch what he has become. And my children now have their father." Another woman compared the past pain and heartache of her husband's betrayal to memories associated with the difficulties of childbirth. "I can remember the pain of labor and how badly I felt giving birth, but it's become a faded memory to me. You do forget the intense pain associated with a betrayal. There is healing. I would never trade my husband for what he is today."

Many couples can testify that the healing of the Savior has come into broken, damaged relationships and made them whole once again. Truly, the Savior can bring about "beauty for ashes" in relationships once damaged by sin (see Isaiah 61:3). In fact, many couples have come to believe, despite the hardships they've been through, that they would not forgo past trials because of the knowledge of the Savior that they've gained through difficult experiences. They will be eternally grateful for the miracle of the atonement that has healed damaged relationships and made them beautiful and whole once more.

NOTES

1. C. Terry Warner, "Why We Forgive," Audiotape (Salt Lake City: Deseret Book, 2000).
2. David E. Sorensen, "Forgiveness Will Change Bitterness to Love," *Ensign*, May 2003, 12.
3. Joseph Smith, *Teachings of the Prophet Joseph Smith*, ed. Joseph Fielding Smith (Salt Lake City: Deseret Book, 1976), 227.
4. Charles Wesley, "Jesus, Lover of My Soul," in *Hymns of The Church of Jesus Christ of Latter-day Saints* (Salt Lake City: The Church of Jesus Christ of Latter-day Saints, 1985), no. 102.
5. Howard W. Hunter, "Reading the Scriptures," *Ensign*, November 1979, 64.

CHAPTER THIRTEEN

From Victim to Agent: Rising above a Spouse's Pornography Problem

Lili De Hoyos Anderson and Christian B. Anderson

Discovering a partner's pornography problem plunges you into a whirlpool you did not choose and over which you feel no control. But the turmoil doesn't have to last forever. A spouse cannot control her partner or the pornography problem itself, but she can learn to respond in ways that help her rise above the pornography problem, no longer a victim, but an agent. As an individual turns from victim to agent, not only does she become a stronger, healthier individual, but the spouse is left with complete responsibility for his involvement with pornography. Thus he may be more likely to begin serious efforts to conquer the problem. In fact, the spouse's ability to combat the problem will increase, since

NOTE: *Most of these remarks are addressed to wives of men who have an involvement with pornography. Certainly there are also women who have a pornography problem, although this is less common. Many of the ideas discussed in this chapter apply to either male or female spouses. There are some concepts, however, that are more specifically applicable to women whose husbands struggle with this problem.*

more energy will be going into conquering the problem rather than into an exhausting marital conflict.

When a wife finds out about a husband's pornography problem, she feels victimized. In a way, she is being victimized. A pornography problem, sometimes defended as a "victimless crime," in fact claims many victims. Direct impacts on the marriage can include loss of emotional intimacy, increase in sexual demands, diminished sexual interest, unfaithfulness, loss of common interests and concerns, loss of sensitivity, and dysfunction in the relationship (including loss of trust).

When needs are threatened at a serious level, the typical human response includes hurt, pain, grief, anger, stress, and other negative emotions. The more important the need and the more serious the threat, the deeper the hurt. A wife needs to feel loved; she needs to feel her marriage is safe; she needs to feel that she and her husband feel the same way about significant behavioral and lifestyle choices. Certainly, if actively involved in the Church, a wife also needs to feel that her husband is a worthy priesthood holder ready to bless family members and to perform ordinances for the children. She needs to feel that she and her husband are "equally yoked," both worthy of full fellowship in the Church and of temple recommends, and equal in their desire to progress toward the celestial kingdom, where the potential for an eternal marriage exists. A husband's choice to indulge in pornography jeopardizes all of these, posing a huge threat to his wife's needs, which helps to explain how deeply hurt and angry a wife may be.

Sometimes husbands express surprise at how deeply hurt and angry their wives are about the husbands' involvement with pornography. Understanding a basic gender difference can help husbands understand how serious a threat the pornography is for wives. It has been said that "men are like microwaves and women are like crock pots" when it comes to physical desire. That is, woman are typically slower in building up feelings of sexual desire, while men can reach a state of sexual arousal very rapidly. One reason for this difference is that, for women, generally, physical desire depends a great deal on satisfying levels of emotional intimacy. Simply put, for women, satisfying sex is tied into a satisfying relationship. (Women who develop pornography problems are typically drawn to pornographic images in the context of a relationship. Women may immerse themselves in steamy romance novels with explicit sexual content, but the sex is presented in the context of a relationship. Another way that women get involved in pornography is through chat rooms on the Internet. Again, the woman is able to imagine the sexual talk in the context of a relationship with the person to whom she is chatting.)

Men are hard-wired differently. They more readily view sex and relationships as separate categories or compartments of life. A wife who is not feeling very happy with her husband because he's not helping with the kids, or because they had an argument about money, comes to bed *not at all* in a romantic mood. When her husband starts to show interest in sex, she may respond, "You're crazy. I'm not even speaking to you." The husband asks, "What does that have to do with it?" The wife can't understand how her husband can be so clueless and insensitive, and the husband is confused because he just doesn't see the problem.

This disparity can be almost comical in a healthy marriage relationship. But when a wife discovers that her husband is involved in pornography, because of the stronger link for women between sex and a positive relationship, she's going to take it extremely personally. The wife sees desire and love as closely connected, and when she learns that her husband is getting "turned on" looking at other women, the rejection is very, very deep. A husband may protest, "It's not about you," but the wife may never be completely convinced.

If a woman is to become more of an agent, rather than remaining a victim, she must first process and resolve the powerful negative emotions that otherwise interfere with making healthy, appropriate choices. Then she will be more able to make rational, healthy, and appropriate decisions, and act on them.

PROCESSING AND RESOLVING ANGER AND HURT

A wife must, if she wants to work through her feelings, first accept those feelings. While this may sound simple, it can be a serious challenge. Acceptance is more than acknowledgement. "Acknowledgement is admitting, being able to say that something is true. Acceptance goes much deeper. . . . Acceptance means receiving on an emotional level what one admits to be true on an intellectual level."[1] We are not suggesting acceptance of the pornography problem but a wife's acceptance of her own anger, grief, and pain. Many LDS women struggle with accepting their anger. They may acknowledge that they are hurt and angry, but they often struggle with feelings of guilt, shame, unrighteousness, or even spiritual unworthiness because of strongly held beliefs that their angry feelings are wrong.

Consider, however, how such a belief—that being angry makes them unworthy—would place Moses, Job, Nephi, Joseph Smith, and many other prophets under condemnation. The scriptures are replete with examples of angry prophets. Moses expressed anger against the hardhearted and stiff-necked children of Israel (see Numbers 11:11–15). Job expressed anger at God, questioning why he was ever born (see Job 3:11). Nephi was terribly upset about his continuing struggles with human weakness—specifically mentioning that he felt anger toward his brothers (see 2 Nephi 4:17–27). Joseph Smith felt so hurt that he accused God of abandoning the righteous: "O God, where art Thou?" (D&C 121:1). And God and Christ describe their own feelings of righteous indignation as anger.

How then can members of the Church better understand that their own angry feelings are not evil? Let's be clear about this.

First, we are talking about *feeling* anger, not *acting* in anger to hurt others. Second, we are not denying that it's a worthy goal to be free from angry feelings. We are only suggesting that the way to become free of anger is to work through those feelings, not to repress or deny them, and certainly not to turn our ideals into a club with which to beat ourselves.

Note, too, that while acceptance is more than acknowledgement, it is less than approval. While it is important to understand and accept anger at a spouse's involvement with pornography, it is neither necessary nor desirable to approve and encourage those feelings. While hurt and angry feelings do not make us unacceptable to God, certain expressions or actions based on those feelings may.

A trusted listener can be a tremendous help in working through feelings of anger. Talking to someone about our feelings in an open and honest way helps alleviate negative emotions. However, it is not easy to find a trusted listener. Caution in choosing someone who can be trusted with such information is essential. Then, even if we are fortunate enough to have someone completely trustworthy with whom to share, few people are very skilled or effective listeners. Even the most loving and benevolently intended friends or family members may be uncomfortable hearing outpourings of pain and hurt. To "help," they offer advice, which may interrupt and interfere with the expression of negative emotions. Sometimes we can "coach" a confidant into being a better resource by explaining that we just need feelings to be understood and accepted, not approved or endorsed, fixed or solved.

Writing can be another excellent source of emotional release and relief, if done correctly. First, whatever is written for this purpose must be closely guarded to protect others from reading our negative feelings and being hurt by them. Second, this is not a permanent record. This is a workbook journal, and when it has accomplished its purpose it can be destroyed. Third, writing should be unfettered and unedited. This is a means of expelling the ugly, painful emotions that are hurting us. If we try to hold back or clean up what we express, most likely the repressed feelings will intensify, rather than dissipate. If safely expressed, the negative emotions release and reduce in intensity.

Finally, seeking emotional support from God can be very helpful. Again, we must not try to edit what we pray about. As noted, the prophets did not hesitate to express negative thoughts and feelings to the Lord.

Interestingly, social science literature supports the importance of working through anger in appropriate ways. Professional research in psychology suggests that anger, when processed appropriately, can be transformed to sadness or disappointment, and subsequently to forgiveness or holding a person who has wronged us accountable (or a combination of both). This transformation heals a person from being paralyzed by their strong emotions associated with the behavior that has hurt them.[2]

ADDRESSING THE PROBLEM IN A HEALTHY, RATIONAL WAY

In addition to accepting and working through anger, a spouse can turn from being a victim to an agent by addressing the problem in a healthy, rational way. In our observation, this includes several components:

1. Remember That It's Not Your Fault. Men struggling with pornography addiction often stress that they want their wives to remember the following:[3]

1. You're not the source of the problem.

2. You're not responsible for his behavior.

3. You've done nothing to cause him to go to pornography.

4. Repeat numbers 1 through 3, as necessary.

This is a mantra a wife needs to keep repeating when faced with a husband's addiction to pornography. It's not your fault. You did not somehow fail in the relationship. You did not push him toward pornography.

In the Book of Mormon, the prophet Jacob gave a powerful speech rebuking husbands who are guilty of sexual transgression:

"For behold, I, the Lord, have seen the sorrow, and heard the mourning of the daughters of my people in the land . . . because of the wickedness and abominations of their husbands. And I will not suffer, saith the Lord of Hosts, that the cries of the fair daughters of this people . . . shall come up unto me against the men of my people. . . . For they shall not lead away captive the daughters of my people because of their tenderness, save I shall visit them with a sore curse, even unto destruction" (Jacob 2:31–33).

Jacob did not admonish the wives to be more attractive and desirable, more loving, more sexually available. President Boyd K. Packer once said, "That word guilt should go with sin,"[3] our *own* sin. Taking upon ourselves the guilt for others' choices is not healthy or productive and limits our ability to respond appropriately.

Jacob continued: "O all ye that are pure in heart, lift up your heads and receive the pleasing word of God, and feast upon his love; for *ye may, if your minds are firm,* forever" (Jacob 3:2; emphasis added). Having a firm mind requires a clear delineation of responsibility. We are responsible for our own actions, not for the actions of others.

2. Establish and Maintain Firm Boundaries. Most of us are familiar with the concept of "hate the sin, but love the sinner." However, in a world that preaches moral relativism and characterizes the hatred of sin as intolerance, this is increasingly challenging. In sincere efforts to love a sexually addicted husband, a wife may find herself tolerating inappropriate sexual behaviors, including involvement with pornography. Where should lines be drawn? How much right does a wife have to demand that certain behaviors stop? How can such demands be enforced? As you think about the specific boundaries to set for yourself, here are some suggestions:

Don't ignore the signs of your partner's double life.

Don't accede to your partner's unhealthy sexual demands.

Don't tolerate abusive behavior toward yourself or your children.

Don't place yourself at risk for serious disease.

Don't cover up for your partner's behavior by lying or making excuses for him to bosses, coworkers, friends, and family.

Establishing healthy boundaries can be a strenuous task, and it may seem terribly unfair that so much is required of you when the problem was brought into the family by the choices of your husband. As challenging as it may be, however, a great opportunity exists to turn your weaknesses into strengths. This is not about "blaming the victim," it's about learning to be an agent. If you get mugged, it's not your fault. It's the mugger's fault. Nevertheless, if you're getting mugged every day of the week, you're walking down the wrong roads, and you can do something about it. Only children, because of their complete dependence on adults, can be consistently victimized *over time* without their own assent. This is why the Lord makes such stringent statements about those who hurt little children. ("Whoso [offends] one of these little ones which believe in me, it were better for him that a millstone were hanged about his neck, and that he were drowned in the depth of the sea" [Matthew 18:6; see also D&C 121:22].) Adults have more power and choices. The spouse of someone with a pornography problem can gain understanding, develop skills, and establish boundaries to deal with the problem and no longer, in any way, support the behavior that victimized them and others.

To a large extent, human behavior is motivated by the benefit gained, minus the cost exacted, for the behavior. Where there is little cost and relatively high payoff, behavior is not very likely to change. With a pornography habit, the payoff for the behavior is immediate. But the costs—though incredibly steep—may seem easily deferred to the point where a husband may have been convinced by the adversary that he will never have to pay those costs.

Clear communication by a spouse can help a struggling individual become more aware of what his actions cost—and will cost in the future, if he continues on their present course. One young man said, "Ecclesiastical leaders and professional counselors have been encouraging and supportive, but no one has helped me see the consequences of my actions quite like my wife. She has made it clear to me that she will not tolerate my addiction. She loves me and wants to be with me, but she can't stand the fact that I am struggling with this. I know that if I don't overcome this addiction, she will leave me. She would hate to, but I know that she would do it. This instills fear in me. I fear that I will destroy my family and myself if I don't fix this. Talking to her has helped me see the consequences of my actions more clearly. I am more motivated to overcome, not just for my own benefit, but to keep my family, and ultimately, my salvation."[4]

Communication of boundaries may be done between husband and wife or, if no progress results, may need to be repeated with witnesses. Witnesses might include parents of either or both spouses, priesthood leaders, and close friends. Children should *not* be involved in the confrontation, possibly excepting adult children.

Some are concerned that the determination to establish firm boundaries seems unforgiving. However, when we quickly forgive someone who continues to choose behaviors that hurt us, we are not so much exercising a Christlike response as we are assenting to our own victimization and the self-destruction of the sinner. President James E. Faust wrote, "Companionship with evil causes our whole being to die spiritually."[5]

When John Taylor was the prophet, a First Presidency statement included this powerful warning: "The mantle of charity must not be stretched so widely, in our desire to protect our erring friends, as to reflect dishonor on the work of God, or contempt for the principles of the everlasting Gospel. There is an unfortunate tendency in the natures of many to palliate sins by which they are not personally injured, but we must not forget that such palliation frequently increases the original wrong, and brings discredit on the Church and dishonor to the name and work of our blessed Redeemer; in other words, to save the feelings of our friends we are willing to crucify afresh the Lord of life and glory."[6]

SEEKING TO FORGIVE AND TRUST AGAIN

Reunion does not come without a price. Lewis Smedes spoke of this price, saying: "I may forgive you in my heart and free myself from my hatred of you, but before I rejoin you as my friend, I demand a price from you. The price is honesty. The currency of honesty is remorse and conversion. And there is no reunion unless the price is paid."[7]

"Trust requires time—time for a husband to change and grow. Trust requires a track record, a pattern of consistent ongoing trustworthiness."[8] It would be unrealistic to expect a pornography problem to disappear overnight, or in a month, or perhaps even in a year. It is not unrealistic, however, to expect to see real change that progresses over time, even if there are stops and starts and setbacks along the way.

"Trust [also] requires empathy from the husband. He needs to acknowledge the hurt and pain his actions have caused you. And trust requires grief. He must feel genuine remorse for the losses his sin created."[9] As David Augsburger explained, "Forgiveness does not mean returning to business as usual but crafting a new relationship with a level of intimacy appropriate to our level of trust."[10]

A clear message on forgiveness is given in scripture: "I, the Lord, will forgive whom I will forgive, but of you it is required to forgive all men" (D&C 64:10). Eventually, any of us seeking to be acceptable in the kingdom of God must forgive any who trespass against us. However, don't try to force forgiveness too soon, particularly before substantial change has occurred or sufficient time has passed for healing. In order to forgive in a healthy and complete way, we must first be *safe* from the destructive behavior. Safety is achieved through consistently improved behavior on the part of the responsible party or through distancing ourselves from the hurtful behavior, if necessary.

Forgiveness can also be premature if we haven't fully worked through our feelings of pain and anger. "If forgiveness eludes you and you feel stuck in your pain and anger, I encourage you to return to the grieving process. . . . Forgiveness comes as a gift when we've completed healthy grieving."[11] Of course, being cautious not to jump prematurely to forgiveness while a person struggles with learning how to change does not leave us free to seek revenge or be hurtful in other ways. That response would turn the victim into a victimizer, now also culpable.

Even after safety is achieved and emotional processing is complete, it may take a while for healing—and healthy, true forgiveness—to come. Rather than pressing ourselves to forgive because we think we should be ready to do so, we need to give it time. After we have done the necessary preparatory work, the atonement of Christ provides forgiveness to us as a gift, over time. President James E. Faust spoke on this subject, giving this explanation and example:

"The Atonement not only benefits the sinner but also benefits those sinned against—that is, the victims. By forgiving 'those who trespass against us' (JST, Matt. 6:13) the Atonement brings a measure of peace and comfort to those who have been innocently victimized by the sins of others. The basic source for the healing of the soul is the Atonement of Jesus Christ. . . . A sister who had been through a painful divorce wrote of her experience in drawing from the Atonement. She said: 'Our divorce . . . did not release me from the obligation to forgive. I truly wanted to do it, but it was as if I had been commanded to do something of which I was simply incapable.' Her bishop gave her some sound advice: 'Keep a place in your heart for forgiveness, and when it comes, welcome it in.' Many months passed as this struggle to forgive continued. She recalled: 'During those long, prayerful moments . . . I tapped into a life-giving source of comfort from my loving Heavenly Father. I sense that he was not standing by glaring at me for not having accomplished forgiveness yet; rather he was sorrowing with me as I wept. . . .

"'In the final analysis, what happened in my heart is for me an amazing and miraculous evidence of the Atonement of Christ. I had always viewed the Atonement as a means of making repentance work for the sinner. I had not realized that it also makes it possible for the one sinned against to receive into his or her heart the sweet peace of forgiving.'

"The injured should do what they can to work through their trials, and the Savior will 'succor his people according to their infirmities' (Alma 7:12). He will help us carry our burdens. Some injuries are so hurtful and deep that they cannot be healed without help from a higher power and hope for perfect justice and restitution in the next life. Since the Savior has suffered anything and everything that we could ever feel or experience (see Alma 7:11), He can help the weak to become stronger. He has personally experienced all of it. He understands our pain and will walk with us even in our darkest hours."[12]

Struggling with a partner's pornography problem can be a frightening, exhausting experience. However, this struggle doesn't have to continue without hope. Learning and living by the principles discussed here can imbue that struggle with meaning and direction whereby the spouse can move from being a victim to being an agent. If your partner addresses and works to conquer his pornography problem, together you can become healthier, happier, and eligible for continued blessings in your relationship as you progress together. If your partner remains involved in pornography, it does not have to destroy you or your children. Healthy handling of emotions and healthy boundaries can be learned and practiced and safety can be achieved. Whether we move ahead alone or with our partner, we must move ahead. There is a place of peace waiting for us.

NOTES

1. Marsha Means, *Living with Your Husband's Secret Wars* (Grand Rapids, Mich.: Fleming H. Revell, 1999), 33.
2. Leslie Greenberg, *Emotion Focused Therapy: Coaching Clients to Work Through Feelings* (Washington, D.C.: American Psychological Associated Press, 2002).
3. Boyd K. Packer, "A Plea to Stake Presidents," Leadership Training Meeting, April 1, 1988, 4.
4. Anonymous, a student in one of the authors' classes.
5. James E. Faust, "Strengthening the Inner Self," *Ensign*, February 2003, 5.
6. John Taylor, quoted in *Messages of the First Presidency of The Church of Jesus Christ of Latter-day Saints*, 6 vols., ed. James R. Clark (Salt Lake City: Bookcraft, 1965–75), 3:88.
7. Lewis Smedes, *STEPS: The Magazine of Hope and Healing for Christians in Recovery* 8, no. 3 (Fall 1997), 15.
8. Means, *Living with Your Husband's Secret Wars*, 158.
9. Means, *Living with Your Husband's Secret Wars*, 158.
10. David Augsburger, "The F Word," *STEPS: The Magazine of Hope and Healing for Christians in Recovery* 8, no. 3 (Fall 1997), 6.
11. Means, *Living with Your Husband's Secret Wars*, 163.
12. James E. Faust, "The Atonement: Our Greatest Hope," *Ensign*, November 2001, 20.

CHAPTER FOURTEEN

Supporting Those Who Struggle with Pornography: Suggestions for Ecclesiastical Leaders, Family, and Friends

Richard A. Moody

O ver the years, as my colleagues and I have worked with those who struggle with pornography, we have tried to listen and learn from the very people who have sought our help. We have also listened and learned from ecclesiastical leaders and others who love and care about the welfare of individuals who suffer.

Religious leaders, family members, and spouses have a great desire to help and support those who struggle with pornography. Often loved ones may not fully comprehend why pornography is such a desperate struggle. Naturally, family and friends vacillate between showing empathy, patience, and love while dealing with negative feelings and adverse reactions. Understandably, these reactions may include expressing disdain for the offender's actions. These reactions may include ultimatums or condemning the offender by reminding him that his behavior will certainly have adverse effects on his life and the lives of others. Loved ones have difficulty understanding how the struggling individual may even relinquish things of eternal importance, like temple marriages and families; growth opportunities like full-time missionary service;

fulfilling meaningful callings; and educational and career opportunities.

Prayer, fasting, and expressions of concern from family and friends often fall on deaf ears. Pleading and weeping soon turn to anger and frustration. Yet for individuals who battle with pornography issues, nothing you say or threaten them with seems to affect their behavior. You may tell yourselves over and over, "I don't understand it. How can someone jeopardize all that is priceless and eternal to fulfill the basest of pleasures through the means of lifeless, touched-up, artificial computer images?"

My response is that you need not arrive at a logical understanding of this disorder to be helpful. This problem is not only insidious (pornography is everywhere) but it is also elusive—the struggle with pornography is likely a symptom of other underlying issues. To support those who struggle with pornography, making sense of this issue is not entirely necessary. Instead, we can develop understanding from the heart that invites trust and eventually hope for lasting change. Scripture suggests we should "incline [our] ear unto wisdom, and apply [our] heart to understanding" (Proverbs 2:2).

King Benjamin instructs his people to "open your ears that ye may hear, and your hearts that ye may understand" (Mosiah 2:9).

We must learn to understand with our hearts as we support those who are ensnared by the plague of pornography. For it is only with a more complete understanding, an understanding that includes the application of the heart, that friends, parents, siblings, and spouses are better able to experience the Christlike love that is necessary to support those who struggle, and thereby help them begin the process of change.

As one who earns a living helping people navigate the waters of adversity and challenge, I believe my efforts are rendered useless without the concurrent help of ecclesiastical leaders, family members, and friends. Ecclesiastical leaders offer divinely inspired guidance by the rights and powers bestowed upon them as "judges in Israel" when they were set apart for their callings. Family members and friends provide the essential support and love for those who suffer emotionally, physically, and spiritually. I believe it takes the collective resources of all of us to help those who suffer, particularly if we wish to help them experience lasting change. Following are eight suggestions intended to help us in our efforts to support others who struggle with pornography issues.

REDUCE SHAME

Shame is the fuel that perpetuates the pornography cycle. Pornography is like a drug, providing a momentary "high" and temporarily relieving a person from his pain. In effect, when the "high" is over, the person comes crashing down, feels powerless, experiences more shame, and eventually reengages in the cycle again. Shame often leaves those struggling with pornography problems with a sense of humiliation that limits their ability to reach out to others. Many who struggle mistakenly think that they can keep their burden a secret. They believe that over time they can take care of their problem on their own, repent on their own, and move on with their lives, hoping to spare themselves increased shame and embarrassment. Many also find it difficult to reach out for help for fear that no one will understand them.

Shame can be inadvertently induced by well-meaning people. Significant others may feel that if they point out extreme examples of consequences stemming from pornography use, the sufferer will be motivated to change. I hear and read about how serial killers, rapists, and child molesters have accessed pornography at some time in their lives. Many people believe pornography is the source of these deviant behaviors. I have had pornography users tell me of experiences in which others told them that if they did not take care of their problem they would likely lose complete control and would eventually act out indiscriminately with men, women, and children.

If this were true, the number of sex crimes perpetrated in our community and the world in general would be astronomical, given the number of Internet pornography sites that are continually accessed.

The vast majority of people who access pornography do not turn into hardened criminals. Insinuating that they do, or that they will eventually criminally act out, only fuels the shame. It leaves the pornography user feeling even more alienated. As a result, they may respond by escalating the unwanted sexual compulsions even further.

Shame is also induced when the pornography user is told that his friends and family will be hurt, and that his marriage and salvation may actually be destroyed. Every individual I have worked with is already well aware of the consequences, without reminder— they live with those consequences daily. Most never forget them, and they find that well-meaning reminders only contribute to a downward spiral that may trigger additional pornographic consumption.

Fortunately, godly sorrow is not synonymous with shame. Shame renders one feeling hopeless, while godly sorrow provides the motivation to start the process of repentance. Paul taught, "I rejoice, not that ye were made sorry, but that ye sorrowed to repentance: for ye were made sorry after a godly manner, that ye might receive damage by us in nothing. For godly sorrow worketh repentance to salvation not to be repented of: but the sorrow of the world worketh death" (2 Corinthians 7:9–10). Godly sorrow involves an understanding of the atonement and of the Savior's love for us. Shame does not leave space in one's experience for the love of the Savior.

PORNOGRAPHY ISN'T THE ONLY ISSUE

Most of us have our favorite ways of avoiding the unpleasant inner experiences that show up in our lives. Negative emotions are part of everyone's lives. When these emotions surface, we typically have favorite methods of making us feel better instead of dealing with the negative emotion directly. For some of us, our vice may be chocolate, and we may go on a chocolate binge to repress vulnerable feelings. Some people work harder and longer hours to avoid uncomfortable emotions. Others may develop an eating disorder to gain some sense of control in a world they perceive as out of control.

A similar process operates for those who use pornography on a frequent basis. Many such individuals feel disconnected from people, particularly females, may be stressed out in school or with life decisions, or have family or marital problems. Many also battle depression and anxiety.

Investigating the context that triggers the impulse to indulge in pornography will likely present other problem areas that need attention. Religious leaders and others who are in a position of support may find it useful to investigate problems that the individual may be avoiding through the use of pornography. For example, does pornography distract the person from having a real relationship? If so, what kind of plan can be established to help this person feel more connected to others? Is pornography utilized as a coping mechanism for anxiety and/or depression? What alternative plan could be implemented to deal with emotional distress in a healthy manner?

SEXUAL IMPULSES ARE PART OF BEING HUMAN

Sexual impulses are part of being human and should not be categorized as sin, unless they are inappropriately acted on. Sexual thoughts and feelings emerge in our everyday lives because we are sexual beings. The media bombards us with sexual images every day. As human beings we are sexually attracted to other people. Experiences that heighten our sexual impulses are a part of life. We have other impulses that are built into our humanity: impulses to react to anger, to hunger, and to unpleasant emotions such as anxiety, depression, and stressful experiences are all part of the human experience. Temptation can come in the form of sexual impulses, and experiencing the temptation itself is not a sin. Even the Savior "suffered temptations" (D&C 20:22; Hebrews 2:18; Hebrews 4:14–15). Of course, like the Savior, we must strive diligently to not give "heed" to temptations (D&C 20:22).

Unfortunately, many individuals have grown up to believe that sexual impulses are sinful. Most of the individuals I work with professionally have obsessive qualities that exacerbate their pornography problem. That is, when sexual impulses show up in their experience, they become anxious, may panic, and may engage in avoidant behaviors. They have been told their entire lives to avoid "unclean" thoughts. Many people automatically assume that if they find a person sexually attractive they have already "crossed the line." They then engage in avoidant behaviors as a way to purge anything sexual from their being. This is a battle that cannot be won because we are by our very nature, sexual beings.

AVOIDANT BEHAVIORS ARE NOT THE ANSWER

"Running away" from sexual impulses is not the answer. When we try to "run away" from sexual impulses or "fight off" tempting thoughts, we set ourselves up for failure. Getting caught up in a tug-of-war with the monster of pornography becomes all about overpowering the monster and not about living a purposeful, value-driven life. This is a tug-of-war we can never win. So instead of getting dragged around, we need to learn to "drop the rope" and turn away.[1]

I realize that "dropping the rope" isn't going to make the monster go away. Many of the unpleasant monster-like things we experience in life tend to show up again and again. We don't have to like it. We'd prefer to be rid of such things once and for all. Nonetheless, we become paralyzed if we think we have to become free of temptations and impulses before we can move on with our lives. We can be about the business of living without getting caught up in the battle. Many who struggle bring their lives to a screeching halt as they attempt to pull the monster of pornography into the tug-of-war pit. They then feel that if they can eliminate the problem completely they will become more acceptable human beings and can then get on with their lives. Sounds good, but it doesn't work that way. This is unrealistic and gives the pornography struggle too much power in our lives. For example, many young men say that they do not want to date or associate with a "daughter of God" as long as they have this problem. They deprive themselves of opportunities to make friends and form meaningful relationships with others—important resources that might help them overcome this struggle. Ironically, those who isolate from others until they ultimately "get control" of the problem may fill the void experienced through isolation with a porn binge. Most young men who choose to move ahead with establishing relationships report that becoming emotionally connected to others helps to dramatically reduce the frequency of pornographic incidents.

DEVELOP AND MOVE TOWARD YOUR VALUES

If a person doesn't run away, what other option is there? He can move *toward* whatever he has determined works or may work for him in his life. This means establishing values that give him a sense of purpose and motivation. "Dropping the rope" and moving forward takes introspection. It involves determining what he wants his life to stand for. It helps to be very specific. Areas to explore include[2]:

Marriage/couple/intimate relationships
Family relations

Friendships/social relations

Career/employment

Education/personal growth and development

Recreation/leisure

Spirituality

Citizenship

Health/physical well-being

To help someone move *toward* rather than just *away,* have him write down a description of the person he would like to be in a marriage. What type of relationship would he want to have? Have him focus on *his role* in the relationship. Also have him describe the *qualities* he would want to have as a father, brother, son. Have him describe how he would ideally treat other people in these various relationships. What kind of parent would he like to be? How would he handle conflict in the family? What types of activities would be important for him to engage in as a father and husband?

It is most helpful if the individual can get in touch with what motivates him internally. Coming up with the "right answers" (criteria established by other people or organizations) will have little utility. Have the individual rate on the scale of 1–10 (10 being most important), how important each quality is in his life. Then have the individual rate how well he is doing to realize that quality in his life, considering his current behavior (1–10 scale; 10 means actions are 100 percent congruent with what is valued). Subtract the difference between the two ratings for each area.[3] Help him process how that feels when he sees difference. Talk about what the obstacles are and what they could do to move closer to that quality.

Setbacks—including reengagement in the pornography, intense cravings, depression, and anxiety—are going to surface as he moves in the direction of the qualities he wants in his life. These repeated struggles may seem overwhelming. This is where work with a professional therapist will likely be useful. However, a person needs to be careful who he seeks out. Most mental health professionals have a willingness to understand the context a person is coming from in regard to his values and religious beliefs, and work with him according to that context. However, this is not always true. Ecclesiastical leaders need to inquire about how the therapeutic work is going. After a release of information is signed (a document that gives the therapist permission to speak to one or more persons specified by the client), you might find it useful to talk with the counselor and coordinate how you can support the struggling individual. Professionals can help a client examine the efficacy of the strategies they are using to overcome the problem. A professional can investigate how pornography is used to avoid other significant problems. These other problems become "grist for the therapeutic mill." A therapist can work with an individual to alter his perceptions of himself and others and to examine and adjust behavioral patterns that are not meeting his needs in a healthy manner.

It is important that individuals remain engaged in a journey toward a valued direction, even when they encounter barriers. Consider the following analogy:

"You are standing at the edge of the ocean. The tide sometimes moves in and the water almost is over your head. At other times, the tide is low, and your feet barely get wet. You don't have any control over how high or low the water is at any point in time. What you can do, however, is mark a point on the horizon and head that way. It may be that in places the water will get very deep, and at those times, it would be easy to lose your way if you were only paying attention to your immediate surroundings. But as long as you keep your eyes on that spot on the horizon, you can keep moving in the chosen direction, no matter how deep the water gets."[4]

Values are represented by the beacon of light that we move toward. If we become consumed by our immediate surroundings, which may include the sexual impulses, it is easy to stop progress.

If, on the other hand, we know that we can move in a valued direction even though these impulses are going to continue, our lives can start working for us.

A few years ago I was involved with temple work when I had the sudden thought, "The temple is a place where I cannot experience Satan's influence because it is the house of the Lord." Just at that moment an inappropriate image entered my mind. I began to get caught up with the struggle to purge the thought by reciting scriptures and singing hymns in my mind. No longer was I attending to the matters of temple work. I was caught up in furiously finding the right hymn or the perfect scripture to replace the unwanted image. Ironically, this approach was making the image more and more at home in my mind. It wasn't until I took the stance of just observing myself having an inappropriate thought that I was able to give up the struggle. I said something to myself like, "Isn't it interesting that of all the places that I can have this thought, I am having it in the house of the Lord." Once I was able to get to that place of observation, the struggle left and I was able to refocus and return to the reason why I had gone to the temple in the first place. As I focused on my "beacon of light" I found myself able to overcome obstacles that would otherwise hinder me from my goals.

FIND MEANING IN THE JOURNEY

The journey to recovery is just that—a journey. It is not necessarily some destination to be reached. We have become very outcome-oriented in our society. Being in control, staying on track, achieving the goal are all messages we send ourselves over and over. We long for the day when we will be able to proclaim, "I have arrived." When we seek to experience change, we want it now. We become demoralized when we are told, "You've had this problem a long time, and it will take a long time to overcome it." Helpers for those who struggle with pornography will find it most useful to look at recovery as a process, not an outcome to be reached.

Sometimes our Church culture leaves us feeling that we need to constantly monitor how well we are doing. We may compare ourselves with others and look forward to the day when we arrive at a better state of existence than the one we are currently in. Consequently, well-meaning life initiatives come to a screeching halt when our outcomes are not delivered on the expected schedule. Moving in a direction that is consistent with our values does not require moment-to-moment monitoring of our progress. Many times the journey takes unexpected turns, and we have to keep the faith that overall we are still on course. Consider another analogy:

"Suppose you are taking a hike in the mountains. You know how mountain trails are constructed, especially if the slopes are steep. They wind back and forth; often they have 'switchbacks,' which make you literally walk back and forth, and sometimes a trail will even drop back to below a level you had reached earlier. If I asked you at a number of points on such a trail to evaluate how well you are accomplishing your goal of reaching the mountaintop, I would hear a different story every time. If you were in switchback mode, you would probably tell me that things weren't going well, that you were never going to reach the top. If you were in a stretch of open territory where you could see the mountaintop and the path leading up to it, you would probably tell me things were going very well. Now imagine that we are across the valley with binoculars, looking at people hiking on this trail. If we were asked how they were doing, we would have a positive progress report every time. We would be able to see that the overall direction of the trail, not what it looks like at a given moment, is the key to progress. We would see that following this crazy, winding trail is exactly what leads to the top."[5]

Elder M. Russell Ballard compared our life's journey to that of the pioneers: "Life isn't always easy. At some point in our journey we may feel much as the pioneers did as they crossed Iowa—up to our knees in mud, forced to bury some of our dreams along the way. We all face rocky ridges, with the wind in our face and winter coming on too soon. Sometimes it seems as though there is no end to the dust that stings our eyes and clouds our vision. Sharp edges of despair and discouragement jut out of the terrain to slow our passage. Always, there is a Devil's Gate, which will swing wide open to lure us in. Those who are wise and faithful will steer a course as far from such temptation as possible, while others—sometimes those who are nearest and dearest to us—succumb to the attraction of ease, comfort, convenience, and rest. Occasionally we reach the top of one summit in life, as the pioneers did, only to see more mountain peaks ahead, higher and more challenging than the one we have just traversed. Tapping unseen reservoirs of faith and endurance, we, as did our forebears, inch ever forward toward that day when our voices can join with those of all pioneers who have endured in faith, singing: 'All is well! All is well!' (*Hymns,* no. 30)."[6]

C. S. Lewis said: "No amount of falls will really undo us if we keep on picking ourselves up each time. We shall of course be very muddy and tattered children by the time we reach home. But the bathrooms are all ready, the towels put out, the clean clothes in the airing cupboard. The only fatal thing is to lose one's temper and give it up. It is when we notice the dirt that God is most present in us: it is the very sign of His presence."[7]

Most important, those who play a supportive role need to emphasize that man cannot embark upon the journey without the help of our Savior, who makes the ultimate destination of eternal life possible. Without the atonement of Jesus Christ, all efforts to bring about change for ourselves and others are for nothing. The Savior of mankind is the only one who completely understands our suffering. And he is the only one who is in the position to make change last forever.

NOTES

1. See Steven C. Hayes, Kirk D. Strosahl, and Kelly G. Wilson, *Acceptance and Commitment Therapy: An Experiential Approach to Behavior Change* (New York: Guilford Press, 1999), 109.

2. See Hayes, Strosahl, and Wilson, *Acceptance and Commitment Therapy*, 224–25.

3. See Kelly G. Wilson and Amy R. Murell, "Values Work in Acceptance and Commitment Therapy: Setting a Course for Behavioral Treatment," in Steven C. Hayes, Victoria M. Follette, and Marsha M. Linehan, eds., *Mindfulness and Acceptance: Expanding the Cognitive-Behavioral Tradition* (New York: Guilford Press, 2004).

4. Steven C. Hayes, Sue M. McCurry, Niloofar Afari, and Kelly Wilson, *Acceptance and Commitment Therapy: A Therapy Manual for the Treatment of Emotional Avoidance* (Reno, Nev.: Context Press, 1991), 36.

5. Hayes, Strosahl, and Wilson, *Acceptance and Commitment Therapy*, 222.

6. M. Russell Ballard, " 'You Have Nothing to Fear from the Journey,'" *Ensign*, May 1997, 59.

7. C. S. Lewis, as quoted in Terry W. Glaspey, *Not a Tame Lion: The Spiritual Legacy of C. S. Lewis* (Nashville, Tenn.: Cumberland House; Kansas City, Mo.: Andrews and McMeel, 1996), 189.

CHAPTER FIFTEEN

How Ecclesiastical Leaders Can Help Those with Pornography Problems

Rory C. Reid, Dan Gray, and Jill C. Manning

lthough the epidemic of pornography that plagues our society is alarming, it should not surprise us. Prophets have repeat-edly warned about this impending danger of the last days. Joseph Smith taught that sexual impurity would be "the source of more temptation, buffetings, and more difficulties . . . than any other."[1] President Ezra Taft Benson labeled sexual immorality as "the plaguing sin of this generation."[2]

Some leaders may not feel they have much to offer, but those who successfully abandon pornography often say the counsel offered by their religious leaders was a significant part of what empowered them to give up their habits. This chapter will provide information for leaders to consider in this important work.

UNDERSTANDING THE PROBLEM

Although pornography problems include sexual behavior, pornography problems are rarely about sex. Pornography creates a mood-altering experience that provides a temporary escape from the present moment. If an individual wants to alter his mood, we should be curious about what mood he is trying to escape.

Pornography is frequently used as a form of emotional avoidance of unpleasant, uncomfortable, or awkward feelings. These undesirable emotions can be triggered by many events, but more specifically they are fueled by the way a person chooses to interpret an event. For example, marital conflict suggests two people see something differently. However, a person may also interpret such conflict to mean he or she is inadequate, a failure, or unlovable. The person may experience a chronic feeling of shame, isolation, or emotional detachment. Pornography, often coupled with masturbation, can provide a temporary escape from such emotional pain.

The emotional roller coaster of payoffs and consequences associated with a pornography habit creates a high degree of ambivalence about change. Individuals feel torn: they want to quit but they don't want to quit. Sometimes working through the initial ambivalence can be a critical aspect of change. If a religious leader gets ahead of an individual's readiness to change or assumes responsibility to "fix" the problem before a person has worked through his own ambivalence, a tug of war may develop, often placing the religious leader in favor of change and the individual in favor of the status quo. We must remember the philosophy of our Heavenly Father, who "will facilitate, but He will not force."[3]

It's important to explore the breadth of issues that may be related to a person's pornography problems. When success is measured solely by abstinence from the sexual behavior, other changes that indicate a person is progressing may be disregarded. Not only that, but temporary behavior change that doesn't address the roots of the problem may be mistaken for deeper repentance and a change of heart. Although commitment to change is often sincere at the time, relapse is likely to occur if underlying issues are not addressed.

In situations like these, religious leaders can unwittingly become part of an abstinence-relapse cycle. When a person feels shame after acting out, he may confess as a way of relieving his shame. He starts to feel better and remains safe for a time until the next slip, which is again followed by a phone call to his leader. It is important to be aware of whether you have become a part of an individual's cycle and to be cautiously optimistic about an individual's repentance process in the context of how many "confessions" he has made.

Elder Richard G. Scott has spoken about the road people follow when they develop pornography habits:

"One of the most damning influences on earth, one that has caused uncountable grief, suffering, heartache, and destroyed marriages, is the onslaught of pornography in all of its vicious, corroding, destructive forms. . . . This potent tool of Lucifer degrades the mind, heart, and the soul of any who use it. All who are caught in its seductive, tantalizing web, and remain so, will become addicted to its immoral, destructive influence. For many, that addiction cannot be overcome without help. The tragic pattern is so familiar. It begins with a curiosity that is fueled by its stimulation and is justified by the false premise that when done privately, it does no harm to anyone else. Lulled by this lie, the experimentation goes deeper, with more powerful stimulations, until the web closes and a terribly immoral, addictive habit is formed."[4]

Because the "tragic pattern is so familiar," we may routinely assume that anyone using pornography is "addicted." This is not always true. People do not always go through the stages of escalation with their pornography consumption to rougher, more kinky or bizarre types of material, nor do they always act out behavior depicted in pornography. Some people may stay fixed on a particular type of pornography for years. Others may use pornography infrequently, perhaps every few years or when the opportunity presents itself. While we realize that any consumption of sexually explicit material should be a focus of attention since it affects spirituality, those people who are not preoccupied with pornography or actively searching for it may not have severe problems. Effective interviewing when assessing a pornography problem can help distinguish between someone who has developed a habit and someone who has not.

LABELING INDIVIDUALS WITH PORNOGRAPHY PROBLEMS

Just as every person who drinks alcohol is not an alcoholic, it is also inaccurate to label everyone who uses pornography an "addict." We should be cautious about labeling people. Harold Brown has written, "We should also be careful about labeling people as homosexuals, abusers, alcoholics, or other such labels, because labels often subtly imply an identity or condition over which there is no longer personal control or responsibility and which may cause someone to lose hope that they can make choices to stop inappropriate behavior and change their lives."[5]

Those in favor of assigning labels do so in part to break through the denial and minimizing that those entrenched in pornography often use to avoid responsibility. Admitting that one is "addicted" can be a catalyst for a person to assume responsibility for their behavior and humbly admit that they need assistance.

ASSESSING THE SEVERITY OF A PROBLEM

It is important to understand what has brought a person to your office. Was their behavior discovered or disclosed? Be curious about what events have led him or her to you at this time in his life. Why not six months ago and why not six months from now? Is this the first time he has talked to a religious leader about this problem?

The following questions may help you assess the severity of a problem:

How do they define pornography?
When were they first exposed to pornography, and how frequently have they used it since that time?

What types of pornography have they consumed:
heterosexual, homosexual, child pornography?

Do they masturbate to the pornography? How often?

Has the pornography become harder, rougher, more kinky or
bizarre over time?

How many times have they unsuccessfully tried to abandon
their behavior?

Do they try to hide and keep their behavior a secret? Who
else knows, and how did they find out?

What have they tried so far? What helps? What makes
things worse?

Talking about a pornography problem can be an embarrassing
and humiliating experience. It takes a lot of courage for someone
to initiate such a conversation. A spirit of compassion and understanding helps keep the discussion from feeling like an interroga-
tion. If an individual is being resistant you might say, "I can see
you're not ready to talk about this. Maybe we could revisit this next
week."

Laying a foundation for the discussion can be helpful. You
might say, "In order to determine what resources may help you
most, I need to ask you some questions about your situation. Please
let me know if some of the questions seem too intrusive." The
principle here is to avoid heaping additional shame upon the individual. The individual may need help differentiating between
appropriate guilt, which says, "my behavior is bad," and excessive
shame, which may lead them to conclude, "I am bad."

AMBIVALENCE ABOUT CHANGE

You may want to explore the individual's ambivalence about
change. Often, people don't consider the advantages of the status
quo and the disadvantages of change; it's important that they do so

in order to understand what they'll be giving up if they succeed. Here are some possibilities that can facilitate a discussion:

Perceived advantages of continuing behavior. Form of escape; it helps me relax; a type of emotional avoidance to cope with stress or other problems in life; it is reliable, predictable, and something I can control; it feels good and doesn't require being intimate with another person.

Costs of continuing behavior. Expensive habit; it impairs healthy relationships; loss of self-respect; loss of spirituality; time consuming; lost productivity; affects marriages and employment; high degree of internalized shame; it's an isolative behavior; fear of being caught; leading a double life; deception and dishonesty; distorts expectations.

Costs of changing behavior. Counseling can be expensive; cravings will be uncomfortable; fear of what lies ahead; uncertainty about how change will be; pain of dealing with reality.

Advantages of changing behavior. Healthier intimacy; restoration of self-respect and spirituality; no longer need to be afraid; increased productivity; elimination of inner conflict, guilt, and shame; congruence with moral beliefs; genuine and true to self; freedom from bondage.

Exploring the factors that contribute to ambivalence helps most people realize that change is going to be hard and will require effort and commitment. It also helps them understand why they've had so many unsuccessful attempts to abandon pornography on their own.

LETTING THE INDIVIDUAL OWN THE PROBLEM

People must initiate change in their own lives if it is to be genuine and lasting. If they are to succeed, *they* must own the problem. In order to clearly establish this expectation with a member, you might say at some point during an initial interview, "Now that I know about your struggle, how can I be of the most help to you?"

The problem remains theirs, even though they've shared it with you. What is *their* "recovery plan," and how do you fit into it? What guidance and revelation have they sought in the matter? Be cautious about offering quick advice or suggestions.[6]

A problem common among those who struggle with pornography is an over-reliance on external sources of influence instead of the guidance of their own values, impressions, and conscience. Leaders can encourage such individuals' growth by gently encouraging self-reliance when they try to hand over the reins of their lives.

WORKING WITH THERAPISTS

If a person has tried unsuccessfully multiple times to abandon his behavior, he may benefit from help from a qualified counselor. If this course is agreed upon, continue to be involved. Encourage your ward member to sign a "release of information" form at the therapist's office, allowing the therapist to communicate with you about the member's treatment. This will enable the three of you to work as a team. This teamwork broadens the support for the individual and allows an exchange of ideas and suggestions.

SUGGESTED READINGS

M. Russell Ballard, "Purity Precedes Power," *Ensign,* November 1990, 35–37.

Harold C. Brown, "The Marvelous Gift of Choice," *Ensign,* December 2001, 47–52.

Bruce C. Hafen, "Beauty for Ashes: The Atonement of Jesus Christ," *Ensign,* April 1990, 7–14.

Spencer W. Kimball, "God Will Forgive," *Ensign,* March 1982, 2–7.

Neal A. Maxwell, "According to the Desire of [Our] Hearts," *Ensign,* November 1996, 21–23.

———, "Notwithstanding My Weakness," *Ensign,* November 1976, 12–14.

———, "Repentance," *Ensign,* November 1991, 30–32.

———, "'Repent of [Our] Selfishness' (D&C 56:8)," *Ensign,* May 1999, 23–24.

Rory C. Reid, "The Road Back: Abandoning Pornography," *Ensign*, February 2005, 47–51.

Richard G. Scott, "Do What Is Right," *Ensign*, June 1997, 51–56.

——, "Finding Forgiveness," *Ensign*, May 1995, 75–77.

——, "Finding the Way Back," *Ensign*, May 1990, 74–76.

NOTES

1. Joseph Smith, in *Journal of Discourses*, 26 vols. (Liverpool: Latter-day Saints' Book Depot, 1854–86), 8:55.

2. Ezra Taft Benson, "Cleansing the Inner Vessel," *Ensign*, May 1986, 4.

3. Neal A. Maxwell, "According to the Desire of [Our] Hearts," *Ensign*, November 1996, 22.

4. Richard G. Scott, "The Sanctity of Womanhood," *Ensign*, May 2000, 36.

5. Harold C. Brown, "The Marvelous Gift of Choice," *Ensign*, December 2001, 52; see also Thomas S. Monson, "Labels," *Ensign*, September 2000, 2.

6. See Boyd K. Packer, "Self-Reliance," *Ensign*, August 1975, 85.

CHAPTER SIXTEEN

How Ecclesiastical Leaders Can Help the Spouse of Someone with a Pornography Problem

Jill C. Manning and Rory C. Reid

When we encounter problems with pornography in marriages, our attention is naturally drawn to the individual who is consuming pornography in an effort to stop the problematic behavior. In the majority of cases, the husband is the consumer, and subsequently he becomes the recipient of our attention and support. Although these men do require help, the impact of pornography is never limited to the individual user. Attending to the needs of others who are in the pornography user's sphere of influence—especially the spouse—is imperative if we desire to be truly helpful and support long-term change and resolution of problems. The following suggestions may facilitate such efforts.

Be sure to include the spouse in the support you extend and any treatment you arrange with professional counselors. Research indicates that when spouses are involved, the outcomes are much better and results are seen much sooner. Many women report

NOTE: *For the purpose of simplicity, it will be assumed that spouses are women and their husbands are the individuals struggling with a pornography problem.*

feeling left out of the process, despite struggling with their own issues pertaining to the pornography use. A combination of individual and couple meetings is helpful, allowing both partners to meet with their religious leader both alone and together. These meetings will also provide the leader a richer perspective.

Do not assume pornography impacts all families exactly the same way. Ask wives how this problem has affected them emotionally, spiritually, financially, physically, and socially. Listen attentively and give them a safe place to talk. Allow wives to express the intense range of feelings they may be experiencing such as betrayal, anger, confusion, mistrust, shame, rejection, inadequacy, worthlessness, and depression. Avoid giving advice early on in the process, unless it is specifically requested. It is also acceptable to indicate you're not sure about what to do and would like some additional time to think about the situation.

The discovery of a pornography problem threatens the hopes and dreams women have for a celestial marriage. This is often as devastating to them as a real-life affair. In the wake of a pornography discovery or disclosure, women commonly experience decreased feelings of self-worth, confidence, body image, and attractiveness. It is imperative that women understand this problem has nothing to do with their attractiveness or sexuality. Men often become involved with pornography long before they marry. Regardless of who these men married, they would most likely be struggling with this same problem. When these truths penetrate a women's heart, they begin to regain their confidence and often become a more effective helpmeet in their husband's recovery process.

Help wives establish boundaries by identifying what specific behaviors make them feel uncomfortable. For example, they can say, "I will not participate in sexual behavior that makes me feel demeaned or uncomfortable in any way." Although it is not her responsibility to stop her husband's pornography use, limits such as these communicate that a wife is taking back control of her own life in areas that may have been affected by her husband's pornography problems.

In addition to the husband connecting with a support network, it can be helpful for wives to seek support. This might include a professional counselor, a trusted friend, or a religious leader. Husbands sometimes become angry when wives seek such support because more people become aware of their problem. It is helpful to remind these men that their choice to use pornography has consequences, and they are not at liberty to dictate how their wives work through their own healing process.

Some wives will choose to end their marriage, particularly when their husband's transgressions have been particularly egregious. President David O. McKay taught that "there may be circumstances which make the continuance of the marriage state a greater evil than divorce."[1] President Gordon B. Hinckley has stated, "There may be now and again a legitimate cause for divorce. I am not one to say that it is never justified."[2] President James E. Faust added that if a just cause for breaking the covenant of marriage existed, it should be "nothing less serious than a prolonged and apparently irredeemable relationship which is destructive of a person's dignity as a human being."[3]

Women who wait a year or so after the time of discovery to make a decision about the status of their marriage are often grateful they didn't decide right away. We have also seen women stay in marriages that are destroying them emotionally and spiritually. In some cases, children are at risk of being exposed to pornography and living in a toxic environment. A temporary separation may give each party some time to consider the serious nature of the situation. Women often experience a great deal of doubt and ambivalence about dissolving the marriage or initiating a temporary separation. Ultimately, the choice is hers, and if a woman decides to divorce, she will need continued love and support from a religious leader.

Wives should not be pressured into forgiving a partner too quickly. Women need time and permission to work through the emotional pain resulting from pornography problems. If wives are pressured to forgive prematurely, their "forgiveness" is likely to be superficial, and resentment will fester over time. Furthermore, it would not be wise for trust to be immediately restored before a husband grows in his capacity to be worthy of it.

Resist the temptation to rescue or "fix" a woman's problems. Agency should be respected. Encourage women to seek personal revelation about their situation. Sometimes the best thing you can say is, "I'm not sure. What do you think you should do?"

If there are women in your ward or stake who have worked through similar issues and are currently doing well, you may consider inviting them to become a support for other women. In many communities, professional therapists facilitate groups for women that provide education and support.

The gospel provides the unwavering assurance that healing is possible. When women receive adequate support, they are better able to survive and thrive despite this trial.

NOTES

1. David O. McKay, in Conference Report, April 1945, 141.
2. Gordon B. Hinckley, "What God Hath Joined Together," *Ensign*, May 1991, 74.
3. James E. Faust, "Fathers, Mothers, Marriage," *Ensign*, August 2004, 3.

CHAPTER SEVENTEEN

Discussing Pornography Problems with a Spouse

Rory C. Reid and Dan Gray

CONFRONTING A SPOUSE WHO USES PORNOGRAPHY

Despite being touted as harmless entertainment, pornography use can be devastating to a marriage. It is not harmless, and if there is a problem you have a right to confront it. We hope the following suggestions will help those who have found themselves in the awkward and often painful position of confronting a spouse who has a pornography problem.

Though it may be difficult to do, accurately discerning whether or not a spouse is struggling with pornography is an important first step in confronting and coping with the suspicions you may have. Below are several signs that may indicate a problem with pornography:

- Loss of interest in sexual relations or insatiable sexual appetite
- Introduction of unusual sexual practices in the relationship
- Diminished emotional, physical, social, spiritual, and intellectual intimacy

- Neglect of responsibilities
- Increased isolation (such as late-night hours on the computer); withdrawal from family
- Irregular mood swings, increased irritability
- Unexplained absences
- Preference for masturbation over sexual relations with spouse
- Unexplained financial transactions
- Sexual relations that are rigid, rushed, without passion, and detached

Although further information should be gathered, if these signs are present in marriage, it is possible that there is a problem. Chapter 9 of this volume, "Confronting Pornography on the Internet," describes how to determine if a computer has been used to access pornography. If you suspect a problem but are unsure, communicate your concerns to your spouse. Listen and be prepared to give him the benefit of the doubt. If there is actually a problem, it will usually come to light in time.

It is difficult to know how to react appropriately after discovering a problem. Emotions are often charged, and unintended things may be done or said. The offending partner may react to the emotions of the spouse rather than hearing what she is trying to communicate. Enlisting the support of a Church leader or a therapist may make the confrontation less difficult. When confronting a spouse, consider the following:

Don't enable. Denial or avoidance can become a form of enabling the behavior. Ignoring the problem is the same as condoning it.

Don't accommodate. Making excuses for a spouse is accommodating the inappropriate behavior. Inappropriate behavior does not need to be tolerated.

Establish and maintain healthy boundaries. You are not to

blame for the problem and need not tolerate abusive or injurious reactions when confronting a spouse. This also means saying no to any sexual requests that you may feel are inappropriate or make you feel uncomfortable.

Don't reinforce distorted beliefs or thoughts. Often the offending spouse will offer excuses to rationalize his behavior or as an attempt to deflect blame. Excusing the inappropriate behavior only reinforces and enables.

Show understanding without condoning the behavior. Provide support without supporting the offensive behavior.

Communicate assertively. Clearly communicate your feelings, thoughts, and concerns. Express how you feel and what you expect. Focus on the problem behavior and consider the rights and feelings of your spouse.

Effective communication moderates conflict, but it does not eliminate it. Great marriages involve couples who have learned how to respectfully resolve conflict.

Overcoming a pornography problem is a long and difficult process that takes months and even years to accomplish. Often it requires professional help. This is a problem that can be overcome, but don't expect your relationship to heal overnight.

DISCLOSING A PORNOGRAPHY PROBLEM TO A SPOUSE

Many individuals struggling with pornography problems want to tell their spouse, but they fear that disclosure will place their marriage at risk. In reality, studies indicate the majority of marriages stay intact if both partners are willing to work through the problem together. When you disclose, you may find the following recommendations helpful.

If you're hesitant, often a Church leader or a therapist can provide encouragement and support to help you follow through.

Remember that over 90 percent of spouses want to know. Furthermore, 96 percent of spouses who disclosed report later that it was the right thing to do.

The consequences you fear are a necessary part of the healing process. The pain you feel through this process will serve as a reminder to facilitate the changes you want to make.

Regardless of what decisions your spouse makes in response to your disclosure, you are doing the right thing by taking the first step toward developing healthy intimacy in your life.

If you choose not to disclose, there is a high probability your spouse will eventually find out. If the disclosure is forced at that point, the consequences will usually be more severe than if you take the initiative to disclose.

Remember that your spouse's pain is not caused by your confession, but by the actions you are disclosing. The decision not to disclose isn't about protecting your spouse. It's an excuse to protect yourself from your spouse's reaction.

Disclosing your behaviors will not be painless. In fact, it may be one of the most difficult things you ever do. However, delaying it will not make it easier. Trust that the burden you carry will be lifted, and accept that disclosure will change your life for the better. You will survive it.

Consider the following suggestions when the time comes for you to disclose your behaviors to your spouse:

Personal Inventory: Take a complete inventory of all your secret behaviors. List the various excuses you've used to rationalize your behavior and the lies you've told to cover up your activities.

Categorize: Create an outline and categorize your behaviors. For example, viewing pornography and masturbation are two different behaviors. Another category would be dishonesty, where you will list all of the lies you've told in order to hide your activities.

Write Your Disclosure: Write down what you want to say and how you want to say it. Avoid using statements that invoke sympathy or make excuses for your actions. It should not include language that requires or requests forgiveness, because the focus is on *your* behavior. Do not get defensive if your spouse gets angry. She needs to have her feelings validated, not suppressed.

Answer Questions: Be prepared to answer your spouse's questions without getting defensive.

Accept Consequences: Part of being responsible includes accepting consequences instead of avoiding them.

AFTER THE DISCLOSURE

Disclosing your behavior will bring with it a vast array of emotions. You and your spouse may both feel a sense of relief; perhaps your spouse's suspicious feelings have been validated and her intuition has been proved correct. She can stop wondering, and you can stop living a lie. However, your spouse may also feel a wide variety of other emotions, including anger, betrayal, rejection, confusion, despair, abandonment, resentment, alienation, and devastation. She may need time to deal with these emotions, and you will need to give it her. Taking responsibility for the pain you have caused is an important part of the healing process.

Disclosure brings with it a time of change and uncertainty. Couples are faced with many decisions, perhaps including deciding the status of their marriage. It might be helpful to know that many couples who stayed together report that they are glad they didn't make any decisions regarding divorce in the aftermath of the disclosure. Things may even get worse before they get better, and both people must be committed to working on the problems.

Remember, you may not be able to change or control the reactions of your spouse, but you can change yourself and your own unhealthy behaviors. Ask yourself what changes and sacrifices you are willing to make, and then focus on making them. You may need the help of a therapist, support group, or Church leader, but take courage. This is a fight that you can win.

Note: Our appreciation to Brittney Carman, who edited extracts from our book, *Discussing Pornography Problems with a Spouse*, 2d ed. (Salt Lake City: Mental Health Publications, 2005).

CHAPTER EIGHTEEN

Pornography and the Law: Legal Issues for Clergy, Counselors, and Others

Merrill F. Nelson[1]

The battle against pornography raises several important legal issues. For example, is pornography illegal? IIow do free speech protections apply? How is child pornography legally different from adult pornography? What legal requirements apply to clergy and professional counselors who hear of pornography use, and what are the limits of confidentiality? While the answers to these and other legal questions may vary somewhat from state to state, the general principles and guidelines discussed here should prove helpful in most cases. Of course, the discussion here provides no substitute for legal advice in specific cases.

PORNOGRAPHY AND FREE SPEECH

Pornography has long been the target of laws designed to prohibit or limit its production, distribution, use, or possession. Defined generally, pornography includes any visual image that depicts sexual conduct or that is intended to cause sexual arousal. As such, it is considered harmful to the morals and safety of society because it tends to produce illicit or illegal sexual conduct, particularly when the conduct involves minors.

Purveyors or advocates of pornography have challenged legal restrictions, arguing that pornography is a form of speech, protected under the First Amendment to the United States Constitution. Scholars and legal experts have debated whether pornography is protected speech or actually a form of conduct outside the scope of the First Amendment. In resolving these legal disputes, the United States Supreme Court has concluded that while some pornography is protected as a form of expression under the First Amendment, sexual depictions that are considered "obscene" are entitled to no First Amendment protection.[2] The Supreme Court defined "obscene material" as that which (1) "appeals to the prurient interest" in sex; (2) is "patently offensive" in light of community standards; and (3) "lacks serious literary, artistic, political, or scientific value."[3]

Based on this Supreme Court definition, states may prohibit the production and distribution of obscene materials, but not materials considered nonobscene. Neither may the law prohibit the private adult possession of obscene materials.[4] However, different rules apply with regard to children and child pornography.

THE PROTECTION OF MINORS

To protect minors, most state laws specifically prohibit exposing them to pornographic materials. Furthermore, in many states, showing pornography to a child during the course of sexually abusing the child escalates the offense to a higher-degree felony punishable by mandatory imprisonment for an extended period.[5] Statutes protecting minors from pornography are aggressively enforced in the courts.[6]

Federal law also protects minors from exposure to pornographic materials. In the case of *United States v. American Library Ass'n*,[7] the Supreme Court upheld the constitutionality of the Children's Internet Protection Act, which requires public libraries receiving federal funds to install filtering software on their computers to block access to obscenity, child pornography, and other materials harmful to minors.

The law related to child pornography is significantly different from that discussed above in connection with adult pornography. The factual distinction is that child pornography depicts sexual conduct involving children, generally those under age 18. The legal distinction is that children, because of their sexual vulnerability, are accorded greater protection under the law. Child pornography victimizes children in its production, exploits children in its distribution, and threatens children as it whets the sexual appetite of pedophiles and predators who may act out what they see and also spread the material to others. Child pornography is recognized in the literature and the law as one of the greatest evils of our day, and those who propagate or peddle it find no protection under the law.

The Supreme Court has declared that "the use of children as subjects of pornographic materials is harmful to the physiological, emotional, and mental health of the child." Further, the production and distribution of child pornography amounts to child abuse, inflicting harm on the child victims even when the depictions may not be "patently offensive" or meet other elements of the Miller test. The court found no public value in the portrayal of sexual activity by children. Because "the evil to be restricted so overwhelmingly outweighs the expressive interests, if any, . . . no case-by-case adjudication is required." Accordingly, child pornography is categorically "unprotected by the First Amendment."[8]

Unlike its application to adult pornography, the First Amendment permits prohibition of even the possession of child pornography. Because "it is now difficult, if not impossible, to solve the child pornography problem by only attacking production and distribution," a state is justified in "attempting to stamp out this vice at all levels in the distribution chain," including mere possession. Child pornography permanently records the child's abuse. The child's injury is perpetuated when the materials are shared and continues as long as the materials exist. A ban on possession and viewing protects children by encouraging the possessors of these materials to destroy them. Destruction of the materials will also prevent pedophiles from using the "child pornography to seduce other children into sexual activity."[9]

Purveyors of child pornography have sought ways to circumvent the law through the creation of "virtual child pornography" by computer animation or "morphing." Legislative attempts to address this problem have run into difficulty in the courts because no actual children are used in the creation of such material.[10]

Today, in addition to federal laws, all fifty states have enacted and vigorously enforce laws against child pornography. For child pornography statutes in individual states, see National Center for Prosecution of Child Abuse, National District Attorneys Association (www.ndaa-apri.org/pdf/statute_child_pornography_2004.pdf).

CHILD ABUSE REPORTING LAWS

All fifty states have mandatory child abuse reporting statutes. In general, these statutes require designated persons, ranging from "any person" in some states to listed professionals in other states, to inform civil authorities when they have reason to believe that a child has been "abused." While the definitions of "abuse" vary in terminology, they generally include any harm or threatened harm to a child, including sexual conduct involving minors or sexual exploitation of minors. Accordingly, these definitions typically would apply to the exposure of children to adult pornography, as well as to the production, distribution, or possession of child pornography. For child abuse reporting statutes in individual states, see National Clearinghouse on Child Abuse and Neglect Information, United States Department of Health and Human Services (http://nccanch. acf.hhs.gov/general/index.cfm).

These statutory definitions of child abuse include any conduct or omission that involves children with pornography. Generally, the production, distribution, or possession of child pornography is child abuse, whether a child views the material or not. In addition, because abuse includes any conduct deemed "harmful" to children, and state laws declare that pornographic material is "harmful to minors," exposure of children to adult pornography also constitutes child abuse. Accordingly, any person who shows or allows a child to view either adult or child pornography may be guilty of child abuse. As noted above, showing pornography to a child in the course of molesting the child is an aggravated form of sexual abuse. Even leaving pornographic materials where children are likely to see them could be considered child abuse or neglect.

DISCLOSURE OF PORNOGRAPHY USE TO CLERGY

Disclosure of pornography use to a religious leader is encouraged so that the cleric may assist the offender in abandoning the addictive and harmful practice, as well as arrange assistance and protection for innocent victims. Court decisions stemming back hundreds of years have recognized the benefit of sharing difficult burdens with the clergy in order to receive spiritual consolation and direction. As stated in *People v. Phillips*,[11] one of the earliest cases enforcing the confidentiality of communications to clergy:

"[W]hen a man under the agonies of an afflicted conscience . . . applies to a minister of the Almighty, lays bare his bosom filled with guilt, and opens his heart black with crime, and solicits from him advice and consolation, . . . this confession and disclosure may be followed by the most salutary effects upon the religious principles and future conduct of the penitent, and may open to him prospects which may bless the remnant of his life, with the soul's calm sunshine and heart-felt joy."

As a general rule, confidential disclosures to clergy are considered privileged, by both doctrine and by law, and cannot be divulged without consent of the communicant. The privilege statutes mandate confidentiality and prohibit unauthorized disclosure, under possible penalty of law. Thus, clergy have no discretion to breach a confidence; they are duty bound, by law and typically by church doctrine, to hold the confidence inviolate.[12]

The public policy underlying the privilege statutes is to encourage uninhibited disclosure of actual or potential problems so that they can be resolved or avoided, to the benefit of not only the communicant but of the family and society in general. The essential premise of the privilege is the assurance of secrecy, without which the communicant would not be as likely to come forward, thereby leaving the problem in the darkness, without chance of resolution and subject to perpetuation. If clergy can hear the problem, they can help resolve it by encouraging and assisting the communicant to change behavior, to confide in other persons in a position to help, or even to involve civil authorities, as authorized by the communicant if possible.[13]

However, under certain limited circumstances, clergy may have a legal duty to report the information to civil authorities or disclose the information to others in order to protect a child or other potential victim from harm. These sometimes conflicting duties of confidentiality and disclosure can generally be resolved with the cooperation of the communicant.

APPLICATION OF REPORTING LAWS TO CLERGY

When adult pornography use is disclosed to a religious leader, whether by the user or some third party, generally no reporting duty attaches. Even when the cleric receives information regarding the production, distribution, or exhibition of obscene materials, conduct typically prohibited by law, the cleric generally has no duty to inform civil authorities. The law imposes no general obligation to report the commission of a crime, and no such duty is imposed on clergy. In fact, as discussed above, clergy are generally forbidden by law from divulging such confidential information without the consent of the communicant. From time immemorial, clergy have received confidential disclosures regarding even criminal conduct, and both law and policy have recognized the personal and social utility of preserving the confidence. No different rule attaches to disclosure of adult pornography use. Of course, the cleric would generally advise the communicant to disclose the conduct to family members or mental health professionals who could help overcome the problem, but civil authorities would not become involved unless criminal conduct comes to their attention through other channels.

Again, different rules apply to child pornography and child exposure to pornography because of the compelling interest in the protection of children. When information involving children and pornography is disclosed to a clergy member, the cleric may have a legal duty to report the information to civil authorities, depending on the specific provisions of the state child abuse reporting law.

Child abuse reporting statutes vary widely in their application to clergy. Several states, including New York and Washington, exclude clergy from their list of mandatory reporters, thereby exempting clergy from any reporting duty, regardless of whether the abuse information they receive is privileged. For example, in the Iowa case of *Wilson v. Darr*[14] the court held that a priest was not liable for failing to report child abuse because clergy are not included as mandatory reporters in the reporting statute. Lawmakers in these states have made the policy judgment that requiring clergy to report child abuse "could serve to dissuade parishioners from acknowledging in consultation with their ministers the existence of abuse and seeking a solution to it."[15]

The majority of states, including Arizona, California, and Idaho, impose on clergy a conditional duty to report child abuse, exempting information that falls within the clergy privilege, whether from the offender or confidentially from others. For example, in the Pennsylvania case of *Hutchison v. Luddy*[16] the court held that a clergyman had no duty to report abuse information received confidentially from the victim's family and other clergy. Accordingly, the states in this category would not require clergy to report confidential information regarding pornography-related abuse.

A small minority of states, including Utah and Nevada, allow clergy only a partial privilege-based reporting exemption, requiring clergy to report child abuse unless the information is received confidentially from the offender. Accordingly, abuse information, including that related to pornography, must be reported when it is received from any source other than the offender.

Several other states, including Oklahoma and Texas, require clergy to report defined child abuse, including that related to pornography, regardless of whether the information is privileged. These states either expressly or impliedly abrogate the clergy privilege with respect to child abuse information. For example, in the Texas case of *Bordman v. State*[17] the court held that the defendant could not assert the clergy privilege to suppress evidence of his confession of child abuse to his pastor.

Even when clergy have no statutory duty to report child abuse, they may still have a common law duty to protect the child through notice to others. For example, in *J.A.W. v. Roberts*[18] a young man informed three different clergy members that he was sexually molested by his foster father. The court recognized a common law duty of the clergy to report based on their "special relationship" with the victim. Accordingly, religious leaders who hear of child pornography use may have a common law duty to protect known or likely victims through notice to others, such as a spouse, parent, or civil authorities, even when they have no statutory duty to report.

DISCLOSURE OF PORNOGRAPHY USE AND APPLICATION OF REPORTING LAWS TO MENTAL HEALTH PROFESSIONALS

Assistance of mental health professionals is typically necessary, and should be encouraged, to help offenders stop their addictive use of pornography, as well as to aid potential child victims of exposure to pornography. Therapists working with pornography offenders and victims generally do so within a framework of statutory privilege, preventing disclosure of confidential information. However, therapists are also subject to mandatory reporting laws and a general duty to protect others from known harm. Accordingly, when pornography use amounts to child abuse, therapists have a duty to report or notify others.

All states recognize a statutory therapist privilege that precludes the therapist from disclosing confidential information without the consent of the client. For example, the Utah Code, section 58–60–114, provides that a "mental health therapist" may not disclose "any confidential communication with a client or patient without the express consent" of the client or the client's parent or authorized agent. A "mental health therapist" includes any licensed psychiatrist, psychologist, social worker, or professional counselor. However, this privilege statute, like those in other states, also sets forth express exceptions for child abuse information and the therapist's duty to warn.

As with clergy, mental health professionals generally have no duty to report pornography use that does not involve children. Even when use of adult pornography constitutes a crime, mental health professionals generally have no duty to report that crime to civil authorities. In fact, under the typical therapist privilege, a mental health professional is generally prohibited from disclosing confidential information, even when related to criminal behavior. Reporting duties do, however, come into play when the therapist receives information of pornography use that amounts to child abuse or that presents a threat of harm to children or others.

The child abuse reporting statutes in all fifty states require mental health professionals to report child abuse. In the typical statute, mental health professionals are either expressly listed as mandatory reporters or impliedly included in a universal reporting requirement. In addition, the therapist privilege is either expressly or impliedly abrogated for the purpose of child abuse reporting and investigation. For example, *People v. McKean*[19] held that the therapist privilege did not apply to a social worker who reported incestuous conduct disclosed by a client. Accordingly, therapists generally have a legal duty to report child abuse information, which would include the exposure of children to adult pornography and the production, distribution, or possession of child pornography.

Because of the statutory duty to report child abuse information, therapists may advise clients of this duty at the inception of the professional relationship. However, no such prior warning is required by the law.[20] Even a therapist who reports child abuse after prior assurances of strict confidentiality is justified under the reporting statute and immune from liability for the disclosure if made in good faith.[21]

On the other hand, a mental health professional who fails to comply with statutory reporting requirements may be subjected to criminal penalties. For example, in *State v. Motherwell*[22] the court affirmed the conviction of non-clergy religious counselors for failing to report child abuse as "social workers." In addition, a therapist who fails to report child abuse may face civil liability in damages for further abuse that a report could have prevented.[23]

In addition to statutory reporting duties, mental health professionals may also have a common law duty to warn or protect an identifiable victim from imminent harm. This duty was recognized in the leading case of *Tarasoff v. Regents of Univ. of Cal.*,[24] which held that a therapist had a duty to warn a third party of threatened harm from the client. This duty has been extended to therapists who receive information regarding child sex abuse and child pornography.[25] This professional duty to warn or protect others from known harm is now codified in most states. Even when this duty is limited by statute to actual threats of "physical violence," as in Utah, such a limitation does not affect the overriding statutory duty to report child abuse to civil authorities.[26] Accordingly, a therapist who learns that a child has been or could be victimized by any form of pornography generally has a duty to make a civil report to protect the child from further harm.[27]

CONCLUSION

Pornography is one of the most pernicious evils of our time. Laws are framed to prevent its propagation, particularly in the interest of protecting children from its harmful influence. These laws are enforced by the courts to the fullest extent permitted by the Constitution. Parents and other responsible adults must make every effort to oppose the spread of pornography in all its forms. Clergy and therapists, especially, must use their influence and training to help perpetrators and victims overcome the effects of pornography through counseling and notice to others in a position to help.

***

NOTES

1. Shareholder in the law firm of Kirton & McConkie, Salt Lake City, Utah. Legal counsel to LDS Family Services and the Abuse Help Line of The Church of Jesus Christ of Latter-day Saints. The viewpoints expressed herein are the author's alone and do not represent any policy or position of the law firm or its clients. © 2005 Merrill F. Nelson. All rights reserved.
2. *Roth v. United States*, 354 U.S. 476 (1957).
3. *Miller v. California*, 413 U.S. 15, 24 (1973).
4. *Stanley v. Georgia*, 394 U.S. 557 (1969).
5. See U.C.A. § 76–5-404.1; *State v. Burke*, 675 P.2d 1198 (Utah 1984):

conviction for showing pornographic magazines to young boys while induc-
ing them to disrobe.

6. E.g., *State v. Helms,* 40 P.3d 626 (Utah 2002): conviction for showing
pornography to teenage boys.

7. 539 U.S. 194 (2003).

8. *New York v. Ferber,* 458 U.S. 747, 758–64 (1982).

9. *Osborne v. Ohio,* 495 U.S. 103, 110–11 (1990). See also *State v. Miller,* 104
P.3d 1272 (Utah App. 2004): conviction for sexual exploitation of a minor
based on possession of child pornography; *State v. Morrison,* 31 P.3d 547
(Utah 2001): conviction for downloading child pornography to computer.

10. *Ashcroft v. Free Speech Coalition,* 535 U.S. 234 (2002): federal law prohibit-
ing virtual child pornography violates freedom of speech.

11. N.Y. Ct. Gen. Sess. (1813), quoted in "Privileged Communications to
Clergymen," 1 Cath. Law. 198, 204 (1955).

12. E.g., *Scott v. Hammock,* 870 P.2d 947 (Utah 1994): privilege precluded
bishop from disclosing even non-penitential communication of child abuse.

13. See generally Jacob Yellin, "The History and Current Status of the Clergy-
Penitent Privilege," 23 *Santa Clara L. Rev.* 95 (1983); Seward Reese,
"Confidential Communications to the Clergy," 24 *Ohio St. L.J.* 55 (1963).

14. 553 N.W.2d 579 (Iowa 1996).

15. *State v. Motherwell,* 788 P.2d 1066 (Wash. 1990): "members of the clergy
counseling their parishioners in the religious context are not subject to the
reporting requirement."

16. 763 A.2d 826 (Pa. Super. 2000).

17. 56 S.W.3d 63 (Tex. App. 2001).

18. 627 N.E.2d 802 (Ind. App. 1994); see also *Kendrick v. East Delavan Baptist
Church,* 886 F. Supp. 1465 (D. Wis. 1995): clergy breached statutory and
common law reporting duties.

19. 418 N.E.2d 1130 (Ill. App. 1981); see also *Commonwealth v. Souther,* 575
N.E.2d 1150 (Mass. App. 1991): by abrogating therapist privilege, the law
favors child protection over patient confidences; *Walstad v. State,* 818 P.2d
695 (Alaska App. 1991): abuse report by psychotherapist did not violate
privilege statute; *People v. Battaglia,* 203 Cal. Rptr. 370 (App. 1984): testimony of social worker is not privileged in prosecution for child abuse.

20. See *Hennington v. State,* 702 So. 2d 403 (Miss. 1997): state social worker
was not required to provide "Miranda warning" prior to discussion of suspected abuse.

21. See *Gross v. Myers*, 748 P.2d 459 (Mont. 1987); see also *Fewell v. Besner*, 664 A.2d 577 (Pa. Super. Ct. 1995): therapist who reports child abuse in violation of the professional privilege is shielded from liability under the immunity provisions of the reporting statute.

22. 788 P.2d 1066 (Wash. 1990).

23. See *Hickey v. Jefferson County*, 985 F. Supp. 66 (D.N.Y. 1997); *Stecks v. Young*, 45 Cal. Rptr. 2d 475 (App. 1995): failure to report may subject mandated reporter to both criminal prosecution and civil liability.

24. 551 P.2d 334 (Cal. 1976).

25. See *Bradley v. Ray*, 904 S.W.2d 302 (Mo. App. 1995): therapist had common law duty to warn civil authorities that client was sexually abusing his stepdaughter.

26. See U.C.A. § 78–14a-102.

27. See generally Marjorie B. Lewis, "Duty to Warn Versus Duty to Maintain Confidentiality: Conflicting Demands on Mental Health Professionals," 20 *Suffolk Univ. L. Rev.* 579 (1986).

PART 3

Overcoming a Pornography Problem

CHAPTER NINETEEN

There Is a Way Out

Philip A. Harrison

How can I hope to convey the miracle that has come into my life? It is a story of hope conquering despair and purity overcoming depravity. I rejoice with Nephi: "Behold, the Lord hath redeemed my soul from hell; I have beheld his glory, and I am encircled about eternally in the arms of his love" (2 Nephi 1:15). Although telling it in one chapter seems impossible, I will try to give you an idea of the journey I have been on and how sorrow and hopelessness have been turned to praise and rejoicing.

I never saw myself as a rebellious sort of person. I was raised in the Church. In fact, my ancestors came to Utah with the Martin Handcart Company. When I was young, Primary was held during the week, and I attended so regularly that the memory of the one time I skipped Primary and went to a friend's house and ate ice cream stands out as a glaring exception. I usually enjoyed going to church and didn't give my parents much trouble. I never smoked (except for the time I tried to roll my own cigarette out of some shredded cedar bark like I had heard of kids doing—it was a total disappointment) and I never drank (except for the time two older ladies brought a gallon of apple cider back to the grocery store where I worked because it was "turning." I tried it, but it didn't have much of a kick). In summary, I have never been inactive in the Church or even questioned the truth of the gospel.

However, all this was not enough to prevent me from having some problems in my personal life. As a child and teenager, I suffered from my share of loneliness and insecurity. I was not as capable in sports or other achievements as other kids. I didn't ride a bike or swim until years after my friends did, and I felt in many other ways that I was "not as good," or "not good enough." After I reached puberty, I learned to comfort myself occasionally with masturbation. Little did I dream that this little practice would become part of an addictive pattern in my life that would take years to overcome. At the time, the topic of sex was mysterious and exciting. While there wasn't much pornography available in the 1960s in Provo, Utah, friends introduced me to enough to give me a taste and plant the seed for later indulgence. Although Church leaders have always warned us about pornography, I was young and foolish and didn't believe that it was truly dangerous. Sex was a world I could retreat into in order to forget my troubles. At least, that's what I thought. I hope today's youth will heed the warnings of their Church leaders more earnestly than I did.

Dragging the weight of these shameful practices along with me, I struggled through my teen years. As I dated, I faced additional temptations and made some mistakes, but I sincerely tried to not let things go too far. I repented and abstained long enough to go on a mission and get married in the temple. Like other men I have talked to, I assumed that getting married would solve everything. How could pornography be a temptation once I had a legitimate outlet for my sexual urges? However, once the newness of the sexual relationship within marriage began to wear off, much to my devastation, so did my resolve never to return to my previous habits. Pornography was steadily becoming more available, and I began indulging again. We moved from Utah to a state where pornography was rampant, which fanned the flames of my addiction.

It's so awkward and embarrassing to go to the bishop to confess these sins. Even so, I started talking to my bishop as a teenager, and through the years I continued in an effort to be accountable and get help. Each time I confessed, I sincerely wanted to quit. I wish I had been completely honest with my bishops, but I wasn't always as forthcoming as I could have been. It is a hallmark of addiction that we minimize to others (when we talk at all) and even to ourselves just how bad the problem is. But at the same time, I truly did want to be free of sin. I sincerely tried to become clean and stay clean. My bishops continued to labor with me, and I have been able to hold a temple recommend most of my life, although there have been times when I stayed away from the temple because I didn't feel worthy.

I have always loved the Church and the gospel and was happy to serve when I was called as the elders quorum president in three different states. I taught priesthood lessons, teen Sunday School classes, the Gospel Doctrine class, and even the Family Relations class. These callings taught me a lot about many gospel subjects, including marriage and parenting. Through all these years I wanted to help people, and I hope I have done some good along the way. The Lord has blessed me richly, but because I only let him into my life in a limited way I was still unable to conquer my own demons.

Over time I became the equivalent of what alcoholics call a periodic drunk. I would act out, then my conscience would bother me, and I would "repent" and quit—at least for a few weeks or months. Eventually, however, tensions would build up, discouragements would accumulate, and I would seek relief in my addiction once again. I practiced a sort of serial repentance. Rationalization became a way of life. During one period I tried to tell myself that using pornography wasn't that bad if I refrained from masturbating.

Unfortunately, addiction is progressive, and eventually I abandoned that boundary as well.

As this maddening cycle continued and the decades passed, I began to lose hope. When I discovered Internet pornography in the 90s, that quickly became a huge part of my addiction. Being able to look at all the pornography I wanted, for free and in private, was like pouring gasoline on a fire. No longer did I have to stand at a magazine rack, pretending I was looking at a wholesome magazine. Thus I became totally ensnared by the adversary, the father of lies, all the while thinking that I had at last found freedom! What a tragic deception! This "freedom" only served to bind me more tightly and to destroy my last vestiges of hope. As my indulgence continued to increase despite my efforts to stop, I started to feel that I would never get free of my entrapment in sexual misbehavior. As defeat piled on defeat, I began to imagine what it would be like to stand before the stake high council and lose my Church membership over this terrible habit I found myself powerless to stop. I realize today that the adversary was carefully trying to persuade me to accept excommunication as inevitable for me.

FINDING THE TWELVE STEPS

Despite the demoralizing weakness that plagued me much of my life, I now see the hand of the Lord acting throughout my lifetime. My parents weren't perfect, but they were loving, responsible people and tried to be good parents. I had good teachers at church and caring leaders who were truly involved with the youth. A few months prior to leaving on my mission I met Kathy, a wonderful, faithful young woman, and I received a powerful witness from the Spirit concerning her. We married soon after I returned home, each totally committed to learning how to live together in peace and love. The Lord blessed us with great happiness, although I now realize that without my addiction we could have had an even better marriage and I could have been a much better husband and father. I know it was a blessing from God that my addiction didn't cause more damage than it did.

Through the years, Kathy had her own challenges. Early in her life she developed the habit of comforting herself with excess food, and although she was very trim when we got married, her weight began subsequently to climb. Nothing she tried made any lasting difference for her until she found Overeaters Anonymous, an organization that had adapted the original twelve steps of Alcoholics Anonymous to the problem of compulsive overeating. Kathy began attending OA meetings every week while I watched the children. At one time she felt the need to attend two meetings a week, and although I thought that seemed a bit excessive and maybe unnecessary, I still watched the children and supported her. It proved to be an investment that would pay me back a thousand times over. As Kathy learned about the twelve steps through OA, she began to apply the principles in her life and then to share with me what she was learning. As I listened, I could see that the steps were completely compatible with the gospel; they were simply an expanded explanation of faith and repentance and encouraged one to live closer to God. Still, I wasn't willing to admit that I needed these same principles in my own life. It would be years before I could entertain calling my problem an addiction. I was sure that in my case I just needed to get serious about quitting on my own. I just needed a little more time, a little more determination. Even when I learned about Sexaholics Anonymous, a twelve-step organization that helps people overcome sexual addiction, I used the fact that the closest meetings were an hour and a half away as an excuse to put off taking any positive action toward my own recovery. I was not humble enough nor open enough with my wife to make that kind of admission or sacrifice. I continued to suffer in secrecy.

Then, one day in the spring of 1998, Kathy excitedly told me she had learned about a twelve-step organization specifically for

LDS people, integrating the principles of the twelve steps with the principles of the gospel and the scriptures. It was called Heart t' Heart, and there was a meeting just a half-hour from our home. I guess the time was finally right—I had suffered enough defeats in trying to overcome my problem on my own. I knew I needed help, and I was finally ready to listen to the message of the twelve-step program, especially when it was explained in terms of the restored gospel. I began attending weekly meetings with my wife and applying the principles in my life, and immediately things began to change for the better.

While there isn't space to share my testimony of all of the twelve steps, I will introduce you to the first three and how they awakened me to my need for the Savior's atonement in my life. Step One required me to admit that *I* am powerless to change my behavior. I had to admit that I was indeed "addicted" and not just trapped in a "habit." This wasn't really too hard to do—I had the evidence of my whole life in front of me as proof! I had tried many, many times to quit, and while I had sometimes succeeded for a time, I had never been able to "stay quit." I always returned, like a "dog . . . to his own vomit" (2 Peter 2:22). That to me is sufficient as a definition of addiction. I qualified. As the original Alcoholics Anonymous literature states, as a "going human concern," I was "100-percent bankrupt" in regards to my sexual misbehavior.

That brought me to Step Two—a recognition that there was One who had the power to straighten out my life, to lift me out of the mire and muck I had put myself in and set me down in a better place. A major hurdle to my acceptance of this step was accepting the reality that the Lord would do this *for me*. I truly believed that he was willing to help others, but my self-esteem was so low that I thought such help was out of my reach—that I had somehow made myself ineligible for it. How many of us think our sins are of the unpardonable variety when they are really very ordinary, common sins and simply need the Savior's atonement? I bear witness that he really is there for *all* of us if we will sincerely seek him. I have come to know for myself that the Lord is not just the Savior of others; he is my very own Messiah, my own personal Savior. I have come to feel the personal love he has for me.

Step Three was perhaps the most difficult, but as is frequently the case in the economy of God, the most powerful. This step involved turning not only my addiction, but *my whole life* over to the Lord. I began to realize how much I had been trying to live according to my own rules. I learned that I needed to now let *him* rule my life, moment by moment. At first, that surrender involved primarily the temptations associated with my addiction, but in time it came to include everything else in my life as well. I came to admit that I had made a mess of my life and, in fact, needed to be reborn as his son (see Mosiah 5:7), take his name upon me, and become willing to follow him as a small child trusts the lead of his earthly father (see Mosiah 3:19).

An old AA slogan that I've come to appreciate goes like this: "I can't; He can; I think I'll let Him." It's a good shorthand summary of steps one, two, and three. I have found that implementing these steps of submission to truth and to the Lord is a continuous process that I must practice on a daily basis, not just to obtain relief from my addiction, but in order to fulfil the entire purpose of my life here on earth.

As for the rest of the steps, suffice it to say that they involve more detailed repentance, making restitution to those I have hurt, and coming to know and follow the Savior more consciously. Following all these steps has brought me to a place of willingness to follow the Lord that I had never known before. While I don't do it perfectly, continually attempting to surrender my will to his has indeed brought me relief from the addiction that held me captive for so many years.

Through the Heart t' Heart version of the twelve-step model I found a pathway of life-changing principles that brought me to a

knowledge of the truth that everyone who desires healing must ultimately come to the Savior. As King Benjamin taught: "And moreover, I say unto you, that *there shall be no other name given nor any
other way nor means* whereby salvation can come unto the children
of men, *only in and through the name of Christ, the Lord Omnipotent*" (Mosiah 3:17; emphasis added). Using these principles to
come to him, I have now been blessed with years of abstinence. I
cannot describe how sweet this remission of sin has been. I doubt
that I will ever be able to sufficiently express my gratitude to my
Savior for this miracle in my life and for the love I have for him as
a result, but I will spend the rest of my life trying.

PROGRESSING IN RECOVERY

Willingness is the key to surrendering to the Lord, and surrendering to the Lord is the key to recovery. I found that when I first
started a program of recovery, I was met by a very stubborn and
unruly will—my own! I had spent so many years doing "what I
wanted to do" that I had a difficult time letting the Lord be in
charge of my life. Another way to say it is that I had blithely surrendered so much of my will to the adversary, I had a hard time getting it back! He doesn't let go of his captives quickly or easily. But
the Lord is stronger, and ultimately, if we will surrender our will to
the Lord, he will fight our battles for us.

Recovery is a process of nursing back to health a feverish and
confused will. Addiction robs us of agency. When I started trying
in earnest to surrender my will to the Savior, I encountered a major
obstacle—*I didn't want to!* On one level, I wanted to change and
stop suffering the pain my addiction caused me, but when it came
down to facing the actual temptation, I wanted the sin more than I
wanted to follow Jesus. So what could I do?

From the first time I heard the AA expression, "be willing to be
willing," I loved it. It made sense to me. I knew that I wanted to be

willing to follow the Lord, but I had to admit I wasn't really willing yet. But I could be willing to be willing. My thoughts took the form of a plea to the Lord and went something like this: "Lord, I am not yet willing to give up _____, but I am willing to surrender my heart to you, and if you will soften my heart and change it, so I don't mind giving up _____, then I will give it up." This is really a "no-lose" proposition. If the Lord changed my heart so I didn't mind giving up whatever it was, then I wouldn't mind giving it up, would I? But I had to give him permission to soften my heart first. I found that when I made this specific surrender of my will, the next time the test came up, I somehow found the willingness to let the Lord direct my choice and make whatever sacrifice he was inviting me to make.

This process helped me get rid of materials I had in my possession that were "triggering," that were a temptation to me. I owned a few R-rated videos, and while they weren't the worst available, they were still a problem. I knew in my heart that I should get rid of them, but part of me was still resisting. However, when I asked the Lord to change my heart, he did. I somehow found the willingness to destroy the R-rated videos. The next surrender involved getting rid of some of the PG-13 movies I owned. And on it went, the Lord taking me by the hand each step of the way.

I like to compare this process to being in a room with many doors, each door representing some bit of progress I could make. Most of the doors may seem pretty difficult or maybe even impossible to open, but after a bit, one of them looks like I might be able to open it. Maybe the door is already open, and all I have to do is walk through it. It is possible, but it still waits on my choice. If I accept the Lord's invitation and go through that door, I find myself in a better place. Then I find another set of doors (some of them curiously like the doors I wasn't ready to tackle before), but in time one of those doors opens, and I am again faced with the decision to move on. This is a continuing process we all must face—

submitting our will to the will of the Savior and the Father. It is the path to recovery, and is even the path to exaltation, if we will let it be. The Lord doesn't ask us to make the journey in one gigantic leap. He makes allowances for where we are and how much we are able to do at that time, even if it is very little. Then he adds his marvelous power to our small, unprofitable contribution, and we are able to take the next step. It has been said that willpower is made up of our will plus his power. That's good enough for me.

I used to think that "enduring to the end" meant getting up on a sufficiently high spiritual plane and then making sure you didn't fall off. More recently I have come to a different understanding. The process the Lord uses to cleanse us is frequently compared to purifying and refining: "He shall sit as a refiner and purifier of silver: and he shall purify the sons of Levi, and purge them as gold and silver" (Malachi 3:3). When a material such as gold is purified, several steps are necessary. The first steps remove the coarsest contaminants, those that are the most foreign to the nature of gold, such as sand and clay. As the word *refine* suggests, subsequent steps focus on removing finer and finer impurities. In the refining of gold, even silver would eventually be considered a contaminant. This is the process the Lord uses with us. As we submit ourselves to him for the purification process, he will "show us our weakness" (see Ether 12:27) that we might come to surrender them to him, that they might be removed from us, the coarsest ones first, then progressively finer ones.

A contaminant that the Lord must have seen as pretty obvious, but one I could not see myself for some time, was the sin of pride. I don't know why I couldn't see it, but pride is an integral part of addiction and, in fact, a component of all other sins as well. As President Benson taught:

"In the scriptures there is no such thing as righteous pride. It is always considered as a sin. We are not speaking of a wholesome view of self-worth, *which is best established by a close relationship with God.* But we are speaking of pride as the universal sin, as someone has described it."[1]

I found I could not get through the first three steps without confronting my pride. Surrendering my pride to the Lord has been like peeling the layers of an onion. I would think I had discovered and discarded my pride, and then, Wow! There it was again, in a slightly different form. Even today I find the need to re-work steps one, two and three with each new form of pride the Lord shows me I still have.

I even discovered a subtle form of pride in the way I went about seeking help from the Lord! At first, I wanted to just ask once for his help and be done with it. It challenged my pride to have to keep coming back and asking over and over again for the Lord to rescue me. But that was exactly what I needed and what the Lord required of me. I experienced a major shift in my thinking when someone introduced me to the Lord's counsel: "Look unto me in every thought; doubt not, fear not" (D&C 6:36). I had never considered that I might take even my unworthy thoughts to the Lord, even though we are counseled: "Yea, and cry unto God for *all thy support;* . . . yea, let *all thy thoughts* be directed unto the Lord. . . . Counsel with the Lord in *all thy doings,* and he will direct thee for good" (Alma 37:36–37; emphasis added). I don't know why I missed understanding this for so long. Even the sacrament prayers that I had listened to every week since childhood encouraged me to "always remember him, that [I] might have His spirit to be with [me]." As I finally started listening to this message, I realized how essential a complete and continuing daily, sometimes even hourly, dependence on the Lord was to my being freed from addiction. I needed to seek the Lord in "all my thoughts" and "all my doings." I needed to plead for his help with each temptation that came to me and not try to deal with a single one of them on my own.

As I accepted the need to seek the Lord with each temptation that came, I learned that I still had to surrender my pride in the *way* I asked for his help. I began to realize that when I simply asked the Lord to "*help me* overcome" a temptation, I was still keeping him in the role of my servant, rather than my Savior. I was still taking charge, and therefore reserving much (or even most) of the credit to myself for any success. How subtle pride is! And how different this new idea was of coming to him in complete surrender and asking him simply and humbly, "Lord, I can't handle this temptation. Will you please take it away for me?" In this way I acknowledge my total dependence on him, and at least for that moment I let go of the last vestiges of my pride. I remember he is the one with all power, not I. I admit that if I am freed from temptation, it is because of his grace and power. These are the "depths of humility" (2 Nephi 9:42) that are required to break the stranglehold of addiction. And so, one incident at a time, *instead of surrendering to temptation, I surrender the temptation to the Lord, and he saves me in the moment I do.* The prayer the Lord taught us becomes real for me: "And lead [me] not into temptation, but *deliver [me] from evil:* For *thine is the kingdom, and the power, and the glory,* for ever" (Matthew 6:13; emphasis added).

When I first started applying these truths, my capacity to retain the gift of deliverance was small, and I would often have to ask again—sometimes several times—for deliverance from the same temptation. It was humbling, but what other antidote for pride is there?

A DAILY ROUTINE—THE "MANNA" OF RECOVERY

One of the absolute necessities in *obtaining* and *retaining* deliverance from my addiction has been to have a daily routine that brings me into contact with the Spirit of the Lord. The metaphor of the children of Israel gathering manna in the wilderness is a perfect comparison. I find that my relationship with the Savior must be renewed every day, for the strength one obtains on Monday doesn't last through Friday, or even Wednesday, especially in the world in which we live.

The prophets have counseled us from the beginning to make prayer and scripture study a part of each day, but in my pride I had decided I was too busy, until addiction compelled me to be humble. Now I accept the inspired counsel and have proven it to be of great worth—in fact, vital—in my life. I begin each day with a morning devotional. I find a place where I can have some solitude, with as few interruptions as possible. Early morning works best for me, before the demands of the day crowd my heart and mind. Getting up earlier is a small price to pay for the gift of healing that it brings. Putting the Lord first in my day is an important way of emphasizing the pre-eminence of that relationship in my life. Without him, I am nothing. Without spending time with him, I am not conscious of his love for me and I do not have the same access to his power in keeping me sober. These are some things I try to include on a daily basis in order to allow him to guide and protect me:

Start each day with a kneeling prayer. This is an important way to express humility and our need for God. We shut out distractions and come before our Maker. I try to talk with my Father in Heaven in personal, heartfelt terms and feel his love for me as his son. He is the perfect Father. If our earthly father has had flaws that caused us problems, our Heavenly Father does not. He loves us with a perfect love and with infinite patience. Coming to him will prove that.

Counsel with the Savior through journal writing. After praying, I write in my journal as a means of communicating with my Savior. I talk with him and tell him my concerns, reverently, but as I would talk with a friend. He has referred to his servants in the kingdom as his friends (see D&C 93:45), and since the Lord is "no respecter of persons" (D&C 38:16), I am bold enough to think I can also be his friend.

Listen for his counsel in response. I find that if I am willing to exercise faith in asking and am ready to record the answer, the answer will come. Doing this in writing seems to hold so much more power than simply "listening." If I have prepared myself through prayer, set aside a special time, and am ready to write down the answer, I receive much more—more answers and clearer answers.

"Capture" from the scriptures. I open the scriptures and find a place I feel the Lord would like me to read. I soon find a passage that speaks to my heart, one in which I can see a message that relates to my own life and struggles. I copy that passage into my journal and then "capture" from it. That is, after each significant phrase, I insert my own comments on how the verse applies to me. In other words, I "liken [the] scriptures unto [myself]" (see 1 Nephi 19:23–24). I find that the thoughts that come to me when I do this often give me added insight into my problems and their solution. I often feel that the Lord is telling me what he wants me to get from the scripture, and so I often write the thoughts in his voice. In this way, my journal becomes a personal volume of recorded revelations, designed specifically for me.

Invite him to walk through the day with me. I listen for the Lord to tell me when I have done enough in my morning devotional, and then as I conclude, I ask the Lord to be with me throughout the day. I do not just need him for a few minutes in the morning; "I need [him] every hour," every moment of every day.

Check in with him at intervals during the day. The world is full of distractions, and the adversary will suggest to our minds whatever he thinks will distract us from God. Sometimes just being busy or, like Martha, being "careful and troubled about many things" (Luke 10:41) is a sufficient distraction to make us forget God and thus diminish his influence with and protection of us. Periodically checking in with the Lord throughout the day renews the connection with him and increases *his* influence in my life (see Alma 37:36–37).

Turn to him with each and every temptation that comes my way during the day. If I have begun the day with him, and have walked with him throughout my day, turning to him for rescue when temptations strike is the most natural thing in the world. If I have neglected my relationship with him and feel like he is a stranger, turning to him will be more difficult to do.

These practices have become the foundation of my relationship with the Lord. They have taught me that he cares about me as a person, not just one of the vast multitude of humanity. I feel him guiding and protecting me, and I know through the whisperings of his Spirit to mine that he does not judge or condemn me for my past and has in fact forgiven me for my sins. As a result, shame and fear have left me, and I desire now to bless the lives of others through my testimony, that they might rejoice in him, as I do, and enter into his rest.

WHAT IT'S LIKE NOW

I'd like to be able to tell you that my life is perfect now (perfectionism always was part of my problem!). In fact, although things are not perfect, my life is so much better than it used to be. I don't act out with pornography or masturbation anymore. I am blessed now to be able to count my abstinence in terms of years. As I have turned my will over to the Lord and tried each day to follow his Spirit in every way I can, I have found a peace of conscience, as the Lord promised: "Peace I leave with you, my peace I give unto you: not as the world giveth, give I unto you. Let not your heart be troubled, neither let it be afraid" (John 14:27). When I was in active addiction, I was troubled and afraid—afraid of being found out or of slipping further. All of that is gone now. I know the Lord will keep me safe as long as I continue to stay close to him. I now have a clear conscience. I know the Lord has forgiven me for my sins of the past. All this is a miracle to me, and something I could not imagine a few short years ago.

Is everything easy? Is my addiction "cured"? Things are much easier than before, but I don't consider myself "cured." I still have to deal with temptations, although they do not come as often or as intensely as before. I know now how to tap the Lord's power to overcome. As I continue the practice of daily devotional time to get close to the Lord each morning, and as I surrender to him each temptation as it comes, I am protected through the day, and the temptations are manageable. But they are still there, and I find if I neglect my sessions of daily spiritual nourishment, the temptations become more frequent and more insistent. I know that with just a little indulgence in sin, I could fall back to where I was before, and even farther. For that reason I still call myself an addict. For me it is not a negative label, but a reminder to myself of my need for constant contact with my Savior.

Over time I have realized a profound truth: the same process that helps us access the Savior's power in overcoming addiction—turning our will over to him—also has the power to bring us into full harmony with God and give us access to all the blessings he has to offer. The fact that we can rise from the depths of depravity to ascend to the very throne of God and partake of his goodness and perfection is truly one of the "mysteries of godliness." Our Savior has made all this possible through his incomparable atonement, and through his grace we are made "partakers of the heavenly gift" (Ether 12:7–8). This is all so very much more than just overcoming addiction to pornography or any other sin. It is about eternal life. Some need to be delivered from the depths of sin, others from the prison of complacency—from lives that seem "good enough" but are not quite godly. Either way, our rescue is a miracle from God, and I thank him for it.

NOTE

1. Ezra Taft Benson, "Cleansing the Inner Vessel," *Ensign*, May 1986, 6; emphasis added.

CHAPTER TWENTY

Getting Started: Taking the First Step toward Recovery

Dan Gray, Todd A. Olson, and Becky Harding

Recovering from sexual addiction is not a simple process, nor is living with an addict. In fact, most recovering addicts and their partners agree that true recovery is a process they will be working on for the rest of their lives. We offer the following suggestions to those who are ready to commit to recovery but don't know how to begin. The principles taught herein may also help the spouses of addicts, whether or not their partner is seeking help.

We've all seen what happens when a rock is thrown into a still pond. The ripples expand and spread until they reach the shore on every side. As you follow the principles outlined below, you will find that mastering these simple steps will have a ripple effect on

NOTE: *There are varying degrees of compulsive sexual behavior— from problematic behavior to serious addiction. For the simplicity of this chapter we've chosen to use the terms "sexual addict" and "sexual addiction" rather than "those suffering from compulsive sexual behavior" and "compulsive sexual behavior," respectively. Whatever the degree of your problem, please don't let the terms we have used stand in the way of getting the help you need.*

your life and your addiction and can facilitate your healing in ways you never dreamed possible.

Don't dive in too fast. Addicts and partners of addicts have a tendency to do things in extreme—either all or nothing. The worksheet at the end of this chapter will help you regulate these tendencies and pace yourself so you don't experience burnout, but instead find a healthy moderation coming back into your routine. If you're tempted to do it all right now, remember the words of Mosiah 4:27:

"And see that all these things are done in wisdom and order; for it is not requisite that a man should run faster than he has strength. And again, it is expedient that he should be diligent, that thereby he might win the prize; therefore, all things must be done in order."

Resist the inclination to overanalyze the following recommendations. *Just get started.* When you are further into recovery, you will understand the benefit of each of the steps and of the daily tasks or "dailies," but for right now, just get some good recovery habits in place, which will help you replace bad habits.

STEP ONE: CHOOSE ONE WAY TO COME OUT OF HIDING AND FIND OUT YOU'RE NOT ALONE

Experience has shown that developing a network of support and finding out that *you are not alone* is very beneficial in the recovery process. Talk to someone you trust about your addiction, such as a close friend or a family member. Get involved in a twelve-step program or group.[1] Your bishop or other priesthood leaders can also be a source of support and spiritual guidance at this difficult time. Engage the services of a qualified licensed therapist who has training and experience in the treatment of sexual addiction to help you through this process. Including both spouses in treatment often enhances its effectiveness.

STEP TWO: POSITIVE SELF-TALK

If you're an addict or the partner of an addict, negative self-talk will sabotage and defeat your efforts at recovery. Combat self-defeating thoughts by doing daily affirmations from an affirmation book like those recommended in Step Three. So that you can get started today, we have included a week of affirmations at the end of this chapter (see "Starter Affirmations," page 257).

STEP THREE: SELF-CARE

Choose at least one (but not more than two) "dailies" listed below from each of the three categories: personal, physical, and spiritual. Make a copy of the worksheet that follows the dailies (see page 256), fill in the dailies you have chosen, and commit right now that you will build these positive habits daily. Be conscientious in filling out the worksheet each day, and before long you will be experiencing the ripple effect mentioned above as you watch these positive habits affect every area of your life. (Following the dailies, you will find some examples from recovering addicts and how they have used their dailies to improve their lives.)

·Personal Dailies

1. Keep a journal
2. Repeat daily affirmations

Suggested affirmation books:

Answers in the Heart: Daily Meditations (Center City, Minn.: Hazelden Publishing, 1989)

Melody Beattie, *The Language of Letting Go* (Center City, Minn.: Hazelden Publishing, 1990)

Gordon B. Hinckley, *Stand a Little Taller: Counsel and Inspiration for Each Day of the Year* (Salt Lake City: Deseret Book Company, 2001)

Touchstones: A Book of Daily Meditations for Men (Center City, Minn.: Hazelden Publishing, 1987)

3. Work on personal development
    - Start a new hobby, such as gardening, recreational reading, playing a musical instrument, and so forth
    - Take a community education course
    - Express creativity, such as artwork, writing poetry, and so forth
    - Do recovery reading (15 minutes daily)—see list below

Suggested readings:

Melody Beattie, *Codependent No More: How to Stop Controlling Others and Start Caring for Yourself* (New York: Harper/Hazelden, 1987) (ideal for partners)

A. Dean Byrd and Mark D. Chamberlain, *Willpower Is Not Enough: Why We Don't Succeed at Change* (Salt Lake City, Utah: Deseret Book, 1995)

Steven A. Cramer, *The Worth of a Soul: A Personal Account of Excommunication and Conversion* (Orem, Utah: Randall Book, 1983)

Rod W. Jeppsen, *Turn Yourselves and Live: Is Anything Too Hard for the Lord?* (Sandy, Utah: Vescorp, 1998)

Charlotte D. Kasl, *Women, Sex, and Addiction: A Search for Love and Power* (New York: Ticknor & Fields, 1989)

Mark B. Kastleman, *The Drug of the New Millennium: The Science of How Internet Pornography Radically Alters the Human Brain and Body* (Orem, Utah: Granite Publishers, 2001)

Pia Mellody, *Facing Codependence: What It Is, Where It Comes From, How It Sabotages Our Lives* (San Francisco, Calif.: Perennial Library, 1989) (ideal for partners)

Rory C. Reid and Dan Gray, *Discussing Pornography Problems with a Spouse: Confronting and Disclosing Secret Behaviors* (N.p.: Rory C. Reid, 2002)

Sexaholics Anonymous White Book (available only through www.sa.org)

Sex and Love Addicts Anonymous Basic Test (available only through www.slaafws.org)

Physical Dailies

1. Heathful Living
   - Exercise 30 minutes at least 3 times a week (walk, bike, hike, swim, run, and so forth)
   - Rest and relaxation
   - Get adequate sleep
   - Limit TV to little or none
2. Nutrition
   - Learn about nutrition and plan meals in advance
   - Eat balanced meals
   - Avoid junk food (including sugar and caffeine)

Spiritual Dailies

1. Pray
2. Meditate
3. Read scripture or other religious books
4. Give Church service

Examples of Dailies in Action

1. When John gets up every day, he spends fifteen minutes in meditation, then does an affirmation from *Stand a Little Taller*. Three days a week he swims laps at the YMCA, and once a week he attends a twelve-step meeting.

JOHN'S WORKSHEET WEEK OF JAN. 28

ACTIVITY	SUN	MON	TUE	WED	THUR	FRI	SAT
Meditate (15 min.)	X	X	missed	X	X	X	missed
Affirmations	X	X	X	X	X	X	X
Swim at YMCA		X		X		X	
Attend SA Group					X		

2.   Sally reads the Book of Mormon each day upon arising. She walks with a neighbor every morning and is taking a community education course in preparing healthy meals. Rather than watching TV until midnight, she committed to being in bed by 10:30 P.M. each night. She is seeing a sex-addiction therapist once a week with her husband.

SALLY'S WORKSHEET WEEK OF SEPT. 8

ACTIVITY	SUN	MON	TUE	WED	THUR	FRI	SAT
Read Book of Mormon	X	X	X	X	X		—
Walk with Doreen		X	oops	X	X	X	—
Bed by 10:30 p.m.	10:00	10:15	10:15	10:15	10:45	12:00	11:45
Class at College					X		
Meet with Dr. Taylor		X					

3.   Helen reads daily from Pia Mellody's *Facing Codependence.* At the end of each day she writes in her journal. She also

HELEN'S WORKSHEET WEEK OF MAY 5

ACTIVITY	SUN	MON	TUE	WED	THUR	FRI	SAT
Read Facing Codep.		X	X	X	X	X	
Write in journal	X	X	X	X	X	X	—
Go jogging		20 min.					
Attend S-Anon					X		

attends a weekly meeting of S-Anon, a twelve-step group for part-ners.[2] She would like to get back to her old habit of jogging, but hasn't fully committed to this daily step.

4.   Jared's life was so out of balance, the most he could do was say a prayer once a day. That was his one, sole daily. After three months he had built up the courage to talk to his bishop and he is planning to get started with the online SLAA group.[3]

JARED'S WORKSHEET   WEEK OF NOV. 7

ACTIVITY	SUN	MON	TUE	WED	THUR	FRI	SAT
Pray Daily	X	X	—	—	—	X	—

Although we have given you guidelines and suggestions, it is important that you do not overdo these dailies and that you take them at your own pace. After all, this is your life and your recovery and no one knows your needs and your capabilities better than you do. Start this program today and evaluate your progress over time. (You can use the worksheet found on page 256.) Add or delete activities as needed to keep a healthy balance in your life.

If you have followed all the suggestions in this chapter, you will be involved in some kind of therapy or group—whether it is with a licensed therapist or a twelve-step program (or both). We urge you to continue this therapy and follow through on the commitments you have made toward your healing. To supplement your recovery process we have included some resources at the end of the chapter (see page 258).

WEEK OF _____

ACTIVITY	SUN	MON	TUE	WED	THUR	FRI	SAT

STARTER AFFIRMATIONS

"No trial is joyous for the present but grievous to be borne; but trials yield their blessings, when patiently endured."
—President John Taylor

Today I will be patient with my steps toward recovery. I will focus on the positive desire for wellness that is the core of my commitment.

"We can do no great things, only small things with great love."
—Mother Teresa

Today I will do one kind thing for myself and one for someone else. I will love myself and let myself receive the love that is there for me.

"What we have to learn to do, we learn by doing."
—Aristotle

Today I am willing to learn by doing. I will learn something about myself by following through on my daily plan.

"[May you] discover the greatest friend of all, Jesus the Christ, . . . full of perfect love and boundless compassion, with the power to forgive and forget. May the Spirit bear witness of that love and somehow touch your heart that you may find the courage to take those steps that will bring you peace and tranquility, that will restore your feelings of self-worth and place you on the path to happiness."
—Elder Richard G. Scott

Recovery is a messy business. Today I will give myself permission to experiment with something new in life, even if it doesn't work out. I will learn from the day's business and move on.

"If I were to begin my life again, I should want it as it was. I would only open my eyes a little more."
—Jules Renard

Today I will take the time to be more aware of my interactions with others. I will remember that each day is a gift to me.

"If you tell the truth, you don't have to remember anything."
—Mark Twain

Today I will be honest with myself. I will tell the truth. Lies tie me to the past.

"Let there be space in your togetherness."
—Kahlil Gibran

Today I will detach with love. To let go doesn't mean to stop caring. It means I can't do it for someone else.

RESOURCES

For information on LDS-oriented twelve-step programs in your area, contact your local priesthood leaders or the LDS Family Services office in your area.

Sexaholics Anonymous

For information or to find a group in your area, contact SA at:
Sexaholics Anonymous International Central Office
P.O. Box 3565
Brentwood, TN 37024–3565
Phone: 615–370–6062
Fax: 615–370–0882
E-mail: saico@sa.org

Sex and Love Addicts Anonymous

For more information on SLAA, visit www.slaafws.org
Fellowship-Wide Services
P.O. Box 338
Norwood, MA 02062–0338
Phone: 781–255–8825
Fax: 781–255–9190
Email: slaafws@slaafws.org
To find a meeting in your area, go to www.slaafws.org/meetinfo.
html. To join an online meeting, visit www.slaafws.org/online/

For Partners

www.sanon.org
S-Anon
P.O. Box 111242
Nashville, TN 37222–1242
Phone: 615–833–3152
E-mail: sanon@sanon.org

Co-Dependents Anonymous

www.codependents.org
Fellowship Services Office (FSO)
P.O. Box 33577
Phoenix, AZ 85067–3577
Phone: 602–277–7991
E-mail: outreach@coda.org

NOTES

1. See resources at end of this chapter, which include LDS-oriented programs.
2. For help in finding an S-Anon group in your area, see resources at end of chapter.
3. See resources at end of chapter for information on SLAA—Sex and Love Addicts Anonymous.

CHAPTER TWENTY-ONE

Surviving Withdrawal: Laying the Groundwork for a Lasting Recovery

Dan Gray, Todd A. Olson, and Scott Peterson

Be prepared!"—the tried-and-true slogan of the Boy Scouts—is good advice for all of us, but it can have special significance for recovering addicts. In our practice we have found that when faced with the painful and confusing symptoms of withdrawal (which are frequently unexpected), many addicts experience setbacks in their recovery. This chapter will discuss what you can expect and give you some tactics that will help you push through these setbacks and move forward. Just as knowing an enemy's strategy aids an army general in drawing up a successful plan of attack, understanding the workings of your addiction—and what you are up against when you begin the process of withdrawal—will help you proactively combat the challenges that are an inevitable part of recovery.

Entering sexual recovery and the early signs of withdrawal can be baffling, as was the case for Edward N.: "When I finally committed to quit acting out sexually and started into recovery, I began experiencing many of the same things I went through when I quit using cocaine. I just don't get it! I could understand withdrawal symptoms from cocaine because it was something I actually put into my body. But I can't understand how stopping an activity or behavior could possibly have the same effect as stopping my cocaine addiction. Is this normal?"

Edward is not the only recovering addict who has unexpectedly experienced the symptoms of withdrawal from sexual addiction. In fact, when withdrawal symptoms begin to manifest, it's a sign that the addict is truly in recovery. And likewise, Edward is not the only recovering addict to express confusion about the complex and difficult process of withdrawal. In order to answer his question, we need to explain what addiction is and how the definition of addiction has been radically changed over the last few years due to recent research.

WHAT, EXACTLY, IS ADDICTION?

You'll find as many different definitions of addiction as there are books written on the subject. These definitions cover everything from compulsive dependence to casual cravings. In today's society, many use the term *addiction* lightly. Have you ever heard someone say that they were absolutely addicted to chocolate chip ice cream or that their favorite author's books are totally addicting? Are these people actually addicted to ice cream or to a certain author's books? Probably not, but they may be displaying some of the characteristics of addiction.

A good, practical definition of addiction that is frequently used is:

"Addiction is the use of a substance or activity for the purpose of lessening pain or augmenting pleasure, by a person who has lost control over the rate, frequency, or duration of its use, and whose life has become progressively unmanageable as a result."

In more simple terms: If you cannot control when you start or stop a behavior, and if the behavior causes problems for you and those close to you, you're addicted.

You may have noticed that the above definitions are not solely related to *substance* abuse. Until about forty years ago, it was generally assumed that the human body could get addicted only to mood-altering *substances,* which did not go beyond the obvious ingestibles (substances taken into the body), such as drugs, alcohol, food, tobacco, and so forth. But in the 1970s scientists discovered that addiction was related to biochemical changes within the brain. Researchers John Hughes and Hans Kosterlitz targeted tiny amino acid molecules in the brain that are responsible for manufacturing potent, mood-altering chemicals. Known as endorphins, these molecules bear a striking structural similarity to opiates. This discovery—that the brain could produce its own opiates—has led the research community to reexamine the biochemical mechanism of human behavior.

Thousands of studies have since been conducted to explore the relationships between thoughts, feelings, behaviors, and brain chemistry. It has now become obvious that not only can individuals become addicted to ingestible mood-altering *substances,* but they can become addicted to non-ingestible, mood-altering *activities* and *behaviors* as well. Departing from the traditional definition of addiction—a pathological (or unhealthy) relationship with a mood-altering substance—we can now expand this definition to describe addiction as "a pathological (or unhealthy) relationship with a mood-altering *experience.*" Therefore we can draw the logical conclusion that if a person can get addicted to experiences as well as substances, then it follows that the body will experience withdrawal symptoms when the addictive behaviors have been stopped, just as when use of the substance has been discontinued.

SYMPTOMS OF WITHDRAWAL

Because each addict is different, each will experience his or her own individual withdrawal process, but there are certain symptoms that are frequently experienced. For instance, it has been estimated that more than 66 percent of sex addicts suffer from insomnia and other sleep disorders during the process of withdrawal. The most frequent symptoms experienced by recovering sexual addicts include:

Insomnia and sleep disorders
Fatigue and excessive tiredness
Headaches and general body aches
Depression
Irritability
Increased or decreased appetite for food
Increased or decreased sexual desire
Shakiness, tenseness, nervousness
Nausea
Rapid heartbeat
Shortness of breath
Unusual skin sensitivity or itchiness
Unusual genital sensitivity

While many recovering addicts going through withdrawal will experience one or more of these symptoms, some do not. As mentioned above, all will experience withdrawal in their own individual way, depending on several factors, such as the longevity of their addiction and how balanced the rest of their life is. Don S. suffered withdrawal in the following fashion: "I was pretty scared when my therapist told me what to expect in the early stages of withdrawal and recovery, and I wasn't sure I'd be able to face it. Though I am experiencing some insomnia and a loss of appetite, I am also feeling really sad. I mean, I hate being addicted and I'm so glad to be getting rid of this ball and chain, but for some reason I am feeling a huge sense of loss. How could I possibly feel this way?"

To many recovering addicts, giving up their addiction is like giving up an old friend, and saying good-bye to old friends is always hard, even if they've caused you pain. There is often a deep feeling of grief and loss. Although this may seem puzzling at first, it's easier to understand when you look at how you've used your addiction to help you cope. Your addiction does become a comforting friend, the one you've turned to in times of trouble or stress—a friend you've relied on for immediate comfort; one that always responds, never talks back, and never judges. In order to move on with your recovery, you must eventually let these feelings go.

ADAPTING TO WITHDRAWAL

During this early stage of recovery we often liken the recovering addict to a runner who is training at sea level and then runs at high altitude. Moving from sea level to high altitude, the runner will experience pain and discomfort when he runs—it is not an easy adjustment. If he returns to sea level the pain and discomfort disappear; but these symptoms will also disappear at the high altitude eventually, if he toughs it out long enough to adapt. The following story from one of our clients illustrates this painful process of adaptation, but also reveals the rich rewards for those willing to pay the price.

"This time around in recovery I decided I would not only stop my physical acting out, but I would also work on not letting my lustful thoughts linger longer than three seconds. During the first week I developed a splitting headache just close to a migraine. It would not go away. Nighttime was the worst. I couldn't sleep and would toss and turn all night.

"Since I had been told to expect some form of withdrawal symptoms, I had already committed to getting through this stage and not acting out, even though I was tempted many times. I remember the awakening I experienced when I realized that my headaches and insomnia were truly symptoms of withdrawal. It was six weeks into my treatment and I just did not see how I could go on if these headaches didn't stop. I thought if they were really a symptom of withdrawal surely they would have ended by now. I was starting to wonder if I had a brain tumor or some other serious illness. I was literally afraid I was going to die of this pain.

"One night I let down my guard and acted out. Afterward I went right to sleep, and when I woke up the next day my headache was gone. What an awakening! I am truly addicted, I thought. My symptoms went completely away when I acted out. I am happy to report I used this new understanding to commit even more than before to my recovery. I realized I had never gone long enough without sex and lust to get through the pain of withdrawal—but this time I would. Sure enough, my headaches returned a few days later, along with my insomnia, and lasted another six weeks.

"I will never forget those twelve weeks. That was one year ago. I have been sober ever since and have not experienced another headache longer than a couple of hours. I am so glad I had been educated about withdrawal, because I was taught that I would eventually get through it and that I would not die. Having this understanding gave me the hope and courage to tough it out and just live one day at a time until I could see the light at the end of the tunnel."

Like the pain and difficulty of the runner trying to adapt to a higher altitude, an addict must tough it out initially and face the pain and anxiety head-on before he can adapt to living without his addictive behavior. We call this "leaning into the pain," which means directly acknowledging and facing the discomfort of withdrawal, knowing that you will live through it and that you will come out stronger than you were before. The natural tendency, as in the story above, is to succumb to the desire for a "fix" when the brain's reward center is crying out to be drugged. But if you will lean into the pain, acknowledge and face it head-on, you will allow your body and mind to detoxify and finally rid themselves of the withdrawal symptoms and the overwhelming desire to sexually act out.

Every addict must pass through this phase of recovery in order to progress. The benefits of such trials was spoken of by the Apostle Peter: "That the trial of your faith, being much more precious than of gold that perisheth, though it be tried with fire, might be found unto praise and honour and glory at the appearing of Jesus Christ" (1 Peter 1:7).

THE BRAIN AND THE THREE STYLES OF ADDICTION

Your brain contains billions of nerve cells, known as neurons, that use electrical signals to communicate with each other and keep the body functioning. Helping these electrical signals along are special chemicals called neurotransmitters. There are many different types of neurotransmitters, among which are epinephrine (adrenaline), endorphins, dopamine, serotonin, and norepinephrine.

Each neurotransmitter has different functions and causes different reactions within the body. Adrenaline, for example, stimulates heart activity and increases the body's metabolic rate, causing symptoms such as heart pounding and sweating. Endorphins are connected to emotions. Dopamine is known as the "feel-good" chemical.

By repeatedly activating these particular neurotransmitters in your brain through sexual stimuli or acting out sexually, you have created certain pathways in your brain that lead you to either the rush of adrenaline; the calm, peaceful feeling of endorphins; the other-worldly escape of dopamine; or all of the above.

There are three different styles of addiction into which people generally fall, categorized by the neurotransmitters associated with each style. It is interesting to note that these addictive styles also cross over into chemical addictions.

Arousal. Individuals who lean toward arousal dislike boredom and crave the rush of adrenaline that accompanies certain activities. Sex is used as power and there is usually a strong need for control. We have seen cases where the mere sound of the whir of a computer fan is arousing. Those also prone to drug addiction would choose stimulants such as cocaine or amphetamines because they activate the neurotransmitters in the adrenaline family.

Satiation. Opposite the arousal addicts are those who avoid excess stimulation because they are already in a state of hyper-arousal. This group seeks calm and sedation, and their goal is to reduce the discomfort stemming from either external events or internal conflict. Endorphins supply the neurotransmitter boost for this type, and depressants, such as heroin, alcohol, and binge-eating, would be the drugs of choice for this category of addicts. The desired effect is the relaxed, secure feeling found, for example, after a good meal, an alcoholic beverage, or sexual release.

Fantasy. The neurotransmitters dopamine, norepinephrine, and serotonin are associated with fantasy-seeker addicts, characterized by preoccupation with fantasies and dreams, compulsive artistic expression, or various forms of mystical experience. These addicts would favor hallucinogens such as LSD, mushrooms, marijuana, and peyote.

While persons addicted to drugs, alcohol, or other substances generally tend to fall primarily into only one of these styles, sex addicts typically take on every one of the styles at different stages of the addiction cycle, which means many different brain chemicals can be involved. This is what makes sex addiction so powerful and why it takes such a concentrated effort to overcome.

INSTINCT VS. CONSCIOUS LIVING

A client we will call Terry S. suffered from a problem that is very common among addicts of all types. He stated, "I really want to get better and beat this addiction. I have every good intention; but sometimes I just feel absolutely powerless over my urges, especially on days when I face a lot of stress at work (which is most of the time). I hate to admit it, but there are times when I feel like my brain is on auto-pilot and I can't stop myself from rushing to my computer to start surfing my old favorite porn sites." Even people who have struggled with overeating will relate to Terry's instinctual drive to reward himself for the hardships he is facing (or the stress, or the disappointment, or the boredom, and so forth). In clinical terms, he is driven by the part of the brain known as the limbic system. The limbic system is instinctive and is what motivates all human beings to seek pleasure and avoid pain, as well as to activate the "fight or flight" response in times of danger. In a very real sense, it is responsible for our well-being, survival, and self-preservation.

In contrast to the limbic system is the cerebral cortex, the part of our brain that can override instinct, which is what separates us from the animal kingdom. The cerebral cortex helps us to reason and make healthy choices. It is where we process information and learn how to widen the gap between stimulus and response. When we understand both these facets of our brain structure, it becomes clearer that the goal of all human beings, not just those suffering from addictions, is to learn to activate the cerebral cortex in order to control our instinctive behavior and thus live more productive lives.

It is within the cerebral cortex that we find the key to controlling—and extinguishing—addictive behavior. By activating the cerebral cortex, or the voice of reason, we can bring about more lasting behavioral changes, rather than the quick-fix the limbic system is programmed to bring about.

As mentioned above, after repeatedly activating these particular neurotransmitters in your brain through sexual stimuli or acting out, the pathways you have created in your brain are still there, still waiting to offer you the rush of adrenaline; the calm, peaceful feeling of endorphins; the other-worldly escape of dopamine; or all of the above. While some may seek to recover by cutting off all neuro-transmitter paths, this method would not bring about true recovery. Joe J. described his struggle with his continued desire to act out this way: "I have been very strong in my desire to quit going to strip clubs. I made a commitment to my wife that I wouldn't go, and so far I've been successful at keeping my commitment. But I think about it all the time. Some days are better than others, but I am never far from my obsession with acting out. Sometimes I can even feel my heart start beating way too fast, and I actually get aroused just thinking of it. Why, when I quit doing it months ago, won't these feelings go away?"

While many addicts, such as Joe J., feel that just stopping the behavior should also control those instinctive urges, we want you to know that simply shutting down the stimulation of the reward center of the brain will not constitute recovery. True recovery will only take place when the brain chemistry is provided sufficient healthy stimuli to maintain appropriate levels of prolonged chemical pleasure. The addict must replace the addictive behavior with health-promoting activities; he can no longer rely on the singularly explosive experience of the sexual high, but must learn new methods of sustaining healthy pleasure.

You must be proactive in your approach to recovery by seeking out healthy activities that provide natural highs and learning to rely more on your reasonable cerebral cortex and less on your instinctual limbic system. The addictive behavior must not only be stopped, it must be replaced by something healthy. So, how do you do that?

You can start by taking charge of the choices you make and not letting your brain run on auto-pilot. We call this "conscious living"—being constantly aware of the choices you make. Advance planning is the key to conscious living, and it can be applied effectively to even the most minute details of your life. In fact, we suggest you practice conscious living by scheduling these small details in advance. For example, we recommend that our clients reduce the amount of television they watch by planning exactly what programs, if any, will be viewed each day. Have your plan firmly in mind before you even turn on the TV. We likewise apply this same concept to our clients' eating habits. By planning each day's meals and snacks in advance, the tendency to "graze" all day long or to binge-eat is minimized. Clay A. described his conscious living by stating, "Ever since I made the conscious decision to be aware of what I'm really doing in my recovery, I've managed to be more proactive rather than simply being on 'cruise control' all the time. I channel-surf less, I'm eating better, and it's easier to avoid taking that 'second look' because I've decided in advance what I'm going to do."

THE THREE STYLES OF RECOVERY

We propose using the same neurotransmitters that you're primarily attracted to—which may vary throughout your recovery process—in healthy ways. You do this by seeking new hobbies, sports, or activities that you enjoy and then practicing and developing these new interests until they become rewarding, life-enriching, lasting passions. In other words, it should not be your goal to cease feeling pleasure altogether, but rather to activate these same neurotransmitters in moderate levels instead of in the massive doses experienced during addictive behaviors. The key here, however, is to activate the neurotransmitters by participating in health-promoting activities rather than by sexually acting out or indulging in other addictive behaviors.

For more clarity on making the healthy lifestyle changes suggested above, we have adapted the three styles of addiction to become the three styles of recovery. It will be necessary to integrate all three styles into your recovery plan in order to achieve the balance you have previously lacked. If you experience resistance to incorporating a particular style into your life, it is probably the area that you need to work on the most, so don't shy away from any of the three.

Arousal becomes **Excitement.** Those who dislike boredom and seem to run on adrenaline are naturally drawn to some of the more thrill-seeking activities, such as rock climbing, paragliding, skiing, or any other high-energy athletic activity. But even a fast-paced game of basketball can induce a natural high, and being a spectator at any exciting event can as well.

Satiation becomes **Relaxation.** Those who seek calm and sedation can satisfy this urge by such calming activities as playing chess, reading, or relaxing in a bubble bath or hot tub. In recovery, it is very important to learn how to relax, because many people use addictive behaviors to help them escape a pace of life that is simply too fast.

Fantasy becomes **Creativity.** Taking a craft class, journal keeping, writing poetry, and playing the guitar or other musical instrument are some of the many ways to move toward a healthy style of recovery if you find yourself frequently slipping into a dream world. Tapping into your creative self can help you channel your daydreaming into constructive avenues, like one of our clients who has begun building a cradle for his soon-to-be-born first grandchild.

If you're not sure which style you lean toward, start exploring all three. Many of our clients have found their needs have varied throughout their recovery and have benefited from incorporating activities from all three styles into their recovery plan. It is important to remember that excitement, relaxation, and creativity may not be as powerful as their addictive counterparts. They were not meant to be. Rather, we must seek for a life that is filled with continuous peace, joy, and satisfaction. In Alma 38:12 we read of the godly admonition to live our lives in a moderate fashion: "Use boldness, but not overbearance; and also see that ye bridle all your passions, that ye may be filled with love; see that ye refrain from idleness." We have had clients tell us that after getting out from under the burden of addiction, life becomes more fun. Excitement, relaxation, and creativity can provide longer-lasting, more satisfying ways of making life enjoyable.

SUMMARY

Being prepared to face the challenging symptoms of withdrawal head-on may be the key element that makes *this time* the time you will succeed in recovering from your addiction. In the words of noted author and physician Archibald J. Cronin, *"The virtue of all achievement is victory over oneself. Those who know this victory can never know defeat."* So, once again, we urge you to be prepared. Learn about addiction and how it affects the neurotransmitters in your brain. Study the three styles of addiction and experiment with the three styles of recovery. Don't give up. What you will gain, victory over yourself, will be well worth it.

CHAPTER TWENTY-TWO

Relapse Prevention

Rod W. Jeppsen

Elder Neal A. Maxwell reminded us: "Even yesterday's righteous experience does not guarantee us against tomorrow's relapse. A few who have had supernal spiritual experiences have later fallen. Hence, enduring well to the end assumes real significance, and we are at risk till the end!"[1] In this spirit, I offer the following fifteen suggestions for preventing relapse.

PUT MINOR MISTAKES IN PROPER PERSPECTIVE

A lapse is a momentary fault or a break in the continuity of our healing. Even though a break has occurred, it does not mean that we are not still on the path to healing. We can choose whether a lapse is momentary or whether we allow it to cause a relapse—a more extended detour from the right path.

When you falter, take a few moments alone and ponder how far you have come in your healing process. Accept a lapse as part of the healing process. A brief lapse is no reason to resort to a former way of life.

Satan wants you to believe the lie that a lapse is evidence that you have made no progress and that you will never be able to change. That is simply not true. In the process of healing you've been acquiring new thought patterns, better communication with others, increased responsibility for your behavior, and more. After a lapse, give yourself credit for all the little things you have done right that have put you on the pathway to healing.

We have all had the experience of driving to a new place and missing a turn along the way. The missed turn put us on a temporary detour. We may have lost a minute or two of driving time or even several minutes. Did we say to ourselves at that moment, "Oh, now I can't go on since I have made an error. I guess I'll just have to turn around and go back home"? Of course not! Although it can be frustrating when we lapse, just as it's frustrating when we make a wrong turn while driving to a new place, the fitting response is the same: simply proceed to get back on track and learn from the mistake. President Brigham Young said, "There is not a single condition of life that is entirely unnecessary; there is not one hour's experience but what is beneficial to all those who make it their study, and aim to improve upon the experience they gain."[2]

REMEMBER THAT CHANGE CAN OCCUR GRADUALLY OVER TIME

Healing is a process made up of trial and error and a few wrong turns. Healing is not an event, but occurs over a period of time. During our healing we learn and progress "line upon line, precept upon precept" (2 Nephi 28:30).

How long will it take us to improve our talents and abilities? Sometimes we lose hope because we are not realistic about how change takes place. President Hinckley said: "Those changes may not be measurable in a day or a week or a month. Resolutions are quickly made and quickly forgotten. But, in a year from now, if we are doing better than we have done in the past, then the efforts of these days will not have been in vain."[3]

What are some realistic changes you can work for in the next thirty days? Sixty days? Nine months? In the next year?

President Spencer W. Kimball counseled: "The principle of repentance—of rising again whenever we fall, brushing ourselves off and setting off again on that upward trail—that principle of repentance is the basis for our hope. It is through repentance that the Lord Jesus Christ can work his healing miracle, infusing us with strength when we are weak, health when we are sick, hope when we are downhearted, love when we feel empty, understanding when we search for truth."[4]

REMEMBER THE SOURCE OF YOUR STRENGTH

Recovery and healing are a partnership with Christ. Like most partnerships in mortality, after a while we may forget how much the other partner contributes to the success of the partnership. In the business world we often think we can do without those who helped us get where we are. We may begin to focus on ourselves and forget about the major contributions from others. We must never forget about Christ, his goodness, mercy, and love. Through him, miracles continue.

ANTICIPATE FUTURE STRESSORS

We have to know ourselves well enough that we know what creates stress in our lives. Stressors might include medications, unresolved emotional issues, relationships, school, work, retirement, and more. Using pornography to hide from emotional stressors does not work. Identify your stressors, anticipate when they will come, and have a set plan to diffuse and resolve them in healthy ways.

SERVE OTHERS

Service to others helps us to avoid relapse. It allows us to think of someone else besides ourselves so we are not susceptible to self-pity and despondency. Service gets us out of ourselves and into the lives of other people. We develop feelings of caring and empathy as we serve others and try to see life through their eyes.

Developing feelings of empathy for others is important to our healing, particularly when our behavior has been abusive. The rule is this simple: Selfishness is deeply rooted in unhappiness, but service to others brings feelings of success and happiness. When we are unhappy, we are usually thinking about how everything affects us instead of how everything affects others. Elder Richard G. Scott said, "Father in Heaven gives us the plan of happiness, which engenders the abandonment of selfish interests and provides happiness through service to others."[5] Using pornography was a self-focused life pattern. If we want to change the pattern, we must develop the habit of focusing on the welfare of others.

BUILD RELATIONSHIPS

Having a strong support system is critical to avoid relapse. A support group can consist of family members, bishop, and friends who provide a good influence. By affiliating with others, we are less likely to feel isolated and alone. Unwanted feelings of isolation and loneliness can be diffused with a strong support system.

Part of our compulsive pornography and masturbation problem is hiding from and avoiding family, Church leaders, and professional help. We cannot underestimate the value of a strong support system. Family, friends, and Church leaders are usually our best resources. We need and should want to have a place we can just talk about our emotions, anger, and frustration without being judged, criticized, or trying to have someone fix us. At the same time we want gentle love and guidance to keep us focused when our thinking is irrational.

Affiliation with other trusted individuals brings positive feelings of acceptance and love. Elder Neal A. Maxwell, speaking about repentance, said, "Genuine support and love from others—not isolation—are needed to sustain this painful forsaking and turning!"[6] Here are some ways we can build supportive relationships:

Make it a priority to stay in touch with family, friends, and others with whom you have developed healthy relationships.

Initiate meeting new people at social events, classes, seminars, and firesides.

Promote healthy relationships by remembering birthdays and other special events.

Be willing to share your thoughts, feelings, and emotions so that others can feel connected.

UTILIZE SUPPORT GROUPS

Some support groups can be very worthwhile and extremely helpful, but other so-called support groups actually reinforce compulsive sexual behaviors. If you choose to attend a group, be very selective. Do your homework; know something about the goals, mission statement, or objectives of the group. Finding out what others have learned who have attended can help you make a decision. In general, we recommend that you attend several times before making a decision on whether or not the group can help you. However, let the Spirit guide you, and if you have uncomfortable feelings from the group even initially, it is okay to stop attending.

It's helpful to consider both the advantages of attending a group and the potential concerns. Advantages include that a group can:

foster openness and make it easier to share inner feelings instead of remaining isolated.

provide the opportunity to associate with others who share the same problems.

help members realize "I'm not in this alone."

provide opportunities to feel acceptance.

provide the opportunity for members to recognize in others
both the irrational thinking patterns and the pain, sorrow,
and guilt connected with compulsive sexual behaviors.

help participants see in others the benefits of abstinence.

provide a "reality check," which is particularly needed since
most who choose compulsive sexual behaviors live in an
unrealistic world.

Potential concerns about a support group includes that it may:

have a negative "personality."

become a participant's main source for spiritual guidance,
replacing prayer or Church meetings.

detract from the time and energy an individual devotes to
family.

replace ecclesiastical leaders as the individual's forum for
confession.

plant unhealthy seeds in the participant's mind as other members describe relapses.

lead a participant to give undue weight or authority to the
statements of other members.

become a source of interaction that substitutes for closeness
with spouse, family, and Church.

ASSERT YOURSELF

Being assertive and taking care of ourselves are important tools
for avoiding relapse. Assertiveness means standing up for ourselves
and expressing our thoughts and feelings in appropriate ways that
do not violate the rights of others. How often do you stand up for
yourself? Do you often let others walk over you?

Self-assertion can prevent us from developing the resentments that often fuel inappropriate sexual fantasies and behavior. Here is an example: A friend calls and asks you to help someone move. You are in the middle of a deadline at work. Although you have freely helped others move in the past, your own best interest tells you to stay at work and finish this project. How do you handle the friend's call? Be honest and open in an appropriate way. "I'm sorry, I'm not able to help this time. I have a huge deadline at the office and need to work late." Even if you do not have a work deadline, if you know that one more commitment could push you over the edge, you might need to say, "I'm sorry. I would really like to help, but I have other commitments." You do not need to explain that you need to take care of yourself.

If we do not watch out for ourselves and our own self-interests, we can easily develop feelings of resentment, anger, and self-pity and invite undue stress that can trigger relapse. Our needs are important too. Appropriate self-assertion is not the same as selfishness. It is knowing ourselves well enough that we take action to maintain our well-being. Self-assertion means that we accept full responsibility to care for ourselves.

MAKE AND KEEP PERSONAL CONTRACTS

Making a written contract with ourselves puts our commitments on paper. Talk is cheap; let's see how committed we are to change by writing what we are going to do on paper. A written contract can define our boundaries, help us stay focused, give us something to review frequently, and remind us about our commitments.

Here are some statements that others have included in their personal contracts:

I will say my prayers each day.
I will read and ponder the scriptures each day.

If I look at someone and have inappropriate thoughts, I will
quickly say a surrender prayer and not continue to look.

I will discontinue my cable TV service.

While dating, I will not French kiss.

While dating, I will not go into my date's bedroom for any
reason.

Every Sunday I will read this list and recommit myself to following this contract.

What is important for you to include in your contract? You know yourself and your compulsive sexual behavior patterns. Write up your own personal contract and then sign it. What day and time each week will you review your contract? How will you reward yourself when you adhere to the contract or discipline yourself for non-compliance?

ESTABLISH BOUNDARIES AND DEVELOP SELF-MASTERY

Healing requires boundaries that are solid and firm. We draw a line and commit ourselves not to cross. If we want healing, there can be no exceptions. The process boils down to self-mastery, obtained through our relationship with the Master. If we turn to the Lord and not away from him, the experiences we have in life can help us develop self-mastery. There is no way around good old hard work and effort, asking every step of the way for the Lord's help. President Thomas S. Monson explained this process: "The battle for self-mastery may leave a person a bit bruised and battered, but always a better man or woman. Self-mastery is a rigorous process at best; too many of us want it to be effortless and painless."[7] We are promised that the reward will be worth the effort. Elder Russell M. Nelson said: "The enormous effort required to attain such self-mastery is rewarded with a deep sense of satisfaction. More importantly, spiritual attainments in mortality accompany us into eternity."[8]

PRACTICE EMOTIONAL CLEANSING
THROUGH WRITING

We can keep a personal daily journal apart from our formal record of life's important events—one that allows us to put our thoughts, feelings, and emotions on paper. Writing has proven very helpful in the process of getting out of ourselves the troubled emotions bottled up inside. Writing gives us permission to express our feelings. We may feel safer writing on paper our thoughts and feelings than talking with someone. When we write experiences or feelings down they seem more real. We do not concern ourselves with grammar, spelling, or punctuation. We start writing and just let the thoughts, feelings, and ideas flow. It's our journal, so we can cross words out, write between lines, and underline or mark the journal in other ways. Writing in journals and being honest and open on paper is like taking infections out of the body. We have emotional infections in ourselves when we have unresolved feelings of anger, resentment, bitterness, rejection, abuse, and more.

We can kill our emotional infections early on by writing in our journal every day. It is a cleansing, healing process. Infections in the body usually begin in a small area and spread over time. Emotional infections are no different. By daily self-monitoring of our thoughts, feelings, and emotions we can cleanse our emotional "pus pockets" and be more emotionally healthy. We can track where we are with our emotional well-being and hold ourselves accountable. As we go back to our feelings journal, we can read what we wrote the previous day and evaluate whether we are taking responsibility for ourselves and our actions. For example, one man was feeling like a victim when he wrote, "My boss is such a jerk. He got mad at me for no reason at all." The next day when he read it again he took responsibility by committing to ask his boss for more details on what he expected of him in his work responsibilities.

We can also use therapeutic writing to communicate with others. Being honest on paper by writing a letter may be easier for us than talking to someone. We may never even mail the letter.

PRACTICE SELF-REFLECTION

Often we need to step outside ourselves and try to look at ourselves objectively in the "big picture." Writing is one helpful tool. By doing this we can usually see more clearly our place in life and the many facets to our existence. As we study our lives and reflect on our strengths and weaknesses, we can learn from the past and make choices to improve our lives now and in the future. President Spencer W. Kimball said, "Self-mastery . . . is the key, and every person should study his own life, his own desires and wants and cravings, and bring them under control."[9] Many times we rush through life and do not take time for self-reflection. There is great value for us to schedule time each week to take an inner inventory. Elder M. Russell Ballard counseled: "I encourage you to take time each week to be by yourself, away from television and the crowd. Have your scriptures with you and as you read, ponder, and pray, take an honest look at your life. Evaluate where you stand with the promises you have made with Heavenly Father."[10]

During moments of self-reflection, we should honestly ask ourselves some very poignant questions. Elder M. Russell Ballard said, "All of us must come to an honest, open self-examination, an awareness within as to who and what we want to be."[11] Here are some questions to consider:

How well do you really communicate with others?
How do you really do under stress?
Do you usually accomplish your goals?
How well can you solve problems?

How do you respond when someone tells you no?

Does your anger get out of control?

Do you find yourself being contentious?

Being honest with ourselves and recognizing that there are other issues that may be related to our compulsive behavior is critical to healing. These can then be addressed by building skills in these other areas of life, and not just working to prevent relapse to a tempting sexual behavior.

OFFER SURRENDER PRAYERS

Perhaps the most effective preventive measure is a surrender prayer. Learning to say surrender prayers, even frequently, can be helpful. Let's say a man in the grocery store checkout line in the middle of the summer sees a scantily clad woman. Here is a sample surrender prayer: "Heavenly Father, there is one of thy daughters. She is beautiful. She has feelings and emotions. There are days when she is sad. There are days when she is lonely. There are days when she cries. May she find in thee what she is looking for in this life. May I respect her in my thoughts and actions as thou doest. I love thee, Father, and am grateful for the beauty thou hast created."

A simple surrender prayer does several things. First, we recognize the woman as a daughter of God and not an object. She is a human being with feelings and emotions. Next, we thank God and express our love for what he has given us. While selfishness and lust go together, gratitude and love also go together. The surrender prayer is an act of gratitude, and that is one reason it works. We choose one or the other throughout the day by how we choose to think about humankind. Will we choose lust or love? By using a surrender prayer, this man can choose to see this woman through the eyes of love, which is the way God sees her.

We can surrender not only our view of things, but also our will.

We can ask God what we need to do next to continue to progress in overcoming our problem.

Lamoni's father understood this principle of surrender: "O God, Aaron hath told me that there is a God; and if there is a God, and if thou art God, wilt thou make thyself known unto me, and I will give away all my sins to know thee" (Alma 22:18). How do we give away all our sins? Surrender. Surrender and healing go together. Keeping inappropriate thoughts and acting out go together. Elder Neal A. Maxwell expressed this surrender process: "If faithful, we end up acknowledging that we are in the Lord's hands and should surrender to the Lord on His terms—not ours. It is total surrender, no negotiating; it is yielding with no preconditions."[12]

We can surrender inappropriate thoughts, harsh feelings toward others, and selfish wants in favor of serving others. We begin by developing more faith in Christ instead of trying to do it all alone. Our dependence on God gives us the power we need to heal. It is a partnership between us and God. To heal we need his help.

TOLERATE THE UNFAMILIARITY THAT COMES WITH CHANGE

The old cycle of compulsive behavior is so familiar to us; we know how to react to guilt and shame by blocking it out with the drug of lust. However, the peace, calmness, and serenity found in healing are emotions that may feel unfamiliar. One woman said, "I feel so different now. I don't know what I'm supposed to do next. I don't have the emotional baggage anymore, but I've carried it for so long that I feel like something is missing."

As we change our behavior, we enter new, uncharted emotional territory. Knowing that others have gone through the uncharted waters, relied on the Lord, and achieved healing gives us great hope for ourselves. We sometimes are afraid of these new positive emotions because we have not experienced them before—at least not for a very long time. It is important that we be honest with ourselves, recognize these new feelings, and accept that they will eventually become comfortable so that we don't sabotage this new life.

If we are honest with ourselves, fear may come with other unfamiliar new feelings as we choose the healing path. We have used silence, lies, and dishonesty to hide, and it will be scary to come out of our hiding place. Elder Richard G. Scott said: "When you are honest with yourself, you may feel afraid. To change will require you to take an unfamiliar path, and it is uphill and narrow."[13]

FOCUS ON WHAT YOU ARE BECOMING

While on the journey to healing, what will we have become? The Prophet Joseph Smith was commanded to translate the Bible. That was the beginning. One might suppose the ending would be to finish the translation, but the Lord did not require a complete translation of the Bible. In the process of translating the Bible, Joseph Smith received eight powerful revelations that are vitally important to the doctrine of the restored gospel of Jesus Christ. Eight sections of the Doctrine and Covenants are the result of revelations received during the process of Joseph's efforts to translate the Bible. The question I've pondered is this: What did we (as a Church) receive or become in the process of the Prophet Joseph Smith translating the Bible?

At times we focus too much on the end results rather than what we should be learning and becoming in the process. Elder Dallin H. Oaks expressed:

"It is not enough for anyone just to go through the motions. The commandments, ordinances, and covenants of the gospel are not a list of deposits required to be made in some heavenly account. The gospel of Jesus Christ is a plan that shows us how to become what our Heavenly Father desires us to become. . . .

"How can we measure our progress? The scriptures suggest various ways. I will mention only two. After King Benjamin's great sermon, many of his hearers cried out that the Spirit of the Lord 'has wrought a mighty change in us, or in our hearts, that we have no more disposition to do evil, but to do good continually' (Mosiah 5:2). If we are losing our desire to do evil, we are progressing toward our heavenly goal.

"The Apostle Paul said that persons who have received the Spirit of God 'have the mind of Christ' (1 Cor. 2:16). I understand this to mean that persons who are proceeding toward the needed conversion are beginning to see things as our Heavenly Father and His Son, Jesus Christ, see them. They are hearing His voice instead of the voice of the world, and they are doing things in His way instead of by the ways of the world."[14]

We like to focus on tangible lists, but it may be more realistic and more consistent with gospel principles to track our healing progress by the virtues we have acquired along the way. Are we more teachable, humble, or sincere? Do we pray with more intent? Have we decided to turn our will over to God? Have we got unstuck and made some progress? Do we have more godly sorrow? Have we lost some desire for sin? Can we extend more charity to others? If the answer is yes, then we have made progress on the journey toward overcoming our obsession and compulsion.

It is my hope and prayer that this journey will be a successful one for you.

NOTES

1. Neal A. Maxwell, "Thanks Be to God," Ensign, July 1982, 51.
2. Brigham Young, in *Journal of Discourses*, 26 vols. (Liverpool: Latter-day Saints' Book Depot, 1854–86), 9:292–93.
3. Gordon B. Hinckley, "'An Humble and a Contrite Heart,'" *Ensign*, November 2000, 88.
4. Spencer W. Kimball, "Give the Lord Your Loyalty," *Ensign*, March 1980, 4.

5. Richard G. Scott, "Removing Barriers to Happiness," *Ensign,* May 1998, 86.

6. Neal A. Maxwell, "Repentance," *Ensign,* November 1991, 31.

7. Thomas S. Monson, "In Quest of the Abundant Life," *Ensign,* March 1988, 4.

8. Russell M. Nelson, "Perfection Pending," *Ensign,* November 1995, 86.

9. Spencer W. Kimball, "The Abundant Life," *Ensign,* October 1985, 6.

10. M. Russell Ballard, "You Promised," *New Era,* February 1994, 7.

11. M. Russell Ballard, "Keeping Life's Demands in Balance," *Ensign,* May 1987, 13.

12. Neal A. Maxwell, "'Willing to Submit,'" *Ensign,* May 1985, 72.

13. Richard G. Scott, "Finding the Way Back," *Ensign,* May 1990, 74.

14. Dallin H. Oaks, "The Challenge to Become," *Ensign,* November 2002, 32, 34.

CHAPTER TWENTY-THREE

Revitalizing Recovery Following Relapse

Mark H. Butler

The best relapse responses are those that encourage the quickest possible return to a recovery frame of mind, feeling, and being. Responding to relapse in a way that fosters repentance requires love and compassion, truth and wisdom, spiritual sensitivity and discernment. Both the addicted person and others who love him ("loving others") must cultivate these virtues.

Following relapse, discouragement and despair nip at the heels of the person seeking to escape addiction and often at those of loving others as well. These feelings undermine desire and discipline, thus threatening to deepen and extend the relapse period. Therefore it is essential to respond to relapses in a way that helps you renew desire, revitalize recovery, and fortify yourself for the future. In this spirit, I offer the following suggestions.

REFUSE TO GIVE UP

The propaganda of despair takes several forms, but its endgame is always the same—to persuade you to lay down all resistance and surrender! "What's the point in resisting. I'll never overcome this." "There's no point in stopping now." "It doesn't matter what I do now." The diabolic subtlety of the propaganda of despair is that underlying all the seeming sorrow is nothing less than a shrewd rationalization for continuing relapse—"I've blown it, so why keep trying to resist?"

Nevertheless, what you do from here *does* matter. By rallying hope and standing firm you can limit your losses and contain the damaging fallout from relapse. It does matter whether you take one drink and then stop, or surrender to a drunken stupor. It does matter whether you succumb for an hour or binge for a week. It does matter whether you exit after looking at just one picture or indulge in the entire catalog. It does matter whether you walk in and then walk right out or stay for the entire tour. It does matter whether you buy it and burn it the same day, or compile and store a supply, just in case. Obviously, containment following relapse is never equal to avoiding relapse, but it is far better than binging away recovery gains.

Every ounce of resistance counts! Even once the walls have been scaled, you can fight house to house. It is far easier to defend the city, and still easier to fight in the streets, than to retake your own house, your own soul after completely abandoning it to appetite and addiction. Thus, the opening rallying cry for reinstating recovery is, "Stop! Stop now!"

FIGHT FOR YOUR HEART

Relapse response focuses on dousing the fires of addictive appetite with the recovery resolve of a true heart. Like a fire that has burned hot for a very long time, addiction takes time to completely douse. Hot coals of appetite burn beneath the ashes of addiction, ready to burst into flame again if fanned by personal weakness, worldly temptation, or the adversary's wiles. Recovery requires thoroughly dousing the embers and coals until the steam and smoke of appetite no longer hiss and curl with heat. Now and again, hot spots can flare up.

After stopping relapse dead in its tracks, the battle for your heart begins. It is a heart divided that makes you vulnerable to the siege of temptation and onslaught of appetite, and the enemy will not be long contained if the heart is not rallied for battle.

At the point of capitulation, many addicted persons hear the echo of Elijah, who challenged, "How long halt ye between two opinions? if the Lord be God, follow him: but if Baal, then follow him" (1 Kings 18:21). Perhaps stricken by conscience, "the people answered him not a word" (1 Kings 18:21). The words of James, "A double minded man is unstable in all his ways" (James 1:8), also ring true to the experience following relapse. As these words of the prophets attest, your heart is your high ground in the battle against addiction, and it must be retaken.

Winning the battle for the heart begins by once again bearing truthful testimony to yourself concerning the destruction of addiction. Truthful testimony is what we tell ourselves and what we allow ourselves to feel in the private sanctuary of our minds. Relapse is a choice—one not made in the light of truth but in the darkness of lies and self-deception and in the confusing intoxication of euphoric recall of the addictive "high." Consequently, the battle for your heart and for recovery is resumed by countering the propaganda of addiction with truthful testimony.

Review the negative consequences of addiction. Equally important, renew and revitalize the inspiration and desire you have felt for the better life you envision without addiction—an exalted vision of joyful life, love, and relationships. Then, unequivocally affirm the inherent incompatibility of addiction with your loftier, nobler vision. This will help you reclaim your heart from the assault of addiction.

CALCULATE YOUR GROWTH TO KEEP YOUR PERSPECTIVE

Calculate your growth in order to keep your perspective following relapse. Some, in fact, find it useful to track their progress for this purpose. Longer periods of recovery, less severe relapse behavior, shorter periods of relapse, quicker return to abstinence—these mark personal progress. Never use progress as an excuse for, or exoneration of, relapse. But do use your record of progress as an encouraging indication of growth, and with it combat the fatalistic feelings and discouraging thinking that follows relapse.

Amidst your sorrow, remember that relapse does not make a lie of your period of recovery. It erodes, but does not wash away your fortifications or your gains. For those shining days, weeks, or months, your recovery was real, and recovery was reinforced as you recaptured the vision of a better life and fortified your strongholds of virtue. Your recovery is not false, or a sham; *it was merely incomplete.* You would be worse off now—in some cases much worse—if you hadn't abstained during the time you managed to. The territory of your heart and mind reclaimed during the period of recovery has not been all lost. Such talk of defeat only invites hopelessness and rationalizes surrender. Refuse it.

Refuse to retreat further. Ramparts have been breached, but there are yet strongholds you have erected that can serve your defense. Review your successes during the period of recovery, and rally resolve in the confidence that you yet have resources to turn the tide.

CALL FOR REINFORCEMENTS

Among these resources, your allies are most important. The enemy of recovery will seek to separate you from your allies, to divide and conquer. His propaganda discourages us from calling for reinforcements: "You don't deserve her love." "You don't belong with them." "You can't ask for anything now." "You have to fix this yourself." What a cruel paradox it would be if you could only qualify for relationship help, or be worthy to receive it, by being perfect and hence not needing it!

The truth is, if ever there was a time when you need to reconnect rather than isolate, it is now. Relationships renew and strengthen our vision and desire and can bring the respite, refreshment, and encouragement that are so essential to rallying resolve and revitalizing recovery.

Appropriate guilt and shame, while a critical ally of recovery, can also lead to self-defeating alienation and isolation from supportive others. Guilt and shame follow recognition that our actions betray our love, commitments, and covenants to spouse and children. These feelings, of course, are only intensified the closer we come to these others. Hence, the temptation is strong to withdraw from intimate, loving contact with these loved and loving others, in order to distance ourselves from intensified pain, guilt, and heartache. Yet in the process, we remove ourselves from the recovery-promoting influence of these relationships as well. Guilt and shame, humbly responded to, will lead us to reach out rather than to run away.

Alienation and isolation must be avoided, however painful confession and reconciliation may be. There is a healing balm in confession, and a key to the windows of heaven as well as the hearts of helping others. Even as drawing close intensifies your sorrow, it can also fortify your resolve. Properly proportional pain can minister to your repentance and needs therefore to be faced, not shunned. Learning by experience to distinguish good from evil includes facing up to the intimate relationship consequences of addictive choices. Recovery experience testifies to the strength that comes from walking this road in "good company."

FACE UP TO CONSEQUENCES

Therefore, confess your choice to relapse—or more accurately, your *choices,* for a person never surrenders but by degrees—to your spouse or others who are sponsoring your recovery and to those whose stewardship it is to determine any necessary consequences of transgression. Recovery is reinstated more readily—and eventually, relapse will be shunned altogether—as you refuse to hide from or postpone consequences of relapse. Deception unnaturally manages and avoids consequences instead of employing them for repentance. Hiding a relapse from loving others is an attempt to buy addiction on credit—postponing payment for some later day— which only tempts further indulgence and which can all too quickly bankrupt your soul and your relationships. Confessing and facing up immediately to the consequences of addiction is paying cash, which makes you immediately and painfully aware of the full cost of addiction.

The urge to hide needs to be unfailingly recognized as the strategy of our enemy. The road signs to repentance, safety, and revitalization of recovery point unstintingly toward, not away from loving others. Nevertheless, it takes real effort and courage not to flinch or backslide from humbling, even humiliating confession, and from consequences that surely follow.

As you face up to consequences, it is imperative for both you and loving others to remember that consequences are not for punishment, but for learning. Consequences wisely constructed and righteously administered (or, shall we say, ministered) serve recovery learning and repentance. As pain ministers an aversive education toward the protection of our physical bodies, so guilt, suffering, and anguish minister an education for the protection of our souls and our relationships from the destruction of sin.

Learning takes hold best when it is not postponed. An immediate experience of consequences can counter the hedonistic pleasure and high of addiction. Mind, heart, and soul are educated best when the entire package deal of addiction is bundled together in the here and now.

REFUSE TO TURN AWAY FROM POSITIVE INFLUENCES

Still, essential learning does *not* include banishing yourself from righteous influences. Your enemy will assail you with damning propaganda: "You don't belong in church." "You're a hypocrite—your life is a sham and a fraud." "You're not worthy to pray." "You're not going to get anything out of reading the scriptures now, so why bother?"

All these lies belie the truth that yours is an embattled heart, not a surrendered one. Although you are weakened by relapse, yours is yet a divine nature that longs for virtue, goodness, and recovery. As long as a spark of righteous feeling, desire, and resistance remains, fan it and fuel it with every virtuous influence, feeling, and experience you are qualified to access.

I repeat, refuse to separate yourself from any worthy influence for which you are qualified (see 3 Nephi 18:28–29). Refuse to turn aside or turn away from activities that buoy and strengthen your soul—or helpfully chasten and humble you—such as Church attendance, Church service, scripture reading, and prayer. Refuse to evict yourself from either the fellowship or the activities of fellow Saints-in-the-making; those who strive to understand and live the gospel will welcome you with a loving embrace (see 3 Nephi 18:22–23, 25–30, 32).

Do not let relapse lead you to flinch, wince, or waver in your commitment to wholesome, virtuous, good activities. There is more power for recovery in living the thirteenth article of faith than we ever foresee. The enemy of recovery is never helped more than when you respond to the discouragement of relapse by surrendering on all other fronts as well. You must hold fast these strategic positions and strongholds from which a strong counterattack can be mounted. Positive influence in other areas of your life—and there are many—are literally the high ground from which you will regain the ground lost in relapse. Be steadfast and stubborn, even obstinate, in holding fast that which is good (see 1 Thessalonians 5:21). Reinstate, renew, and revitalize recovery by continuing to seek after those things that are "virtuous, lovely, or of good report or praiseworthy" (Articles of Faith 1:13).

Lay aside relapse by taking up your scriptures and your prayers—and every other positive spiritual and relationship resource—regardless of how empty, belated, or hard a gesture and exercise that may seem in the present moment.

CONTAIN THE DAMAGE, RESIST AFFILIATED LOSSES, SEEK STRENGTH IN JOYFUL LIVING

Such spiritual sustenance is all the more essential in the days following relapse, because the seismic upheaval of relapse can all too readily trigger a tidal wave of associated transgressions. Severe spillover or outward rippling of consequences can include increased irritability and irresponsibility in the home, with increased marital distress and conflict; it can include diminished work performance; it can include general spiritual degeneration and malaise, with a severe ebb of testimony. Spillover is in fact so predictably associated with relapse that a husband's sour mood and surly behavior becomes the wife's sure signal that relapse has occurred or is in the offing.

These affiliated losses can reverberate backward again, increasing risk for further relapse. It is critical, therefore, to work to contain the damage of relapse by refusing to succumb to affiliated transgressions. Exercise the discipline necessary to avoid projecting your pain or inner turmoil on to others, whether by blaming them for your actions or by simply venting your pain on them.

Alongside sustaining strongholds of virtuous influence in your life, sustain your own virtue as well—your redeeming virtues. Work hard to prevent addiction's consequences from infecting and corrupting any more of your life. While accepting chastening, don't entertain or accept thoughts that your life as a whole has gone bad. Punitive penance is not part of real repentance.

Be as happy as you can possibly be. Don't heap upon yourself more suffering than accumulates naturally from your relapse. Pray that God, by the Holy Spirit, will make you sensitive, discerning, and keen concerning your choices. Then trust that there is enough pain inherent in your indulgence of addictive appetite to lead to real regret, and sufficient sorrow to invite repentance.

The instruction and assurance of the scriptures is pertinent here: "There is a law, irrevocably decreed in heaven before the foundations of this world, upon which all blessings are predicated—And when we obtain any blessing from God, it is by obedience to that law upon which it is predicated" (D&C 130:20–21). Within the limitations imposed by your addictive behavior, if you obey the law, you qualify for the blessing—in spite of the fact that there are other areas of your life yet needing reform. If you are obeying the law of love with your children, you are entitled to the blessings attached thereto. If you are obeying the law of work, you are entitled to the blessings linked thereto. If you are living the law of service in your neighborhood, you qualify for the blessings attending that obedience. If you are living the law of friendship and fellowship with your neighbors, you can rightfully claim the blessings associated therewith. If you are living the law of love and kindness with your wife in every other way, the blessings attending that law need not be erased or refused, although they will certainly be diminished.

By all means, live all these laws, and use your obedience as redeeming virtues to springboard renewed obedience to this other law as well. In humility and contrition, submit to the consequences of your actions, but don't go beyond the mark and deny yourself any of the joy and subsequent strength and will to which your redeeming virtues entitle you.

The Lord's declaration suggests that disobedience and transgression will bring the loss of respective blessings naturally and lawfully associated with any commandment. The punishment of sin is sufficient. We don't need to add to it arbitrarily. No one, I believe, punishes their way to a change of heart and enduring virtue.

NEVERTHELESS, A WITNESS AND A WARNING

Nevertheless, accept that there will be limits to carrying on life as usual. Unrepented sin will eventually consume the whole of a person's life. Further, there are dire dangers if the principles discussed in this chapter are distorted and misapplied in practice, justifying an attempt to live life as though nothing at all had happened. Some, instead of healing the pain through sincere repentance, try to live in denial of it. Trying to wall off the painful reality of addiction by deceiving yourself and others leads to spiritual numbing and deadening, not healing. Sin always brings only two possible choices—either repent, or harden (see Jacob 6:5; Alma 12:33; 12:37; 34:31; 3 Nephi 21:6; 21:22)—emotionally, psychologically, spiritually, relationally, and physically.

Repeated relapse attended by attempts to contain addiction's consequences, rather than containing addiction itself, requires ossifying and petrifying a portion of the heart, mind, and spirit as a suitable, callused container for the pain. While marginally successful in terms of deadening the pain, this coping strategy permits the development of terrible incongruence, hypocrisy, and moral dissonance, shrinking and withering the soul. Terrible transgressions can develop in a life deadened to the pain and guilt, sorrow and suffering of sin.

The Spirit is never deceived, and the ability to enjoy its

influence and to worthily participate in and benefit from sacred, spiritual opportunities diminishes. Further, if this schism of the soul continues, in process of time a behavioral chasm opens up. Personality is fragmented and dire dissociation develops. What this means is that a person becomes capable of enacting a deadly double life. But like the picture of Dorian Gray, the deeds of the soul are etched indelibly on the portrait of our lives, and whether in time or eternity, eventually we and others will see ourselves as we really are.

Estrangement and dissociation—separation and alientation from others, and separation and alienation within ourselves—are the companion consequences of chronic addiction and unrepented sin. When these occur, we then observe unimaginable internal and behavioral contradictions, pendulum swings of such magnitude they leave us aghast—the priesthood holder who views pornography and practices seduction on the Internet on Saturday and then stands Sunday in an office of significant stewardship; or the husband who attends the temple with his wife on Saturday after patronizing the strip bar the night before. When someday these separated parts of life are again pieced together, the contradiction and collision will be painful beyond belief. Do not risk hardening, for it may take you to a place where you can no longer conceive of repentance, because of the terrible truth it entails.

Therefore, keep relapse response inexorably repentance-bound. Do not let patience and tolerance become accommodation and indulgence. Beware of self-deception regarding your ability to enjoy the influence of the Spirit and to worthily participate in sacred, spiritual opportunities. Since addiction impairs judgment, do not take it upon yourself to render judgment, but submit to the judgment of worthy others following *full* confession—which includes the complete history of addiction, within which the current relapse is but a small part.

Fragmentation of the soul is an accommodation to sin, but it leaves parts that remain at odds with each other. And a soul at odds with itself will never know peace or joy. In time, petrification spreads and the person will cease feeling altogether. Therefore, you must not, in choosing and striving to be as happy as you can possibly be, seek to unnaturally escape from or postpone the inevitable consequences of addictive behavior. You must not keep relapse a secret from loving others on the pretense of sparing them and containing addiction to some small, dark corner of your life.

Thus, the kind of positive, put-it-behind-you-as-soon-as-you-can focus advocated here includes first a full confession and facing up to natural consequences. There is no premature foreclosure or outright avoidance of a spouse's tearful, sorrowful, or indignant response. Helping your spouse to heal from the pain inflicted by your addiction is part of your recovery process. There is no self-righteous insistence that you have put it behind you and so they must, too. Instead, there is acceptance and submission. There is understanding that loving others' conveying of natural consequences is completely necessary. There is no avoidance of necessary restitution. you don't attempt to live in denial.

UNDERTAKE A FORENSIC ANALYSIS

Finally, once preventative attitudes and behaviors are reconstituted and reinstituted, take the time to reevaluate. Undertake a forensic analysis of your relapse. This is not a self-condemning review, but a learning review and inventory.

Pay particular attention to the earliest warning signs of your impending descent into addiction. Note and confront the winking rationalizations used to justify "innocent" gateway behaviors and first steps. Witness to yourself the truth that without indulgence of these, relapse would likely never have happened. Recommit to come completely clean in order to *become clean,* to "give away all

[your] sins"—even the so-called little ones—"that [you] may be raised from the dead, and be saved at the last day" (Alma 22:18).

Take a learning perspective and then determine to *learn* from your experience. Learn about your relapse; learn about yourself; learn for recovery.

CONCLUSION

Tragically, relapse all too often leads to relapse, in a descending cycle, like a sinkhole into a dangerous subterranean labyrinth. The cold, wet, darkness of relapse threatens to snuff out the light in your life. Squinting into the darkness or groping around to try to fathom the contours of the cave is futile.

However faint the light in your life may seem after relapse, it is nevertheless the key to your escape. When you have relapsed, to "hold fast that which is good" (1 Thessalonians 5:21) is not to pretend that you have not descended into darkness, but is to keep your eyes steadfastly fixed on the ray of light beaming from above. We must shelter the flickering light within as well—shelter it from the dripping darkness, and fan it into a flame again. Only then can light chase away the dark shadows of fear, give encouraging warmth, and provide the direction we need to navigate our way out of addiction.

The Savior said to the woman taken in adultery, "Go, and sin no more" (John 8:11). Speaking millennia later to Latter-day Saints, the Lord reaffirmed his counsel, saying, "Go thy way and sin no more" (D&C 24:2). I believe that for those seeking recovery from addiction, to "go thy way" means to go on, to go forward, to "hold fast that which is good" (1 Thessalonians 5:21), in order that they may be strengthened to repent and "sin no more." Our Savior and Redeemer once again points and prepares the way for our repentance and redemption. Thus may each of us rise up, go his way, and sin no more.

CHAPTER TWENTY-FOUR

"No More Disposition to Do Evil": Abandoning Pornography through a Mighty Change of Heart

Rory C. Reid

After experiencing a mighty change of heart, the people of King Benjamin exclaimed, "We have no more disposition to do evil, but to do good continually" (Mosiah 5:2). People who struggle with pornography problems should be curious about this Book of Mormon story. How does a changed heart become a catalyst for behavior change? I'm convinced that a mighty change of heart occurs when we make sincere and genuine efforts to feast upon the words of Christ by the power of the Holy Ghost. The process of learning and living the word of God subsequently sanctifies us from unrighteousness and purges our hearts and minds from the harmful effects of pornography.

LEARNING TO LOVE THE TRUTH

Individuals consume pornography because they feel like it, and they will probably continue to use it unless they feel more compelled to do something else. The irony in this pattern is that most men who develop habitual pornography problems believe their behavior is wrong. They know it violates the law of chastity and jeopardizes their ability to feel the Spirit. This belief, however, is often insufficient to elicit a change in behavior. Subsequently, understanding and insights about behavior usually fail to change behavior. Consider the surgeon who smokes despite his understanding of the harmful consequences of his habit. Commenting on this pattern in human behavior, President Brigham Young observed, "Do you think that people will obey the truth because it is true, unless they love it? No, they will not. . . . It is evident that many who understand the truth do not govern themselves by it; consequently, no matter how true and beautiful truth is, you have to take the passions of the people and mould them to the law of God."[1]

Sometimes we exhaust too much mental energy thinking or talking about problems. This can lead to "looking beyond the mark" (Jacob 4:14). It can also inadvertently provide more attention to the very behavior we are trying to abandon. If the adversary can get us to intellectualize the process of changing behavior, our ability to see the "small and simple things" (Alma 37:6) may be impaired. Although insights and awareness help facilitate change, the change itself is usually fueled more by what we feel than what we know. Elder Neal A. Maxwell taught that "knowing gospel truths and doctrines is profoundly important, but we must also come to love them. When we love them, they will move us and help our desires and outward works to become more holy."[2]

CONVERSION: A CONVICTION OF THE TRUTH

Most Latter-day Saints who struggle with pornography habits know the gospel is true. They have a testimony but have yet to be converted to the truth. A testimony is only part of the process of becoming converted. Someone who possesses knowledge of the truth possesses a testimony. But conversion requires more. After a three-year companionship with the Savior, a witness of many miracles, seeing the Lord transfigured, hearing the voice of the Father, and a knowledge that Jesus was the Christ, Peter was reminded by the Lord that he had yet to become converted (Luke 22:32).

What does it mean to be converted? President Joseph Fielding Smith said, "People are converted by their hearts being penetrated by the Spirit of the Lord when they humbly hearken to the testimonies of the Lord's servants."[3]

Conversion is a conviction of the truth that leads us to repent and obey God's commandments, and it subsequently leads to a remission of sin. President Marion G. Romney explained this process of becoming converted: "Converted means to turn from one belief or course of action to another. Conversion is a spiritual and moral change. Converted implies not merely mental acceptance of Jesus and his teachings but also a motivating faith in him and his gospel. A faith which works a transformation, an actual change in one's understanding of life's meaning and in his allegiance to God in interest, in thought, and in conduct. In one who is really wholly converted, desire for things contrary to the gospel of Jesus Christ has actually died. And substituted therefore is a love of God, with a fixed and controlling determination to keep his commandments."[4]

Thus, one measure of our conversion is the presence or absence of our desire to do what is right. This desire to do what is right evolves from how we feel about gospel truths and must be distinguished from "good" feelings. There are many things that feel good that are not necessarily right. Looking at pornography and masturbating feels good, at least for a time (although God will not always suffer us to take happiness in sin, as we learn in Mormon 2:12), but it doesn't feel right. Conversely, things that feel right do not always feel good. Often doing the right thing is unpleasant or uncomfortable. The Savior came to understand this principle more intimately when he partook of the bitter cup. Gethsemane felt *right* but the bitterness of what he endured certainly did not feel *good* (see D&C 19:15–19).

As we learn to discern between our feelings and the feelings

God would have us experience through a mighty change of heart, we become cleansed and sanctified from all unrighteousness (see D&C 76:41). The feeling that accompanies conversion is often a quiet assurance that the course we are pursuing is right and pleasing to the Lord. Such conversion is facilitated and fortified by the Holy Ghost and is fueled by our conviction of the truth.

FEASTING UPON THE WORDS OF CHRIST

Each of us must learn to move beyond the black and white words in holy writ. We must learn how to "feel his words" (1 Nephi 17:45). Reading alone is insufficient to produce meaningful experiences with personal scripture study.[5] There are many who *know* the words but "seeing see not; and hearing they hear not, neither do they understand" (Matthew 13:13; see also 1 Corinthians 2:9–16). They are forever "learning, and never able to come to the knowledge of the truth" (2 Timothy 3:7). President Boyd K. Packer taught: "The Holy Ghost communicates with the spirit through the mind more than through the physical senses. This guidance comes as thoughts, as feelings, through impressions and promptings. . . . The scriptures teach us that we may 'feel' the words of spiritual communication more than hear them, and see with spiritual rather than with mortal eyes."[6]

If we believe the word of God has a more powerful effect upon our minds than anything else (see Alma 31:5), we must also conclude that the words can purge our minds of the harmful effects of pornography. Individuals who say scripture study and prayer are ineffective in helping them abandon pornography often do not follow the pattern outlined by the Lord for effective scripture study. President Boyd K. Packer has said: "The study of the doctrines of the gospel will improve behavior quicker than talking about behavior will improve behavior."[7] This study of the doctrine involves more than an intellectual activity. It involves being receptive to the promptings of the Spirit so we can experience the power of the word. This occurs most often when we immerse ourselves in scripture study. Elder Neal A. Maxwell taught: "On very thin pages, thick with meaning, are some almost hidden scriptures. Hence we are urged to *search, feast,* and *ponder* (see John 5:39; Alma 14:1; Alma 33:2; Moro. 10:3; 2 Ne. 9:51)."[8]

To feast upon the words of Christ is to *learn* and *live* the principles found in the scriptures, the sermons of our living prophets, and truth received by the power of the Holy Ghost. The scriptures teach us, "Be ye doers of the word, and not hearers only" (James 1:22). We must carefully study and extract principles from the scriptures that apply to our unique situations in life. Nephi taught, "Liken them [the words of Christ] unto yourselves" (1 Nephi 19:24).

Elder Richard G. Scott counseled: "As you seek spiritual knowledge, search for principles. Carefully separate them from the detail used to explain them. Principles are concentrated truth, packaged for application to a wide variety of circumstances. A true principle makes decisions clear even under the most confusing and compelling circumstances. It is worth great effort to organize the truth we gather to simple statements of principle."[9]

The power of the word is manifest in our lives when we *live* the principles we learn through our personal study of the words of Christ. God will add to our efforts the strength and desire necessary to follow through with our righteous intentions as he observes our commitment to do what is right. Through this process, God embraces us as we embrace his word.

CULTIVATING THE COMPANIONSHIP OF THE HOLY GHOST THROUGH SINCERE SCRIPTURE STUDY

As we develop meaningful scripture study, our lives are blessed with the power of the Holy Ghost. President Ezra Taft Benson taught, "Immerse yourselves in [the scriptures] daily *so you will have the power of the Spirit.*"[10] Similarly, President Spencer W. Kimball noted: "I find that when I get casual in my relationships with divinity and when it seems that no divine ear is listening and no divine voice is speaking, that I am far, far away. If I immerse myself in the scriptures the distance narrows and the *spirituality returns.*"[11] As we qualify for the companionship of the Spirit, we will find additional reservoirs of strength to resist temptation and, like the people of King Benjamin, have "no more disposition to do evil, but to do good continually" (Mosiah 5:2).

Dedicating ourselves to serious scripture study requires sacrifice and time. Elder Richard G. Scott has taught: "It may be difficult to begin, but pick up the scriptures and immerse yourself in them. Look for favorite passages. Lean on the Master's teachings, on His servants' testimonies. Refresh your parched soul with the word of God. (See 2 Ne. 4:15–16.) The scriptures will *give you comfort and the strength to overcome.* (See Hel. 3:29–30.)"[12]

Anything short of dedicated effort will not yield the desired results. Elder Merrill J. Bateman of the Seventy taught, "A casual, infrequent exposure to the scriptures will generally not open the door to the whisperings of the Spirit."[13] Qualifying for the whisperings of the Spirit is the essence of feasting upon the words of Christ and will become the key to abandoning a pornography habit. As we cultivate the companionship of the Holy Ghost through feasting upon the word, our hearts and minds will focus more on righteous desires.

LOOK TO GOD, LEARN, AND LIVE

Feasting upon the words of Christ, feeling the spirit of their truth, and applying them in our lives—this is the process of experiencing the mighty change of heart. It is a change that ultimately leads to receiving Christ's image in our countenance. Alma described this process and highlighted the discrepancy between the natural man and those who yield their hearts to God. He used words like *captivity, bondage, deep sleep, chains of hell,* and *mist of darkness* to describe our lives without God's word. Conversely, he speaks about souls being "illuminated by the light of the everlasting word" and songs of "redeeming love." The way has been prepared and, like Moses, our modern-day prophets can show us the way to be healed from the poisonous serpents that seek to destroy us. Each person can abandon the belief that change is too hard if they will "look to God and live" (Alma 37:47; see also Numbers 21:8–9; 2 Nephi 25:20).

SANCTIFICATION: A PROCESS, NOT AN EVENT

The Savior is capable of erasing or reversing the harmful consequences of sin. Scripturally speaking, he "blots" them out (see D&C 109:34) and our scarlet sins "shall be as white as snow" (Isaiah 1:18). As we continue to press forward, feasting upon the words of Christ, the Spirit will purge our hearts and minds from the distorted truths internalized by the consumption of pornography. Such cleansing of the inner vessel can apply to our mind, body, and spirit. This transformation creates a new heart, a new mind, and a renewed spirit centered in Christ and his gospel. The process of becoming sanctified takes place throughout our lives. Of course, abandoning pornography doesn't need to become a lifetime endeavor, but just as pornography habits are not developed overnight they are not abandoned overnight. Elder Bruce R. McConkie observed: "Being born again is a *gradual thing,* except in a few isolated instances that are so miraculous that they get written up in the scriptures. As far as the generality of the members of the Church are concerned, we are *born again by degrees,* and we are born again to added light and added knowledge and added desires for righteousness as we keep the commandments."[14]

Joseph Smith also taught the need for patience with the process of becoming one with God: "We consider that God has created man with a mind capable of instruction, and a faculty which may be enlarged in proportion to the heed and diligence given to the light communicated from heaven to the intellect; and that the nearer man approaches perfection, the clearer are his views, and the greater his enjoyments, till he has overcome the evils of his life and *lost every desire for sin;* and like the ancients, arrives at that point of faith where he is wrapped in the power and glory of his Maker and is caught up to dwell with Him. *But we consider that this is a station to which no man ever arrived in a moment.*"[15]

RECOGNIZING THE CHANGE

Many individuals struggle to know if they have received a testimony of the remission of their sins. They wonder if their heart has changed and if they have become sanctified. To discern in these matters we must cultivate familiarity with the Holy Ghost. As we yield our hearts to God and submit to his will, each of us will *feel* different. This feeling is a personal and sacred experience. If we are used to looking outside ourselves for validation, such understanding and awareness may take even more time to cultivate. Those who have experienced a mighty change of heart tend to be more softened and tender. Their behavior and mannerisms are characterized by humility. They possess a calm and peaceful assurance. In the meantime, avoid becoming frustrated when the path is not lit every step of the way. The important thing is to keep progressing, rather than wondering whether we're "there yet." Like Nephi, sometimes we must continue moving ahead without knowing what lies before us (see 1 Nephi 4:6–7), and so we must press forward with patience and rely upon the Lord to guide us in our journey.

MAINTAINING HIS IMAGE IN OUR COUNTENANCES

Alma asked the poignant questions, "Have ye spiritually been born of God? Have ye received his image in your countenances? Have ye experienced this mighty change in your hearts? . . . If ye have experienced a change of heart, and if ye have felt to sing the song of redeeming love, I would ask, *can ye feel so now?*" (Alma 5:14, 26; emphasis added).

King Benjamin similarly admonished his people to "always retain a remission" of their sins (Mosiah 4:12).

Helaman endowed his children with the names Lehi and Nephi so that they might remember their rich heritage and the works of their forefathers. He suggested that one way to retain a remission of sin and remain true and faithful is to *remember.* Among the things to remember he suggested:

"O remember, remember, my sons, the words which king Benjamin spake unto his people; yea, remember that there is no other way nor means whereby man can be saved, only through the atoning blood of Jesus Christ, who shall come; yea, remember that he cometh to redeem the world.

"And now, my sons, remember, remember that it is upon the rock of our Redeemer, who is Christ, the Son of God, that ye must build your foundation; that when the devil shall send forth his mighty winds, yea, his shafts in the whirlwind, yea, when all his hail and his mighty storm shall beat upon you, it shall have no power over you to drag you down to the gulf of misery and endless wo, because of the rock upon which ye are built, which is a sure foundation, a foundation whereon if men build they cannot fall" (Helaman 5:9, 12).

We too must remember how merciful the Lord has been and look to God for our salvation. Daily, consistent time spent feasting upon the words of Christ can help us maintain the mighty change of heart and instill within us each day the renewed commitment to choose the right.

WHERE TO START

If you're unsure where to start, begin today by spending thirty minutes prayerfully studying your scriptures, specifically the Book of Mormon. Remember Nephi's admonition to "feast upon the words of Christ; for behold, the words of Christ will tell you *all things what ye should do*" (2 Nephi 32:3; emphasis added). President Ezra Taft Benson said:

"There is a power in the book which will begin to flow into your lives *the moment you begin a serious study* of the book. You will find greater power to resist temptation. You will find the power to avoid deception. You will find the power to stay on the strait and narrow path. The scriptures are called 'the words of life' (D&C 84:85), and nowhere is that more true than it is of the Book of Mormon. When you begin to hunger and thirst after those words, you will find life in greater and greater abundance."[16]

CONCLUSION

Rarely have I seen someone successfully abandon a pornography habit without also having made a recommitment to spirituality. As we seek to acquire strength to overcome pornography through the word of God, we can experience a mighty change of heart. This will occur as we *feel* the meanings of the words by the power of the Holy Ghost. This same Spirit will give us the understanding of what we must do and the strength to do it. I echo Nephi's testimony that feasting upon the words of Christ will truly teach us *all things* we should *do*—including those things necessary to overcome a pornography habit. We can receive strength through God's word and through his Spirit. At some point in this journey we will arrive at a point where our hearts are changed and we are sanctified from all unrighteousness. Then, we will truly feel no more disposition to do evil, but good continually.

Suggested Readings

The following readings may be helpful in further exploring the process of becoming sanctified through feasting upon Christ's word.

M. Russell Ballard, "His Word Ye Shall Receive," *Ensign*, May 2001, 65–67.

Merrill J. Bateman, "Coming unto Christ by Searching the Scriptures," *Ensign*, November 1992, 27–28.

Ezra Taft Benson, "A Mighty Change of Heart," *Ensign*, October 1989, 2–5.

———, "The Power of the Word," *Ensign*, May 1986, 79–82.

D. Todd Christofferson, "Justification and Sanctification," *Ensign*, June 2001, 18–25.

Spencer J. Condie, "A Disposition to Do Good Continually," *Ensign*, August 2001, 13–19.

Loren C. Dunn, "Fire and the Holy Ghost," *Ensign*, June 1995, 22–26.

Bruce C. Hafen, "Beauty for Ashes: The Atonement of Jesus Christ," *Ensign*, April 1990, 7–13.

———, "If with All Your Hearts Ye Truly Seek Me," *Ensign*, October 1984, 71–74.

Robert D. Hales, "When Thou Art Converted, Strengthen Thy Brethren," *Ensign*, May 1997, 80–83.

Howard W. Hunter, "Reading the Scriptures," *Ensign*, November 1979, 64–65.

L. Lionel Kendrick, "Search the Scriptures," *Ensign*, May 1993, 13–15.

Spencer W. Kimball, "How Rare a Possession—The Scriptures," *Ensign*, July 1985, 3–5.

Robert J. Matthews, "Finding Answers to Our Problems," *Ensign*, February 1974, 30–31.

Robert J. Matthews, "Searching the Scriptures: How to Face Temptation," *Ensign*, August 1973, 68–69.

———, "Searching the Scriptures: What Do the Scriptures Say about the Scriptures?" *Ensign*, May 1973, 22–24.

Neal A. Maxwell, "According to the Desire of [Our] Hearts," *Ensign*, November 1996, 21–23.

———, "Insights from My Life," *Ensign*, August 2000, 7–13.

———, "Willing to Submit," *Ensign*, May 1985, 70–73.

Russell M. Nelson, "Living by Scriptural Guidance," *Ensign,* November 2000, 16–18.

Dallin H. Oaks, "The Challenge to Become," *Ensign,* November 2000, 32–34.

———, "Scripture Reading and Revelation," *Ensign,* January 1995, 7–9.

L. Tom Perry, "Give Heed unto the Word of the Lord," *Ensign,* June 2000, 22–29.

Richard G. Scott, "Acquiring Spiritual Knowledge," *Ensign,* November 1993, 86–88.

———, "Full Conversion Brings Happiness," *Ensign,* May 2002, 24–26.

———, "To Acquire Knowledge and the Strength to Use It Wisely," *Ensign,* June 2002, 32–37.

NOTES

1. Brigham Young, in *Journal of Discourses,* 26 vols. (Liverpool: Latter-day Saints' Book Depot, 1854–86), 7:55.
2. Neal A. Maxwell, "According to the Desire of [Our] Hearts," *Ensign,* November 1996, 22.
3. Joseph Fielding Smith, *Church History and Modern Revelation,* 4 vols. (Salt Lake City: Deseret Book, 1953), 1:40.
4. Marion G. Romney, in Conference Report, Guatemala Area Conference 1977, 8–9.
5. See Howard W. Hunter, "Reading the Scriptures," *Ensign,* November 1979, 64.
6. Boyd K. Packer, "Revelation in a Changing World," *Ensign,* November 1989, 14.
7. Boyd K. Packer, "Washed Clean," *Ensign,* May 1997, 9.
8. Neal A. Maxwell, "Lessons from Laman and Lemuel," *Ensign,* November 1999, 6; emphasis in original.
9. Richard G. Scott, "Acquiring Spiritual Knowledge," *Ensign,* November 1993, 86.
10. Ezra Taft Benson, "The Power of the Word," *Ensign,* May 1986, 82; emphasis added.
11. Spencer W. Kimball, *The Teachings of Spencer W. Kimball,* ed. Edward L. Kimball (Salt Lake City: Bookcraft, 1982), 135; emphasis added.
12. Richard G. Scott, "Finding the Way Back," *Ensign,* May 1990, 75; emphasis added.

13. Merrill J. Bateman, "Coming unto Christ by Searching the Scriptures," *Ensign,* November 1992, 27.

14. Bruce R. McConkie, "Jesus Christ and Him Crucified," *1976 Devotional Speeches of the Year* (Provo, Utah: BYU Press, 1977), 399; emphasis added.

15. Joseph Smith, *Teachings of the Prophet Joseph Smith* (Salt Lake City: Deseret Book, 1976), 51.

16. Ezra Taft Benson, "The Keystone of Our Religion," *Ensign,* January 1992, 2; emphasis added.

CHAPTER TWENTY-FIVE

The Miraculous Process of Change

Mark D. Chamberlain

Sometimes we can't seem to make needed changes in our lives, no matter how hard we try. Fortunately, help is available from the Lord. However, even when we need his assistance, it's easy to go on trying to improve ourselves, working at it as though success depends entirely upon our own efforts, as though the Lord has left us to fend for ourselves in such matters. As a result of our failure to seek divine help as often as we might, we may live much of our lives "running on fumes" spiritually, while a vast reservoir of power remains largely untapped. In this chapter we will explore some of the principles by which we can "with joy . . . draw water out of the wells of salvation" (2 Nephi 22:3) to aid us in our efforts to change.

LEARNING TO RELY ON THE LORD

Vic was helping his son, Jeff, prepare for a mission. Jeff had turned in his papers, but their bishop was holding the application until Jeff could demonstrate a promising pattern of abstaining from masturbation. Jeff was succumbing to temptation once or twice a month, which was a significant improvement. For two years, starting at age 15, he had been caught up in a pattern of viewing Internet pornography and masturbating multiple times a week. Over the last year he had avoided pornography and curtailed his masturbation significantly. Over the last four or five months, however, his progress had reached the present plateau and stalled.

As Vic lovingly and patiently worked with his son, he shared Jeff's hopefulness when he succeeded for a period of time and his discouragement when he faltered. As time went on, however, Vic could see that Jeff's confidence and self-image were too wrapped up in his struggle. He beamed with enthusiasm on good days and became almost despondent on bad days.

As Vic prayerfully sought the Lord's guidance about how he could help, he realized that Jeff was riding this emotional roller coaster not only because of his struggle with sin, but also because of the immaturity of his faith. He started discussing with Jeff the need to place his trust in the Lord and his power instead of putting so much pressure on himself to succeed. Vic assured him that although his failures would always be discouraging, he must not let them destroy his hope. Over time Jeff came to better understand this key gospel truth: the faith that will save us is faith in the Lord Jesus Christ (see Articles of Faith 1:4), not confidence in our own capacities or performance. He came to understand what it means to rely "wholly upon the merits of him who is mighty to save" (2 Nephi 31:19) instead of his own merits. It was a tremendous comfort to know that he didn't have to conquer this habit on his own. Instead of being so fearful and focused on how his daily battle against temptation was going, over time Jeff learned to draw peace from remembering, as Elder Neal A. Maxwell taught, that "Jesus is already victorious in the greatest battle anyway."[1]

As he learned to look to the Savior and draw strength from him, it felt to Jeff as though the weight of the world was being removed from his shoulders. Amazingly, temptation seemed to ease up as he stopped putting so much pressure on himself. He was less likely to panic when he was tempted or berate himself after he succumbed. As his approach to the problem changed, Jeff enjoyed the companionship of the Holy Ghost more regularly. He didn't conquer the problem all at once, but he was more able to treat his failures as opportunities to learn how to handle temptation better in the future.

Seven months after Vic began working in earnest with his son, he sat at the kitchen table with his wife and their other children as Jeff opened his mission call and announced that he would be serving in Guatemala. Later that evening, after celebrating with friends and family, father and son knelt privately together and took turns pouring out the gratitude of their hearts for the miracle the Lord had worked in their lives.

Let's take a closer look at the principles that Jeff and Vic applied, principles that might also help us put aside the sins we have a difficult time overcoming.

1. Be willing to look deeper. While Jeff's sexual sin was certainly a problem in and of itself, the fact that he couldn't overcome it by trying in his usual way indicated an even deeper difficulty—it pointed to a problem in the way he went about trying to solve problems in his life. President Spencer W. Kimball taught: "Jesus saw sin as wrong but also was able to see sin as springing from deep and unmet needs on the part of the sinner." He then counseled that if we hope to change our own habits or help someone else change theirs, we must "look deeply enough . . . to see the basic causes for . . . failures and short-comings."[2] Vic was able to see beneath the surface appearance of things and discover the basic causes of Jeff's ongoing struggle. He took the time to carefully observe and critically analyze the patterns Jeff was caught up in, and his perception was enhanced and fine-tuned by the Holy Spirit.

2. Rely on the Lord instead of trying to change yourself. Before he went through the experience described above, Jeff's faith often faltered when he faced a serious problem. He was easily overcome by fear. In crisis situations he became overly focused on what *he* had to do to make things better. When his initial efforts failed, he would attack the problem again, hoping to succeed by trying even harder. This approach did not work very well. Jeff was like the armies we read about in the Book of Mormon who, once they relied on their own strength, were left to their own strength (see Helaman 4:13; Mormon 2:26). Like Jeff, we can learn to humble ourselves and become more submissive, rather than more willful, in the face of challenges and setbacks.

As long as he tried to change himself, Jeff struggled, because the power to exercise self-control is ultimately not mustered from within but is a gift from above.

"Human nature can be changed, here and now," said President David O. McKay, and then he quoted the following:

"'You can change human nature. No man who has felt in him the Spirit of Christ even for half a minute can deny this truth. . . .

"'You do change human nature, your own human nature, if you surrender it to Christ. Human nature can be changed here and now. Human nature has been changed in the past. Human nature must be changed on an enormous scale in the future, unless the world is to be drowned in its own blood. And only Christ can change it.

"'Twelve men did quite a lot to change the world [nineteen hundred] years ago. Twelve simple men.'"[3]

If we focus primarily on changing our behavior, we will forever be struggling against our natures (see Mosiah 3:19). If we focus instead on becoming "partakers of the divine nature" (2 Peter 1:4), then "doing what comes naturally" will take on an entirely different meaning and staying on track will not be so difficult.

3. Guard against pride and express gratitude. To be partakers of the divine nature, we must approach the process humbly, acknowledging that the qualities we are developing are being received from above and not generated from within. This humility can be difficult to maintain, because once we begin to prosper in an area of life that has been a struggle, it's natural to think to ourselves, "I hope *I* can keep this up." However, success that has come as a blessing from the Lord can only continue as we keep relying on and exercising faith in him. Once our focus on the Savior begins to bring about the changes we have been pleading for, we must keep our gaze centered on him and our eye single to his glory (see D&C 88:67). We have been warned that "in nothing doth man offend God, or against none is his wrath kindled, save those who confess not his hand in all things" (D&C 59:21).

We remove ourselves from the protection of grace when we forget from whence our blessings come and fail to acknowledge the help we have received. By contrast, when we humbly accept our growing freedom from sin as a blessing resulting from the Lord's protection, we remain open to receive even more of the same. Consider the humility Gid and Helaman demonstrated after reclaiming the city Cumeni from the Lamanites. Their armies had worked to exhaustion to accomplish the task, fighting "desperately" and suffering "great loss." Nonetheless, they "justly ascribe[d]" their success "to the miraculous power of God." After describing the sequence of events in the battle, Gid rejoiced, "And behold, we are again delivered out of the hands of our enemies. And blessed is the name of our God; for behold, it is he that has delivered us; yea, that has done this great thing for us." Helaman responded similarly: "Now it came to pass that when I, Helaman, had heard these words of Gid, I was filled with exceeding joy because of the goodness of God in preserving us, that we might not all perish" (Alma 57:19, 23, 26, 35–36).

After his people had humbled themselves and repented, King Benjamin taught them to "always retain in remembrance, the greatness of God, and your own nothingness" (Mosiah 4:11). His plea is that we adopt this perspective *always*, in other words, regardless of how things are going. So when we struggle with sin and our need for repentance is obvious, we are to retain in remembrance the greatness of God and our own nothingness. Likewise, when we feel like our lives are on track and we are living righteously, the same prescription applies: we are to retain in remembrance the greatness of God and our own nothingness. Some things don't change, regardless of how well we think we're doing.

4. Exercise patience and self-respect. We learn from the Apostle Paul that "the fruit of the Spirit is love, joy, peace, long-suffering, gentleness, goodness, faith, meekness, [and] temperance" (Galatians 5:22–23). When Jeff tried to battle temptation in an intense, worried, and self-critical way, the Spirit could not empower his efforts and he was left to his own strength. By contrast, when he cultivated a more patient, gentle approach to life in general, his efforts to avoid temptation and prepare for a mission flowed more naturally and became less of a struggle.

Certain features characterize the way in which our Father in Heaven attempts to influence us. It's no wonder that we don't respond very well when our attempts to control ourselves don't reflect the patient, respectful approach that was described by President Howard W. Hunter:

"God's chief way of acting is by persuasion and patience and long-suffering, not by coercion and stark confrontation. He acts by gentle solicitation and by sweet enticement. He always acts with unfailing respect for the freedom and independence that we possess. He wants to help us and pleads for the chance to assist us, but he will not do so in violation of our agency. He loves us too much to do that, and doing so would run counter to his divine character. . . .

"To countermand and ultimately forbid our choices was Satan's way, not God's, and the Father of us all simply never will do that. He will, however, stand by us forever to help us see the right path, find the right choice, respond to the true voice, and feel the influence of his undeniable Spirit. His gentle, peaceful, powerful persuasion to do right and find joy will be with us 'so long as time shall last, or the earth shall stand, or there shall be one man upon the face thereof to be saved.' (Moro. 7:36.)"⁴

Like the power to influence others, self-discipline can succeed long-term only when it is exercised according to the principles of righteousness (see D&C 121:36).

5. Make keeping the Spirit your highest priority. It is possible for us to overcome longstanding patterns and be healed. However, President James E. Faust has reminded us that "Christ is the Great Physician . . . and the Comforter is the agent of healing."⁵ It is only by the power of the Spirit that we can be insulated from temptation and thus protected from sin. Once we realize, as Jeff did, that our ability to live righteously depends on our having the Spirit of the Lord with us, we are more careful not to offend the Spirit in any area of our lives. When we are struggling to overcome sins that "so easily beset us" (Hebrews 12:1), we can't afford to approach other aspects of life carelessly. If we do, then the heavens withdraw themselves and we are left to struggle on our own, both in the area of life we approached unrighteously and in the struggle against our familiar temptation (see D&C 121:37).

We must approach our efforts to live righteously with the kind of thoroughness described by King Benjamin: "And finally, I cannot tell you all the things whereby ye may commit sin; for there are divers ways and means, even so many that I cannot number them. But this much I can tell you, that if ye do not watch yourselves, and your thoughts, and your words, and your deeds, and observe the commandments of God, and continue in the faith of what ye have heard concerning the coming of our Lord, even unto the end of your lives, ye must perish" (Mosiah 4:29–30).

UNEXPECTED BENEFITS

One day I couldn't find a piece of paperwork I needed. I quickly thumbed through a few of the papers on my desk, but to no avail. I reluctantly determined that I might have to look through everything on my desk and in my briefcase to find it. I decided that until I could find the document, I might as well sort the papers I looked through, organize them by topic, and put them into file folders. This wasn't the way I wanted to spend my time that afternoon, but I needed that paperwork. As it turned out, I finally found the document in one of the last stacks of papers I sorted. Since I had been frustrated early in the process, I was surprised that even after I found the paperwork I needed, I wanted to continue cleaning up the mess.

As I finally made it through the last pile of paper, I felt great. I no longer resented the time my search had required. After all, it was looking for that lost paper that had motivated me to finally organize my office, something that had been hanging over my head for months. Afterward, I was grateful for a lighter briefcase and the extra work space on my desk. Most of all, I enjoyed opening up my filing cabinet and looking through a few file folders when I needed something instead of repeatedly sorting through stack after stack of disorganized papers.

Those of us who are "easily beset" by certain sins might prefer a magic bullet, a single key that could free us once and for all from their addictive pull. Instead, in order to succeed in such struggles, we must bring our entire lives into alignment with the principles and powers of heaven. Perhaps this is one reason God doesn't take away our "thorn in the flesh" (2 Corinthians 12:7) in one grand transformation. While the journey of change can be arduous and at times very frustrating, it can be through this very process that our lives become sanctified.

NOTES

1. Neal A. Maxwell, "Encircled in the Arms of His Love," *Ensign*, November 2002, 16.

2. Spencer W. Kimball, *The Teachings of Spencer W. Kimball,* ed. Edward L. Kimball (Salt Lake City: Bookcraft, 1982), 481, 482.

3. Beverly Nichols, quoted in David O. McKay, *Stepping Stones to an Abundant Life,* comp. Llewelyn R. McKay (Salt Lake City: Deseret Book, 1971), 23, 127.

4. Howard W. Hunter, "The Golden Thread of Choice," *Ensign,* November 1989, 18.

5. James E. Faust, "Strengthening the Inner Self," *Ensign,* February 2003, 5.

CHAPTER TWENTY-SIX

"That God Would Remove These Feelings from Me": Suggestions from Those Suffering from Pornography Addiction

Scott Peterson

arly on, sex addicts discover that six of the twelve steps of Sexaholics Anonymous deal directly with their Higher Power. They soon come to realize that surrendering to that Higher Power is an essential step toward relinquishing the false sense of control they have over their addiction. They must finally recognize that their problem cannot be vanquished by their own efforts, but only with the intervention of the Lord. This is but one of the many commonalities that addicts share on the road of recovery. Through the stories of several addicts, this chapter describes recurring themes and issues in their backgrounds, how they disclosed their addictions, and what steps and strategies have worked as they strove to overcome their dependence on pornography and sex.

BACKGROUND

The backgrounds of addicts, as seen in their families of origin, oftentimes provide great insight as to where and why addictions begin. There are those families whose lives are built on denial, when older family members try to hide problems rather than face them. Much like the emperor's new clothes, everyone pretends everything is all right when it really isn't. The addict at a young age learns to avoid the painful and the obvious, from something as small as never commenting on Grandma's poor grammar to something as devastating as Dad's own sex addiction. Don't see it. Don't speak about it. And never show your feelings. The proverbial elephant in the middle of the living room is never to be discussed.

There are the rigid, authoritarian families. Parents dominate and the children have little, if any, say in decisions. Everything is seen as black or white. Natural child development is very difficult. There are only two directions the addict can choose in such families: Either give up his identity and do exactly as his parents want, or live a secret life about which the family knows nothing. Both result in a distortion of reality, a loss of trust in authority, and low self-esteem.

Sometimes part of the family's rigidity includes a negative attitude toward sex. The addict is taught that sex is bad, dirty, forbidden, or sinful. It can either become exaggerated or a subject that is completely taboo. Such an environment creates early obsessions, resulting in a double life where the addict appears proper and sex-avoidant, but secretly acts out sexually whenever the opportunity presents itself. Life becomes based on lies. The addict pretends what is true is not true and becomes torn between both distorted realities. Living a dual life is part of the foundation of addiction.

There are cases where the addict has been abused and neglected. He is not taught common life skills and ways to care for himself. This increases stress and anxiety and the tendency to self-medicate to deaden the pain of not having his basic needs met.

For instance, boys who learn to never need anything from their parents are faced with feelings of inadequacy whenever they feel young, needy, or otherwise insecure. If masturbation has been their principal source of self-nurturing, it would not be unusual for them to resort to masturbation in order to emotionally care for themselves during those times when they have needs completely unrelated to sexuality.

The addict turns to sexual behavior such as masturbation because it is something that he can control and it cannot be taken away from him. Such compulsive behavior decreases self-esteem, increases distrust in others, and at an early age begins to establish core beliefs based on shame and distrust.

The following are individuals' own stories of their backgrounds and how their addictions began. (Names have been changed in each of the examples.)

James

"I suppose you could say that I lived a model life. I grew up in a large LDS family. I felt safe, loved, and secure for the most part. Nothing in particular stands out as extraordinary as I grew up. I experienced a lot of the struggles of adolescence such as self-consciousness, wanting to be accepted and to fit in, and also falling in love with the cute girls. I was above average athletically and excelled at basketball.

"At a very early age I experimented with my sexual drives and urges. I always knew that somehow it was not right, and I found myself suffering from guilt almost immediately. Most of my curiosity was fulfilled by newspaper ads, Montgomery Ward catalogs, and *National Geographic.*

"At about age twelve, I found some pornography discarded by the side of the road. This really enhanced my sexual interests. The high school locker room was filled with the stuff. Kids would bring it from home or steal it from the local gas station. At the same time I was very involved in my Church activities and callings.

"It was recently pointed out to me that we teach that sex is bad, dirty, and nasty—so we should save it for someone we love. What a contradiction. But that is how I always understood it.

"Somehow I made it through junior high school, high school, and completed a successful mission. I was able to control my appetite on my mission and thought that when I got married that my problem would be solved. Not so. I came home, started school, met a wonderful girl, and married her in the temple. It seemed that I could go for short periods of abstinence, but was never able to overcome the problem.

"Over time, my curiosity for more than magazines led me to strip clubs. Having received a new position at work that required travel, it was easy to visit them. At this point, even though I couldn't see or admit it, I was totally addicted. I was powerless to stop when I wanted. Still, no one knew about my addiction. So everything was still perfect on the outside while it was taking a terrible toll on the inside. I continued down this path while feeling more guilty and empty each time I acted out."

Phil

"I was born into the LDS faith. My parents and all my family have been active. I was active in Church through my child and teenage years. From my early years, I believe that I have had some of the feelings that have contributed to my addiction.

"I served what I considered a faithful mission. After returning and finishing up college, I married a wonderful girl. I completed graduate school. I have a good stable job. I have four wonderful children. I have been active in the Church, holding a number of positions of responsibility. No one would have expected that I would have had a problem with pornography.

"The event that set off my addiction in a major way occurred on a business trip. While channel surfing in my hotel room I accidentally came across some soft-core adult films. I turned the TV off, but the compulsion to watch kept me coming back to take a look. For the next seven-and-one-half years, on and off, I dabbled in pornography. The compulsion was most particularly prevalent on business trips when I would view adult television movies or videos. I also found myself spending time in video stores looking at the back covers of videos, sometimes slipping into the adult section. The Internet provided another way for me to view pornography in private.

"After every experience with pornography I would feel an incredible amount of shame and self-hatred. I cannot tell you how many times I prayed on my knees that God would remove these feelings from me. I would repeatedly promise again and again that I would not 'act out.' Although I would try, I did not keep any of these promises. The urges and compulsions were simply too strong. This repetitive cycle of viewing pornography, feeling shame, and promising not to do it again became so prevalent that I was convinced that I would never be able to break free. My desires for pornography were simply too strong.

"During this period, I also felt the strain of leading a double life. Outwardly, I appeared to be the perfect LDS member following the commandments and doing what was right. But inside, I felt like a different person. I was leading a double life. One of the keys to addiction is secrecy. I could not tell anyone about my secret. I felt that if I did, people would look down on me, be disappointed in me, or even reject me. It is difficult in so few words to express the conflict that I would feel inside. On one hand I was drawn to pornography with its allure and excitement. On the other hand, I hated myself for giving in to these feelings."

Umberto

"I come from a large family of eight children. My parents are converts to the LDS Church. I was baptized when I was fifteen years old. While I knew my parents loved me, my father was gone on business much of the time and it seemed as if my mother was busy with my younger brothers and sisters. I was pretty much left on my own. Since the age of eight I had a great amount of freedom and for the most part raised myself. It was also due to this lack of supervision that I fell prey to my teen-aged uncle's influence. He always had a stash of pornography in his basement that he would gladly let me look at. By the time I was eleven or twelve years old he had taught me how to masturbate to the slick, alluring photographs. Then when I was thirteen or fourteen he would sneak me into X-rated movie houses with his friends. You could say I was addicted to pornography by the time I was fourteen years old. At sixteen I had my first real sexual encounter, with a seventeen-year-old neighborhood girl. All the while my parents, my mother especially, thought I was a good little boy, doing what I was supposed to.

"Just before I turned fifteen my best friend joined the Church. He insisted that I start going to church with him, which I did. I had something of a spiritual awakening and decided to join the Church. But when I was interviewed to be baptized by the missionary, I said nothing about my sexual escapades.

"I stopped my sexual acting out for about three months. But the draw was too strong. It was as if I had to be sexual to feel okay about myself. To keep things more discreet I made friends with a group of other kids in another part of town. I'd spend Friday nights with them, sexually acting out, and then go to church in my own neighborhood on Sundays and go to Young Men's on Wednesday evenings. It was as much a double life as you could lead. Living in a big city made it easy.

"Each year went by and I would lie through my teeth to my branch president. He'd ask if I had a problem with masturbation and I'd say, 'No.' He didn't ask about my relationships with girls because I appeared to be such a good teacher and priest.

"The years went by and I was rapidly approaching nineteen. I wanted to go on a mission but I knew I wasn't worthy. Six weeks before I started my interview process, I went cold turkey. I lied in the interviews, saying I'd done some 'heavy petting' and that I didn't have a masturbation problem. I got my mission call and away I went.

"I had a successful mission except for some trouble with a couple of girls in two of the areas that I served. I didn't say anything to anyone about it, but the indiscretions seemed to place a pall over my entire mission experience.

"After my mission I returned home and entered the local university. In about six months time I was back to looking at porn and masturbating regularly. During this time I met my wife. She'd been raised strict LDS and I treated her completely differently than I did most girls that I had dated.

"We were engaged to be married in an LDS temple. I never told her of my previous sexual encounters and I lied to my bishop in preparation to enter the temple. Three weeks before we got married I had sex with one of my old girlfriends. I went ahead with the wedding as if nothing had happened.

"Being married didn't stop me looking at porn and masturbating. I was so out of control my wife knew something was wrong. I told her it was stress from work and finishing up my degree in school. But it was the deceit and lies, the sneaking around and making excuses, that were tearing me up inside. Yet I couldn't stop myself. I was headed straight for disaster and there wasn't anything I could do about it."

Seth

"I came from an abusive home that was emotionally and physically violent. I survived a lot of trauma from an early age. From my best memories, there were two camps at our house—Dad's and Mom's. It didn't matter whose side you were on, it was still wrong because you had to defend yourself from the other side. You always looked for allies, but they were hard to find. And because of the secrecy of the violence, you couldn't include friends, or other family members, or Church leaders. If you tried, you were considered a traitor. The secret was like a great wound that crippled the family; the family could not heal its own wound, but would not allow others to help.

"If appearances mattered, we were deeply religious, and although people suspected trouble at times, my parents were very involved in the religious community and very active in worship and church functions. We were considered 'stalwarts.'

"As soon as I hit puberty, I was very interested in what my body was doing. I was completely fascinated that these changes could supply such fantastic feelings. And it was one of the few ways I could feel good. So masturbation became an immediate relief, and I quickly became addicted to all the physical feelings associated with it. And of course, because of my religious upbringing, there was a tremendous amount of guilt accompanying it.

"I was plagued with suicidal thoughts from my early teens and often slumped into long-term depression. Years later I married and had children and brought my hang-ups and addictions into our family life. At times I was completely hopeless at the prospects of being able to overcome the gravity of the trauma I still carried with me from my childhood and the immense pull my addictions still had on me.

"By my early 40s I was struggling to get up in the morning and go to work, struggling to balance my religious convictions with my addictive patterns, battling horrific flashbacks of suppressed abuse, and tired of ignoring compounded guilt of an illicit sexual encounter I finally had. I was at the end of my rope emotionally, spiritually, and physically."

SELF-DISCLOSURE

While sex addiction thrives on secrecy, silence, and ultimately shame, disclosing sexual addiction is a delicate matter and should be handled with much forethought and care. Telling a spouse about sex addiction is an extremely daunting task. The offending spouse must be prepared for any number of responses and should be accepting of his wife's anger (short of abusive behavior), pain, disbelief, and suffering. Typically, it is not helpful to share all of the details of one's addiction unless it affects the spouse directly (such as the risk of disease). Studies suggest that it is best to disclose all information at one time rather than piecemeal. Sharing information a little bit at a time increased hurt and decreased trust. It is heartening to note that 96 percent of spouses and 93 percent of addicts reported that making full disclosures of their addictions benefited their recoveries.[1] Here is what two individuals said about disclosing their addiction.

Phil

"I had gone on another business trip and again dabbled in pornography by viewing segments of an adult movie. As always happens after 'acting out,' I felt tremendous guilt and shame. I decided that my life could not go on like this and that I needed help. I felt that the difficulty of facing up to this problem could not be worse than continuing with my shame, deception, and self-hate.

"I must admit that one of the hardest things in my life was to open up to someone about my addiction. It is still hard to talk about it. I talked to my wife about the problems I was having. Instead of rejecting me, she listened and encouraged me to see someone. I met with a therapist who specialized in these problems. That first session was difficult. It was difficult for me to even say the words 'pornography' and 'addiction.' I hated to admit to someone else that

I had this problem and that I was not strong enough to solve it on my own."

Umberto

"Everything finally fell apart when my wife discovered a condom wrapper under the seat of my car. I believe that my being so careless was a cry for help. However, at the time, it seemed it was the worst way I could have asked for it. Needless to say, she was furious. I couldn't stop from blurting everything out—my college single life, the time during our engagement, all the times that I was unfaithful for the short seven months that we'd been married. She kicked me out of the house that night. I went to stay with my parents, telling them only that we were having a fight. It was much later that I told them what the real problem was.

"My wife contacted an attorney and had divorce papers drawn up. In the meantime I had gone to my bishop and confessed everything. He referred me to a therapist and a program that specialized in sexual addiction. The program was for both spouses, so I called my wife and told her what I was doing to begin to address my addiction. I asked her if she would be willing to postpone filing for divorce just long enough to go through the first phase of the program with me. I was shocked but incredibly grateful when she agreed. I'm still not back in the house. I understand I have severely betrayed my wife's trust, but she is willing to let me earn that trust back as we both follow our paths of recovery."

WHAT WORKS

Patrick Carnes identifies, in his book *Facing the Shadow*, several common denominators that addicts share when they are successfully on the road to recovery.[2] Carnes and his associates found that sobriety was but one factor in the several life changes that took place in those that had the most success. Those who were willing to go to any lengths to make their recovery succeed appeared to have made a deeper commitment for a better life. The profile that emerged for such individuals showed that they all did the following:

They had a primary therapist. Regardless of the nature of the treatment program in which they participated, each had a therapist with whom they worked for a three-to-five-year period. During this time they allowed their lives to be examined in detail, letting the therapist get to know them extraordinarily well.

They were in a therapy group. Again, regardless of the setting, those that were successful spent an average of 175 hours in a therapy group over an eighteen-month to two-year period.

They went regularly to twelve-step meetings. Furthermore, they became deeply involved in the program, doing service, sponsorship, and step work.

They addressed any other addictions, as well. They came to understand how their other addictions interacted negatively with one another and attended other twelve-step meetings as necessary.

They worked to find clarity and resolution for their family-of-origin and childhood issues. They worked on the deeper personality issues related to their childhoods and how those affect their present lives.

Their families were involved early in therapy. There appeared to be a large difference in the recovery of those addicts who had the support of their families and those who did not. Often the addict's treatment proved to be the impetus for the treatment of the family as well.

If they were in a primary relationship, the couple went to a twelve-step couples group such as Recovering Couples Anonymous. It was found that those who had a spouse who was committed to recovery as well did the best of all. Where there is a twelve step–based support network for couples, the outcome is usually the most successful.

They developed a spiritual life. It was important that they practice their spirituality on a regular, even daily, basis. It was typically most effective if they were part of a spiritual community.

They actively worked to maintain regular exercise and good nutrition. Those whose recovery truly flourished exercised on a regular basis and made healthy food choices as a critical part of their self-care.

Regarding recovery strategies, here is what several of the men I interviewed had to say.

Carl

"Church and SA meetings: I had to be careful with this one. Since my addictive cycle included running to the bishop for absolution, I had to be careful not to overdo church. I had to make sure I was surrendering and letting the atonement work for me rather than trying to 'white knuckle' my recovery. Whenever I had that feeling that I was being good then usually a relapse was on its way. A better state of mind was 'today is my only day,' 'easy does it,' and 'take the days as they come.' I just needed to let sobriety happen. Forcing or manipulating it just doesn't work.

"I have let church become a spiritual feast. Before, I was either shamed by church or was a zealot. I can see I am on the right path now. 'I will prevail' is one of my favorite slogans. If I fall, I avoid pitying myself. I pick up where I left off and keep going.

"Prayer: I can't surrender unless I ask him to take it away. 'Father, please take this desire to lust from me and give me what my lust is looking for.'

"Journal: This helped me to see progress, get out my feelings, and analyze my addictive cycle. Re-reading and seeing the ludicrous lies that I told and believed was key to seeing the insanity of my addiction. I made a point of re-writing paragraphs to really get honest with how I felt. I would vent in my journal and later laugh at my childishness.

"Exercise: I found that occasionally after I worked out I had a feeling that life was great. At times I felt this connection with my masculinity that was very empowering. My running has become an obsession. Running has also refuted many of the lies that I had bought into during my high school years: my body is flawed; I will die young from a heart attack or stroke; my body is ugly. Furthermore I refuted some negative scripts: I am a loser; I will never achieve anything meaningful; I am a quitter. Ultimately, running says, 'If you patiently work at something then you will learn the lesson it has to teach you.' It teaches and persuades me to pursue difficult things like recovery. It teaches me respect for myself and others.

"Talking to my spouse: Whenever I am completely honest with my wife, I realize how much effort and worry I generated trying to keep my undisclosed actions a secret. She is really on my side. It is nice to know that she cares about me and really wants me to have a lasting recovery.

"Dealing with triggers: 'What am I missing?' I ask this question when I start to become preoccupied with a trigger. 'What great thing in life am I missing right now because of this trigger?' I might miss some cute thing one of my children is doing. I might ignore a need or miss a cue from someone important because of my preoccupation.

"'Monsieur Thenardier': Occasionally I allow myself to see my addict self as Mr. Thenardier from *Les Miserables*. He is despicable, obnoxious, disgusting, and a laughable character. He has a sickly French-laced accent and has missing and rotting teeth. So I laugh at myself when I catch myself stealing a lustful glance and say, in my best Thenardier accent, 'Bonjour, darling, through rotten teeth.'

"'One of millions': Sometimes it is helpful to see a trigger as just one of millions. It's not anything special. A dime a dozen.

"Procrastination: 'I can lust after that later if I choose to then. Not now.'

"Humor: Sometimes it helps to see the humor in all the men turning at a stoplight to watch the woman cross the street. They are like robots. 'You will comply. Resistance is futile.'"

Phil

"First, openness is a key to dealing with pornography addiction. Even today, I find it difficult to discuss my addiction because of what people will think. Yet openness is one of the keys to true healing. Some people may think less of you, but in the end it is only important what God thinks of you and what you think of yourself.

"Second, admitting to myself and others that I am powerless over pornography has been essential for me. Through prayer, discussion, and thought, I came to understand that I could not deal with my addiction alone. I realized that I truly needed God's help to change.

"Third, I spent many hours going through the principles outlined in Carnes's book *A Gentle Path Through the Twelve Steps.* I spent many hours meditating and praying about the things discussed in that book.

"Fourth, I worked to change my behavior and avoid risky situations. When I go out of town, I will talk to my wife about what I will do. When I enter a hotel room, I dedicate that room as a place of purity and peace. I take pictures of Christ and my children with me. I also avoid video stores or do not go alone.

"The final key, after I have done what I can, is the grace of God. Somehow, God touched me and helped me change my behavior. Today I know that even though on occasion I have those desires to view pornography, that through God's help, I and anyone else can change their behavior. I cannot in words express the gratitude that I feel towards God. He has taken a situation that I thought unsolvable and has not only given me hope, but actually changed my behavior. I have learned through personal experience that one's behavior towards pornography can be changed. It is not easy. Change requires humility, being open, having faith in God, trusting that he will help you and sustain you."

Ron

"One way to prevent relapses and prepare for temptation is to try to define all of the triggers that affect our thinking or actions. These triggers can include people with whom we associate, places we go, ways of processing information, and pornographic literature. One of the easiest ways to do this is to backtrack, or to go from the undesired thoughts or activities back to try to find out what it was that started off the chain of events that led to the problem or relapse. It is then valuable to address every item in the chain, from the initial stimulus to the final behavior.

"If I know that looking at pornographic literature will likely lead to cruising, which will likely lead to sexual indiscretion, it is important that I keep myself completely away from such literature. This type of behavior control is a necessary prerequisite to behavior change.

"When I was involved in homosexual activity, I found that I got a rush from standing too close to the 'edge.' I would experiment by going to adult book stores or gay cruising places, rationalizing that I just wanted to see who was there or that I just wanted to look but that I never would do anything. But in my addictive delirium I almost always proved myself wrong. I did not follow my rule of behavioral control.

"How does one effectively modify such behavior and deal with the related excitement and addiction? The answer is painfully simple, but it is one that people involved in addictive lifestyles either fail to recognize or choose to ignore. The answer is to replace the excitement. When faced with the excitement of this type of sex-ual behavior versus leading a dreary, boring life, the addict will invariably return to the excitement. I firmly believe that the answer lies not in suppressing the desire for excitement in life, but in redefining excitement and in locating new avenues to achieve it.

"This is an area where friends who know about homosexual struggles can be helpful. In my experience, when life started to get a little boring and it became tempting to get into the car and cruise, I could, instead, call a friend who knew of my difficulties and ask if we could go play racquetball, go to a show, or simply visit and talk for a while. This strategy would often get me through just one night of difficulty, but it did get me through one night. The old twelve-step motto of 'One day at a time' is all we can ask for and is really all we should attempt. Over time, I found that my crises tended to diminish in both frequency and intensity.

"Addiction literature refers to the acronym HALT—hungry, angry, lonely, tired—as being common precursors of addictive behavior. I would add boredom to this list. Whenever you find one or more of these conditions present, you must be prepared to address it.

"When talking about behavior modification, commitment is key. I made commitments to call friends or support groups when I was having problems. I found that when I followed through with my commitments, my struggles became much easier to handle."

In the final analysis, *what* is done in recovery may not be as important as the fact that *something* is done. One of our veteran recovering addicts has made the observation that he now must put as much time and effort into his recovery as he did his addiction. Recovery simply isn't sobriety. It is a way a life. It is committing to becoming the type of man or woman you want to be. It is being self-approving no matter what the outcome is. It is self-improvement one day at a time. Recovery is active and dynamic. In conclusion, perhaps Seth's words say it best:

Seth

"Get into recovery work. Join a group. Get individual help. Do it like your life depended on it. I went through the exercises. I did the homework. I followed through with recovery work when I couldn't seem to follow through with anything else in my life. I would think that I wasn't getting any better and I would be ready to lie down and die. Then someone in group would stick his finger in my face and *show* me where I had been and where I was now and prove to me that I was making progress and that I really was becoming a whole person. And then I would become upset because he and the other group members would be right and they would take away my reason for feeling like a victim that day. So when those fingers were poked in my face I would first get upset, but then before group was done I would embrace my fellow group members and thank them for being the kind of friends and brothers who were honest enough with me that they could show me my faults and show me how to leave my anger behind and trade it in for true happiness.

"This is what you can expect from recovery: grief, pain, suffering, loss, major life changes. But if you are willing to sacrifice by going through these things—once you give all these things to God, lay them on the altar and turn your back—you can expect to receive far greater things in return. Grief turns to peace. Pain and suffering turn to well-being sprinkled with pleasure. Loss turns to generosity and plentifulness. Major life changes can bring a better life. Recovery has helped me slide into the 'flow' of becoming whole. I have started sleeping at night. I have found love, appreciation, and acceptance among the people I'm with every day. My only intent in writing this is to bring you, the reader, hope. If you have no hope, then rely on mine until you find your own."

NOTES

1. Reported in Patrick Carnes, *Facing the Shadow* (Wickenburg: Gentle Path Press, 2001), 127.
2. See Carnes, *Facing the Shadow,* 268–69.

CHAPTER TWENTY-SEVEN

Addiction and Recovery: One Man's Story

Anonymous

My counselor was pleased with my progress and congratulated me as I finished my final session. I had been a model client. I had been humble and contrite. I had agreed with every concept presented and answered every question with a positive affirmation for the future. Now our eight weekly sessions were completed and I was pronounced healthy and whole.

The last thing I told my counselor was, "I'll be all right as long as I stay away from the Internet. If I ever let that thing get into my life, I'm done for." It was a personal revelation. Oh, how I wish I had listened to that Spirit and obeyed its prompting.

Another addictive cycle was completed, but no one had ever called it addiction. All I knew was that when life started feeling overwhelming, when I started feeling those old insecurities and inadequacies inside, I would be drawn powerfully to find an escape—from my real-world life as a perfect Latter-day Saint husband and father to a secret life of pornography, masturbation, and sexual fantasy.

Eight times in my forty-plus years I had gone through the repentance process. Each time, the intensity and sincerity of my

remorse led to a brief probation and a quick return to full fellowship. Six times in my twenty years of marriage I had left a job, left
a city, and tried to start anew where my sins and shame would not
be known and where I could reestablish my credentials as a model
member of the Church, with a perfect marriage and a fabulous family. Twice I had gone through a brief series of counseling sessions
with glowing projections of success.

Now I had been offered the perfect job—a dream job at LDS
Church headquarters that combined high visibility, good salary,
great benefits, and a wonderful sense of community service. Sure
there would be long hours and a lot of stress, but it was the job of a
lifetime. My wife and I were amazed at the opportunity, but deep
in my heart there was a hint of dread. What if I messed up again?
My wife had forgiven me many times in the past, but she would
never be able to forgive me if I were to blow this chance. But you
don't say no to an opportunity like this. I soon began my new job.

As time passed, I began noticing information about Internet filtering programs that would block pornography. I was intrigued, and
decided to try them out. In spite of all the premonitions of danger,
I installed the Internet in my home and set up a computer in the
basement. Then I began testing the boundaries of the filtering system, seeing what sites would be blocked and what sites could sneak
through. About the same time, the opportunity opened up to get the
Internet at work. As the months passed I started to test the filtering system at work also.

I was drawn in like a fish on a line. I found that no filter could
stop me if I was creative enough and determined enough. The
Internet gave me a powerful illusion of anonymity, and in the insanity that only an addict can recognize, I rationalized that I was actually providing a service by uncovering web sites that could get
through the filters.

As I would spend more and more time downstairs on the
Internet, my wife became more and more dismayed. I became

distant and withdrawn. She became fearful, then angry. As the gulf between us grew larger, masturbation again became a problem. To escape the uncomfortable reality of life, I would allow my mind to fly to all sorts of fantasy. When my conscience bothered me about sexual fantasies, I would substitute heroic fantasies in which I would defeat terrorist attacks or perform great sporting achievements that weren't remotely possible even in my most athletic years.

As Christmas approached, the computer specialists at Church headquarters notified my boss of my Internet misuse. The Church has a zero tolerance policy when it comes to employees and Internet pornography. Church employees have wonderful job security. All that is asked of them is to work diligently and stay temple worthy. I was not temple worthy. I resigned my position so they wouldn't have to fire me.

I told a friend that afternoon, "I am a dead man." I went slowly home and told my wife. As our world crumbled around us, she reacted, not with the expected red-hot anger, but with an ice cold sense of finality that I had never seen. Whatever remnant of love had survived all the years of trials and disappointments seemed to die right before my eyes.

I moved into the basement. My father called from the mission field to try to push my wife to forgive me. All it did was damage my parents' relationship with my wife as well. We tried marriage counseling for a while. The counselor told us to come back after some healing had taken place.

It is ironic that the one ray of hope we could see came when our bishop and stake president refused to let me off the hook and play the game of quick repentance. I was disfellowshipped from the Church. My long-standing practice of minimizing my sins and shrugging off the consequences had come to an end. I could no longer partake of the sacrament. I could not raise my hand and make comments in Gospel Doctrine class or offer a prayer in meetings. I watched silently as my family spoke at my son's mission farewell. I sat outside the Bountiful Temple as my beautiful daughter was married for time and all eternity. Because my priesthood leaders took the disciplining role seriously, the burden of punishing me was lifted from my wife's shoulders. This was a huge relief for our devastated relationship.

Our bishop was a truly kind and loving steward. He was convinced that there was help for us out there somewhere. For days he made phone call after phone call searching for something that could make a difference in our lives. He finally found a treatment clinic that provides individual counseling and a three-phase group program. He arranged for us to attend Phase I of the LifeSTAR Network, a three-phase program for the treatment of sexual addicitions.

The first meeting we attended was filled with intense hurt and anger for my wife. She had initially decided not to attend. She felt that the problems were mine to fix and she would have nothing to do with them. Instead she planned to attend the temple that day, but she was given the strong inspiration that she had to go to the first meeting, and so she did, but with great frustration.

As the weeks passed, we learned principles about addictive behavior that stunned us. For all our education, reading, and counseling experience, we had never even considered the subject. But the symptoms of addiction were all there: the shame-based faulty beliefs, the family of origin structures, and the cyclical patterns, including a hyper-spiritual side to the addictive cycle.

We learned about a concept called "the drama triangle" where spouses engage in an unproductive dance of being the victim, the persecutor, or the rescuer. Each of these roles can be used as a means to try to control each other. Surprisingly, the most powerful of these roles is that of the victim. In the midst of an argument, the partner who can most successfully become the victim is then able to force the other into either being a persecutor (the argument explodes into a fight) or the rescuer (the argument dissolves into apology and impossible promises that it will never happen again). One of the unintended consequences of this "victim dance" is that it can become a powerful trigger of both addictive behavior and codependent behavior.

As we began to understand this concept, my wife and I looked at each other with amazement. For all our college education, gospel study, and supposed adult maturity, we recognized that this was exactly the pattern we had fallen into over and over again during our marriage. We could recreate in our minds argument after argument that followed this very description. It was one of many concepts that brought us to a realization that we had indeed fallen into addictive and codependent patterns and that we needed to be more humble and accept this help.

We found a growing degree of comfort in the presence of other couples who were battling the same war. They were good people, normal everyday people trying to understand how this horrible influence of pornography and sexual addiction had entered into their lives and how they could be free of it. A sliver of hope crept in that there might be a path that could lead toward recovery.

Then one week a panel of recovering addicts came to speak to us. In the group was a dear friend, a respected colleague, who was maintaining his temple worthiness as he battled with his own addictive tendencies. I broke down, sobbing with a mixture of sorrow, relief, and hope. We stayed after the meeting for hours, sharing thoughts and feelings of a lifetime of hiding, struggling, and pretending.

The progress came slowly. But each week my wife and I would learn something worth talking about. As we moved through Phase II and Phase III of the program, we changed the way we communicated. I stopped pursuing, invading her space, and demanding forgiveness. She learned to set appropriate boundaries and let go of the internal shame brought on by the lie that she was somehow to blame for my choices. We stopped the futile "victim dance" of trying to be the victim and blaming each other for the pain we felt. I moved back upstairs, and we found that love had somehow survived after all.

After several months, we began attending an LDS twelve-step support group meeting for those struggling with substance abuse, which taught principles that were just as applicable for my addiction and my wife's healing process. We learned more clearly than ever before how to surrender our addictive and codependent behavior to the Savior and the importance of seeking his healing influence in our lives on a daily basis.

After several months, the Church-service missionaries we were working with piloted a support group program using the twelve-step plan to help both those struggling with pornography and compulsive sexual behavior and their spouses. In this program, the men and women were split into separate groups so that the sharing could be conducted openly and honestly.

There were just three or four of us at the beginning. The group quickly grew to where thirty to forty men and fifteen to twenty spouses were attending. A second meeting night was added, then more. The program has now been expanded to many cities and can be introduced wherever there is an organized LDS Family Services office and proactive local priesthood support.

We found as we moved forward that the "drama triangle" in our lives was being replaced by a healthy triangle of support. Our wonderful, caring priesthood leaders kept in close communication with us. Our professional counselors taught us clear principles, helped us reach deep inside ourselves for understanding, and gave us tools that we could use to interdict the triggers that in the past led to addictive and codependent behavior cycles. Our twelve-step group provided us with a safe and ongoing setting of emotional support where honesty and humility have brought a rebirth of hope. And at the center of this triangle lies the atonement of our Lord and Savior,

Jesus Christ. As we have opened our hearts to him, he has truly sent his spirit into our hearts and healed our wounds and lightened our burdens.

As the months passed, my wife and I were extended a calling to serve as missionaries to lead our twelve-step support group. With nervous faith we accepted, recognizing that our own recovery is still ongoing. For years I used every effort to hide and conceal my struggles. Now each week, I share my story with wonderful men, young and old, who are battling the same addictive patterns. Together we turn to the Savior as we each work our individual steps to embrace the atonement more fully in our lives.

After so many years of hurt, anger and despair, to now see my wife arrive at a point where she can bring a spirit of peace to these meetings, helping other women find hope in the Savior's atonement, is one of the greatest miracles I have ever witnessed. To feel the power of the atonement of the Savior at work in our lives fills our once-battered hearts with incredible joy.

The triggers that used to pull me into addictive cycles over and over again seem more visible now and more easily identified. The daily steps that keep us humble, honest, and focused on the Savior's atonement give our lives a spirit of renewed love and renewed hope. Our home has become a place where love and harmony radiate, and the wars of past addictive cycles fade from painful memory. As we continue to participate in meetings with others who are facing the same struggles we have endured, their stories and their spirits strengthen us and keep our determination bright.

We have sometimes asked ourselves: "Why couldn't we have found these programs years ago when we were first married?" A sister in one of our twelve-step meetings made an analogy that has helped us surrender that frustrating thought. There may have been many pioneers who watched with wonder as brand new steam locomotives brought Latter-day Saints across the plains to Salt Lake

City short years after they had walked the hundreds of miles. They too might have said, "Why couldn't the Lord have given us trains when we needed them?"

In his wisdom, the Lord lets us sometimes struggle and learn through hard experience so that our stories can help others along the way. On more than one occasion, my wife has been asked by a new sister walking into the twelve-step meeting, "Has your husband done this to you?" When she says yes, any defensiveness evaporates, and the new sister has been able to sit down, join in, and begin the healing process.

We try to be good pioneers in a battle that is exploding all around us. We invite all who find themselves in the same battle to join us in turning to the Savior and his atonement and in utilizing this healthy triangle of support: inspired priesthood leaders, professional counselors who have a gospel perspective, and twelve-step support groups where honesty and humility bring a rebirth of hope.

About the Contributors

Lili Anderson, Ph.D., LCSW, received her MSW from UNLV and her Ph.D. from Brigham Young University in marriage, family, and human development. She is currently an adjunct professor at BYU for the College of Family Life. She has a private practice working with individuals, marriages, and families. She and her husband, Chris, are the parents of eight children and have five grandchildren.

Christian B. Anderson, LCSW, is a therapist with LDS Family Services. He and his wife, Lili, are the parents of eight children and have five grandchildren.

Anonymous Author of Addiction and Recovery Chapter. The author is an active member of The Church of Jesus Christ of Latter-day Saints and is currently serving with his wife as a part-time family service missionary in the Addiction Recovery Program–Pornography. (ARP–P) Both served full-time missions in their youth and are grateful to serve again. They are the parents of four children.

Mark H. Butler, Ph.D., is associate professor in Marriage and Family Therapy at Brigham Young University. His area of clinical specialization is recovery from addictive behavior. He and his wife, Shelly, are the parents of five children.

Mark D. Chamberlain, Ph.D., is a Salt Lake-area clinical psychologist specializing in the treatment of impulse-control problems. He is the author of *Wanting More: The Challenge of Enjoyment in the Age of Addiction* and coauthor of *Willpower Is Not Enough: Why We Don't Succeed at Change.* For more information, see his website: www.turningpointi.com.

Evan Christensen is a Microsoft Certified Systems Engineer and works for a Microsoft affiliate. He has worked on a variety of projects integrating the Internet with various information technology applications. He and his wife, Sarah, are the parents of two children.

Victor B. Cline, Ph.D., is a psychotherapist in private practice focusing on marital and family counseling and treatment of sexual addictions. He is a professor emeritus at the University of Utah. Dr. Cline is a well-known researcher and lecturer and has served on many local and national organizations. He has published many articles and books on the topics of parenting, the media, and marriage.

Richard Crookston is the systems administrator for Religious Education at Brigham Young University. He received a bachelor of science in business management and a master's degree in information systems management from Brigham Young University. He and his wife, Luna, reside in Provo, Utah.

Ruth Davidson is coauthor, with Tamara Davies, of *Heal My Broken Heart: An LDS Guide to Dealing with Those Bound by the Deadly Sin of Pornography.* She owns a small publishing company and has written two other books: *I, The Lord, Have Seen Thy Sorrow: An LDS Guide to Dealing with the Pain of Infidelity* and *Through Faith They Shall Overcome: Facing the Daunting Challenge of Forgiving Sexual Sin.* She and her husband, Greg, are the parents of five children.

Tamara Davies is coauthor, with Ruth Davidson, of *Heal My Broken Heart: An LDS Guide to Dealing with Those Bound by the Deadly Sin of Pornography*. She was born and raised on a small farm in southern Colorado and grew up working the family farm. She owns and runs a small decorating business and has won many decorating awards. She and her husband, Brian, are the parents of five children.

Shelley Y. DeVries graduated from Brigham Young University with a bachelor of science degree in education and taught school for sixteen years. She is the cofounder and executive vice-chair of Communities for Decency, a citizens group working to raise decency standards in Utah communities. Shelley has lectured at BYU Education Week and the Protecting Children and Families Against Pornography conference in Salt Lake City. Shelley and her husband, Daniel, have four children.

Dan Gray, LCSW, CSAT, is the cofounder and clinical director of the *Life*STAR Network (Sexual Trauma and Recovery) program of Utah, a comprehensive sex- and pornography-addiction treatment program, providing assistance to individuals, couples, and families. Dan has coauthored several publications, including the book *Discussing Pornography Problems with a Spouse*. He is a Certified Sex Addiction Therapist and often lectures for church, civic, and professional groups. For more information go to www. lifestarnetwork.org. He and his wife, Becky, have four children.

Becky Harding is a writer and editor, specializing in communications and web content. She served on the editorial board of *This People* magazine, for which she wrote a regular column, and has been published or quoted in several national women's magazines. She is currently working with Dan Gray and Todd Olson of the *Life*STAR Network in developing their twenty-unit workbook series, *Recovery from Sexual Addiction*.

John L. Harmer is the author of *A War We Must Win*. In that book he recalls nearly forty years of experience in fighting against pornography. As an attorney and an elected state official in

California, Brother Harmer carried on this battle in the courtroom, the legislative chambers, the public arena, and the media.

James M. Harper, Ph.D., MFT, is the director of the School of Family Life at Brigham Young University. He received his Ph.D. in counseling psychology from the University of Minnesota and his master's degree in marriage and family therapy from BYU. He has authored numerous articles and two books, *Uncovering Shame: An Approach Integrating Individuals with Their Family Systems* and *Sibling Positions and Birth Order in Individual and Family Therapy.* He has served in several ecclesiastical positions and has served as the former president of the Korea Pusan Mission. He and his wife, Colleen, have five children and four grandchildren.

Colleen C. Harrison holds a B.A. and M.A. in English from BYU, with an emphasis in "Personal Life Writing." She is author of *He Did Deliver Me from Bondage,* the study guide used since 1995 in the LDS Family Services Addiction Recovery Program, and founder of *Heart t' Heart,* an LDS 12-Step recovery program. Colleen and her husband, Philip, are parents of a combined family of seventeen children.

Philip A. Harrison is the author of *Clean Hands, Pure Heart: Overcoming Addiction to Pornography Through the Redeeming Power of Jesus Christ.* Phil is the husband of Colleen C. Harrison, author of *He Did Deliver Me from Bondage.*

Rod W. Jeppsen holds a degree from Brigham Young University in financial and estate planning and a minor in communications. He is a financial trainer and coaches individuals on the national stockbroker's exam. Recently Rod received his master's degree in counseling from the University of Phoenix. Rod and his wife, Terry, have three daughters. Rod has served as a bishop and high councilor and is currently his ward's Young Men's president.

Mark B. Kastleman is cofounder and chief training officer for the *Life-Balance Institute,* which provides special training programs for couples, corporations, recovering addicts, law enforcement, hospitals, the U.S. military, and many other groups. As an author and researcher, Mark has written a variety of books including *The Drug of the New Millennium—The Science of How Internet Pornography Radically Alters the Human Brain and Body.* His latest book, *Healing Hearts and Mending Minds,* contains simple daily steps to protect families from pornography addiction and rescue those already trapped. For more information go to www.lifebal.net.

Jill C. Manning, M.S., is currently pursuing her Ph.D. in Marriage and Family Therapy at Brigham Young University. She has practiced marriage and family therapy for several years, and formerly worked with LDS Family Services. Her current professional and academic interests include helping women whose husbands are under the influence of pornography and finding effective therapeutic responses to pornography problems.

Richard A. Moody, Psy.D., is currently an associate clinical professor at the Counseling and Career Center at Brigham Young University. He also maintains a part-time private practice. He obtained his doctor of psychology degree at Central Michigan University, a master's degree in marriage and family therapy from Kansas State University, and a B.S. in psychology from Brigham Young University. Dr. Moody and his wife, Carol, have three children.

Merrill F. Nelson, J.D., is a lawyer in the firm of Kirton & McConkie, practicing civil and appellate litigation. He has represented LDS Family Services and is lead counsel to the abuse helpline of the LDS Church, advising clergy and social workers on various legal issues. He served in the Utah legislature and has written and lectured on legal and social topics. He was an editor of the BYU Law Review and has served on the staff and advisory committee of the Utah supreme court.

Todd A. Olson, LCSW, CSAT, is a psychotherapist in private practice. He is the cofounder and program director of the

*Life*STAR Network, a comprehensive sex and pornography addiction treatment program, providing assistance to individuals, couples, and families. He is a Certified Sex Addiction Therapist (CSAT). Todd provides training for professionals interested in treating sexual addiction and lectures to a variety of audiences on the subject. Todd and his wife, Julene, have five children.

Scott Peterson, LCSW, CSAT, is a licensed clinical social worker and a Certified Sex Addiction Therapist (CSAT). He is in private practice specializing in the treatment of bipolar depression, anxiety disorders, and sex addiction, including those with same-sex attraction. He works with the *Life*STAR Network (Sexual Trauma and Recovery) program of Utah and conducts sex-addiction treatment groups. Scott has coauthored three books relating to self-esteem. He and his wife, Lynne, are the parents of five children.

Rory C. Reid, MSW, is a licensed psychotherapist specializing in the treatment of sexual impulsivity. He is the program director at the Provo Counseling Center and practices part-time at the Salt Lake Counseling Center. Rory teaches part-time at BYU and Utah Valley State College. He presents at many national conferences and has authored several publications and coauthored others, including the book *Discussing Pornography Problems with a Spouse.* He and his wife, Renee, have one son. Online website: www.provocc.org

LaNae Valentine, Ph.D, MFT, is the director of Brigham Young University's Women's Services and Resources. Previously she has been an assistant professor at North Dakota State and Colorado State Universities. She is a licensed marriage and family therapist whose interests include women's mental health issues. She maintains a private practice and also provides group support for wives of individuals who are struggling with pornography at the Provo Counseling Center.

Brad Wilcox, Ph.D., is associate professor in the School of

Education at Brigham Young University. He has presented at Especially for Youth and Education Week programs and has taught maturation clinics and workshops on sexuality and pornography in schools throughout Utah. He is the author of *Growing Up: Gospel Answers about Maturation and Sex* and *Where Do Babies Come From?* He has served as a bishop and is currently president of the Chile Santiago East Mission. He and his wife, Debi, have four children.

Index